Breaking Free

Foreword

I met Vince Maertz during the most chaotic time of my life. I was strung out, full of hate, and hovering on the line between despondency and apathy. Vince and I were rivals, co-conspirators, and friends. The night he was arrested, I remember feeling outraged for the stupidity that caused him to be put in chains. But in the meth world, out of sight is out of mind and when Vince went "inside," my life continued to spiral and our friendship became a fond memory to occasionally revisit.

Eventually, I went to a 13-month treatment program and engaged the opportunity I was blessed with to change my life. I wasn't allowed to access social media during that time, so when I got out and made the transition to ministry school, I looked Vince up and saw that he had been prolifically writing alongside his mother on the blog Breaking Free.

Imagine my surprise when I saw that my angry friend Vince had the soul of a poet, and the story-telling (and grammar) skills to display it.

This book, based on the blog, is significant in that it vividly portrays the daily life of a prisoner and teaches that rarely is a prisoner doing his time alone. In the following pages you will see that redemption is not an immediate process, nor is it a process that costs nothing. The following pages will reveal to you the raw heart of a hurting mother, the thawing soul of an addicted son, and the journey they took hand in hand towards what is, in my opinion, one of the great stories of transfiguration to be told to date.

There is hope to be had for those brave enough to engage the journey to find it.

Anthony Byrne. November 2018
Minneapolis, Minnesota

Introduction

This book represents collected entries from Breaking Free, originally published in blog format. In general, the posts alternate between mother and son as authors. They chronicle observations on daily life in prison, the Prison Industrial Complex, mandatory minimum drug sentencing, what led one man to prison, what it's like being his mom on the outside, the family disease of addiction. It conjectures on the causes of, solutions to, and meaning of it all. Besides the obvious prison reference, the title Breaking Free refers to the suggestion that anyone can find contentment and even happiness, even someone in prison, even someone whose kid is in prison. Anne would say she has lived life to the max. Vince will avoid that reference.

About the Authors

Anne Maertz lives in St. Paul, Minnesota and works for an international human rights organization. Vince Maertz was incarcerated in a state prison, also in Minnesota. They began co-blogging as a project they could work on together, to give themselves a voice, and to provide an outlet through which they could vent their fears, hopes, shame, amusement, and bemusement.

Thanks and Acknowledgements

The authors would like to thank their copy editor, Erin Kessler; their technical advisor, Farhad Anklesaria; and the many readers who have followed them on their journey from addiction, to prison, to redemption.

Selected Comments on the Blog

I sit down every day at my computer and can't wait to read the next post and feel ashamed of myself for pre judging and assuming that Vince wouldn't be able to write so well. This is an amazing story and so well written. - Jane

I want to say something smart, but this is all I can come up with … I read all that you've shared with gratitude that you're not silent. Thank-you for your blog. I read every post. Your and Vince's insight keeps me thinking, on my toes, and hopeful. - Sarah

For months I have been reading your blog~sometimes reading posts more than once so I knew I wasn't missing anything. Thank you for providing insight to prison. (my fiancé is there also) It has helped me tremendously. - Becky

I'm hooked—can't wait to read the next post! - Andrew

What a great project and what courage to be real on the internet with such a painful real life situation. - Debbie

You are an amazing story teller. You should continue to write. - Connie

Just made time to read the most recent entries on your blog & wanted to write how much hope, humility, inspiration & love shone out of your entries. - Rachel

I was beyond moved while reading what you and Vince have written. You have owned your stories—as individuals and as a family—in a way that most of us aspire to. The cycle of abuse is nearly impossible to break, yet you did it. - Kristi

Both mother and son are insightful and relentlessly honest. Kudos to both of you. - Debra

You are living an authentic life. Wish more people could share the realness of their true life experiences. There would a lot less shame, and more answers on how to manage through trauma. - Joni

St Cloud

My Name is Vince

-Vince-

My name is Vincent.

What the fuck is a Blog? Since nobody here knows the answer to that, I'm going to assume it's yet another internet based form of impersonal communication. I can get down with that.

As I sit here contemplating exactly what to write, I notice my roommate out of the corner of my eye punch his towel repeatedly, exhaling through his teeth to make a noise like you might hear in a movie or a video game. He's super pissed that he missed the bake sale so the towel gets punished. It's ok. I thought I heard the towel talkin' shit earlier anyhow.

This is prison life. Live from St. Cloud Men's Reformatorium, B House North, Galley 11, Cell #167. I am Vincent 244296.

Phone Calls of Shame

-Anne-

Editor's … er, mom's note: I don't know what the "bake sale" is. Was there really a bake sale in St. Cloud state prison? Or is it code for something? Is Vince delusional? Or is it just his sense of humor? There's no way to ask him. I can't call him. I could ask him in an email, which he would receive in a couple days. He can't email me back, and the chances of either of us remembering to discuss this in one of our infrequent 10-minute phones call is slim. And it's just not that important. So you will have to live with some lack of clarity, just as I have for years.

****

When I found out Vince would be going to prison, I thought the obvious way to avoid the dreaded collect calls would be to move to another country.

The calls go like this: An unknown number shows up on my phone. When I answer, a cheery computerized female voice begins, "You have a collect call from…" then my son's voice would interject his name, "Vince." Then a different, condemning, shaming voice would say, "…an inmate in the Ramsey County Adult Detention Center," or "Woodbury Workhouse," or "Crow Wing County Jail," or wherever he was.

OK, you might not hear the shaming tone but I do.

The cheerful voice returns and informs me that I will be charged $9.99 for 10 minutes, that the call will be monitored, and that this "service" is provided by Prison Corporation of America. As if it was some patriotic public service, not a scam to rake in billions from a (literally) captive audience and their desperate loved ones. "To accept this call, press 1. To refuse this call, press 2. To permanently block calls from this number, press 3."

Vince hadn't been incarcerated for over 10 years, he had reminded me a few months before. While in his late teens and early 20s, he had been locked up multiple times so that's how I knew what to expect with the phone calls. But the earlier experiences had been short stints for minor offenses, and the calls then had come from jails. Now he was looking at up to five years in a prison. A prison. That sounded so much worse than a "jail." My expectations had been steadily going downhill for years, but this was different; big.

He hadn't been incarcerated for 10 years, but he had hit the skids every couple of years. The last time, about two years earlier, he had lost his job and, since he lived so close to the edge of subsistence, quickly lost his apartment and all his possessions—right down to his underwear and toothbrush.

Fortunately, I had been 9,000 miles away, working for a human rights organization in Nairobi, Kenya. I was concerned about him, but there was nothing I could do —and being surrounded by people who were risking their lives by confronting corrupt police, or organizing LGBT activists, or just trying to avoid being kidnapped by El Shabab on their way home from work, put things in perspective.

So this time, when he was facing four charges of selling heroin, meth, cocaine, and marijuana with a potential 11-year sentence, I immediately applied for a job in Turkey with an organization based in Los Angeles. I figured if I played my cards right I could work in Turkey for four years, travel all over Europe and Asia from there and send Vince a lot of cool postcards, then return to work in L.A. I had it all figured out.

So when I got back to my desk after a meeting and saw I had a call from an L.A. number, I thought "Hurrah!" it was them calling for an interview. For a moment I thought things would actually pan out as I had planned. I was floating toward the emergency exit.

But instead it was "You have a collect call from…"

Bob Barker World

-Vince-

Day 1. Nearly 13 days after my pronounced sentence of 50 months is handed down to me, I am finally chained up, put into an Olmsted County Sheriff's van, and driven through Shakopee to St. Cloud. About a four-hour trip (we stopped to drop of female prisoners at Shakopee Correctional Facility).

I'll skip the intake procedure. But it is nowhere near as invasive as I thought it would be.

An hour after my arrival I'm in my new home. A 6×10 foot combo of cold steel and concrete. I unpack my pillow case which holds everything I need to survive, kind of.

> 3 pair state-issued stretch pants that resemble blue jeans
> 6 pair tighty whities
> 6 pair socks
> 5 white Ts
> 3 blue button-up long-sleeve shirts
> 3 white towels
> 1 washcloth
> Sheet and blanket

And the following Bob Barker [1] products:

Maximum Security Brand 3-in-1 shampoo, shave, and body wash - My advice: don't use it for anything I just mentioned. I can't believe it doesn't say, "Made with real pine!"

Deodorant, a size so small I've never even seen in it a Dollar Store. No scent.

A 4.4 ounce tube of something labeled Mint Paste. I'll assume it's for teeth because it's next to the Safety Brush, which is 4 inches long and flexible so you can't sharpen it and stab somebody, or brush your teeth.

A 3 inch flexible pen. Take your standard Bic pen. Throw away everything except the very middle, then cut that in half. Here we pick paint off the walls and wrap it around that until it becomes useful for writing.

All set up now. My first move, grab the 3-in-1 and a razor (forgot that) and go to town on my month-old beard.

Half an hour later, my wash cloth is covered in blood and hair. And I'm not done. I've left a patch of hair on my chin because that's what all the kids are doing these days. That's when it hits me. I look in the safety mirror and for the first time in my life, I see age. And I realize

9

how much time I've wasted. I'm not a kid anymore. I'm a beat up, 35-year-old con, washed up unsuccessful drug dealer and addict. And I cry. Fuck my life.

The last time I cried was about 7 months ago. It happened about a week and a half after I was arrested. I had slept off the drugs, something struck me funny and I laughed out loud. And I wondered if I could remember the last time I had done that. Then everything came flooding out.

****

I don't meet my first roommate until the next day because he is gone on a writ of Corpus Christi, or something like that. (It's actually called a writ of habeas corpus, Latin for "You may have the body." Creepy, right?) He's exactly my age, fairly down to earth, and in for 5 years on a DUI. We talk. We get along. My first big hurdle. He gives me the rundown on how things work in E House, the intake unit.

Basically, imagine prison, and then don't change anything. That's what you can expect for your first 30 days. That goes for every male in the State of Minnesota; everybody goes to E House in St. Cloud for classification and orientation.

Locked in my cell for the entire day except for three 15-minute meals (3,300 calories per day), and maybe a "flag" period of no more than 50 minutes where we scramble to use the phone, shower, and try to communicate with the Corrections Officers. The C.O.s have a tough job, that's why they're assholes.

The only other times we get out are for passes, i.e. going to the infirmary, dentist, or caseworker.

He teaches me how to make dominoes, dice, and chess pieces, all from toilet paper. They're actually quite functional. He has been stuck in E House for 45 miserable days when he's finally called to move. Lucky bastard.

-Anne-

When I tell my therapist that Vince is in his cell 23 hours a day, she says, "But, on TV they show prisoners sitting around in a big common area, watching TV and hatching their schemes." I have always avoided watching TV shows about prisons and drug dealers. "I think a TV show about a guy sitting in a cell 23 hours a day would make for pretty poor drama," was my analysis.

Feeling Like Florida

-Anne-

Would I really move to Turkey just to avoid the shame factor of phone calls from prison? There's more to it, of course.

Once you are actually talking to your loved one, the call is of such poor quality and they speak so softly, that you can barely make out what they're saying. Why the poor quality? Shouldn't $1 a minute buy you some top-notch connection, considering that I can call England for 1 cent a minute, or free with Skype, and it sounds like I'm in the room with my friend? A great deal of time is wasted by me asking Vince, " What ? I can't hear you–say that again!"

They speak softly, or at least my son does, because he is surrounded by men he wouldn't want thinking he's a pussy if they overheard him expressing some real emotion.

Then, the call is fraught with tension because you're keenly aware that you've got to say everything in 10 minutes, and you've got no idea when you might be able to talk again. There's all the baggage from the past, the urge to say, "You idiot!" and "I'm so scared for you!" and "My heart is breaking" and "You'd better fucking figure it out this time!" all at once.

There are the logistical questions you need to cover, like what is the actual sentence, when you'll be eligible for parole, is this the facility where you'll be for the duration or will they move you?

And of course you are aware that some redneck cop-wanna-be prison guard may be listening to the call.
On this first call he actually had some things to say that I'd been waiting seven years to hear.

It feels like a dream now, that conversation. Like he was under water, his voice so low I only caught half the words. I know he said, "Mom, I know I'm done. I'm done with all those things I was doing that got me in here." He went on, and from the tone of his voice I could tell he was confiding something big…but I couldn't make out his words.

He had been sober for five years, then relapsed seven years before now. Since his plunge from sobriety he had held me at arms' length, saying things like, "You're going to have to accept my lifestyle, mom, or you just won't see me." His lifestyle: drinking a case of beer and bottle of whiskey a day and—this was clear to me now—using all the drugs he's been charged with possess ing: meth, heroin, pot, and cocaine.

I could only make out a handful of his words. Then I caught a whole sentence, "I haven't felt this way since Florida." Florida, where he had lived in a halfway house for a year after four months at Hazelden, his third shot at treatment. Where he had been on medication for bipolar disorder. "I just want to get back to Florida." It was like Florida was a state of mind as much as a place.

"You can!" I exclaimed, "You can go anywhere because you're a cook and you can get a job in 5 minutes."
"I don't know if I want to be a cook any more, Mom."

I had a thought but bit my mom-tongue from saying, "You could finish your degree in prison! You could become a lawyer!" I also didn't ask, "Are you going to AA", "Have you seen a psychiatrist?"

or "Do they have a good library there?" or any other mom-like questions.

I wanted answers but asking could annoy and alienate him, I knew from experience. The 10 minutes were up. We said our "I love yous."

I almost wished he'd never call again.

Katie

-Vince-

December 2013
I had just come into contact with an old acquaintance I'll call Katie after several years of no communication. We used to get high together back when she was still in high school. That and the fact that her father is/was a priest always made me smile.

Although we were never romantically involved, I spent time with her, teaching her the proper ways of my little-known side job. There used to be only two ways to do things. The right way, or the way that could get you killed by Mexicans or bikers. I taught her the right way. Little did I know that would all come into play 8 years later.

Katie had recently cut off her ankle bracelet and become a fugitive. My kind of girl. We hooked up on Facebook and started talking on the phone. I wasn't interested in hiring at the time so I kept my business hidden, but she was fun to get high with.

I was bouncing around from hotel to hotel because I could afford to, and because it wasn't safe to stay in one place more than 2 nights.

December 19, 2013, sometime just before midnight
As evidenced by the fact that Katie had called for a ride from a boyfriend, I came to the conclusion that she still had no desire to sleep with me. What I didn't know, was how her ride would change everything in our lives forever.

December 20, 2013, just after midnight
Katie says her ride is outside the hotel. We say goodbye. Thirty seconds later, pounding on my door. She's back. The car and occupants that came to pick her up are surrounded by police, she tells me. I turn on the police scanner I have downloaded on my phone. First thing I hear is, "…at the Super 8 South." Shit, that was here. I knew I had all the shite hidden from view but that was all I remember thinking about.

Katie gets a call. It's her ride. He says he's been pulled over. What we don't know is that he had told the officers that Katie had a D.O.C. warrant, was in Room 141, and she had meth.

Five minutes pass.

KNOCK, KNOCK, KNOCK!

****

-Anne-

I did the math and reckoned Katie was around 10 years younger than Vince. No saint, but I hoped I'd never run into her parents. Not for the first time, I counted myself lucky to not have a daughter, because she probably would have turned out like Katie, with all the additional perils that come with being a young woman.

Filling Space

-Vince-

August 3, 2014, 8:40 p.m.
My roommate has aspirations to become a M.M.A. fighter. Would you like to know how I can tell? Well. Yesterday after a short flag, he came back in the cell and yelled, "You call that a workout?!" and promptly punched the wall. Then the poor towel.

He's an angry man. Every time he hears someone breathing heavily on the weights that are just below us on the bottom tier, he rushes the 6 feet over to the bars to see what's going on. Always shirtless, he picks them apart. Much like I'm doing right now, to avoid talking about my problems. Yep, he's a fuckin' douche bag.

9:30 p.m.
Another weekend of boredom done. With minimal staff, we have no work, no school, recreation, or activities. Plenty of church available, though! So I spend my weekends reading. I have read quite a lot since I arrived in St. Cloud. I have not gone much further than Tim Dorsey and Dean Koontz, but that is much broader a selection for me than before I got to prison. I am almost to an average of a book a day at an average of 300 pages. I think that's pretty damn good.

Busted

-Vince-

I talked to an investigator for the Olmsted County Public Defender 's Office last week. Now that I have been sentenced, Katie and I are no longer banned from communicating with each other. Part of my plan. This also means that I am allowed to testify on her behalf during her trial. D.A. didn't see me coming! I plead down to 2nd degree possession, which means technically that I'm not a drug dealer. Since she is charged with the same crimes as me, and double jeopardy can't apply to me, I can finally take the rap for all of the dope. Something I probably should have done back in December, but, we don't talk to cops. If they want to put people away, make 'em work for it.

COPS, technically an acronym, Constable on Patrol. I don't know if cop has become an actual word in the English language yet.

KNOCK, KNOCK, KNOCK!

"Katie ____, open up! R.P.D!"

Katie and I stare at each other with blank expressions. She's not ready. But there's little choice. She has a D.O.C. warrant. She has to go if I stand a chance. We say our goodbyes. She opens the door and shuts it behind her. Two minutes later, more knocking.

Pissed off, I open the door. I say, "What?"

"Can you step outside and talk with me, please?" says the officer. I should have said no. I don't know why I did a lot of things the way I did that night. But I stepped out. Big mistake. With my back turned, Katie asks if she can go in the room and get her purse. A cop says, "yeah." Flashlight searching high and low for the purse on the bed, a cop spots a tiny bag of weed on the floor I had dropped earlier. Fuck! The other cop comes out and asks for my consent to search the room. And for whatever reason I will never know, I say, "Go ahead and search." Ugh.

For fuck sake, who ever would look up in a light fixture when looking for dope? Everybody. Especially the cops. Out in the lobby I am casually chatting with officer Lou, who had pulled me over the week before for speeding and let me go, and the officers come out and say, "Who wants to go to jail?" I raise my hand. The cuffs go on. Booked in for 1st degree sale of methamphetamine.

Only murder is higher up in our state as far as sentencing. That's right. Selling more than 10 grams of meth within 90 days in the State of Minnesota is punishable by up to 30 years in prison. Most first-time sex offenders are given probation. Granted, 30 years is for the most extreme meth cases, but all 1st degree controlled substance crimes carry mandatory minimum sentences. Fuck my life.

****

Dear Vince:

I am looking through old photos of you—having a water fight with your auntie in grandma's backyard, at the lake, at your Montessori preschool, you and your little friends in that subsidized housing project we were living in that had a million kids your age, me spinning you on one of those twirling rides at a playground, birthday parties with my terrible lumpy cakes (but I did try!), a seder at the Levine's, religious school (and you are smiling!), camping, birthday pinatas, your Big Brother, weddings, playing in the snow, doing your homework, you doing your volunteer dog walking at the humane society, at Paul Bunyan Land feeding a tame deer, another birthday cake decorated like a baseball (by me, the least sporty person I know!), Halloween costumes, you feeding your new cousin a bottle, our trips to Chicago and New York and Seattle, pet cats, Disney World, posing with your uncle for Boy Scouts, your aunt dressed in a gorilla suit for your 15th birthday surprise party.

And then the photos stop, until you came back from Hazelden and Florida when you were ... 21?

You would think I would just stop caring by now, or as grandma says, "Just don't think about it." She's always said that, about anything unpleasant, not necessarily about you. I wish I could.

I think I wouldn't be human if I didn't ask myself, "What was I missing in all those photos?" He looks healthy. He's smiling in a lot of them. Should I have seen some signs—gotten him to a shrink? Should I have been more strict? Less strict? Was it because we were broke for so long and lived on Ramen and went to food shelves? Was it because I was depressed for so many years—would a child take that as neglect and think it was his fault? Was it the whole awful chapter with [abusive alcoholic but filthy rich ex boyfriend I'll call Kermit]? I take complete responsibility, being desperate to get married and have more kids, at the expense of exposing you to domestic abuse and all sorts of inappropriate shit? Was it how I stupidly told you about the brother you didn't know you had, thinking it would cheer you up, which backfired? God, what an idiot I was!

Maybe I should have never told you how I smoked pot and drank in high school, trying to warn you against them. Again, my parenting backfired, when later you told me you took that as a sign that you could drink and smoke, since I had turned out ok. (Ha!)

I know you've said you were "over" not having a father but maybe you really aren't? I think you tell me what you think I want to hear. Or is your addiction mostly genetics? Me passing down my alcoholic/addict father's genes to you, loaded with your father's alcoholic/addict genes?

Do you really have Bipolar Disorder, as Hazelden diagnosed you? Are the drugs and booze medication?

I can hear you saying, "Oh, mom." You've rarely talked to me about any of this, so I don't know if you've ever given it a thought or if you even think you have a problem.

I hope it is not too awful there. I hope you'll take advantage of whatever resources they offer. I hope you know that I love you, no matter what—always will, always have. You have dug your way out of some very deep pits and you'll do it again. You probably don't feel young anymore but from my perspective you are so you've got time to rebuild.

18

I Love you,
Mom

Boy of Summer

-Vince-

August 4, 2014
Twenty-eight full days in St. Cloud prison. I don't feel cured yet.
But I'm working on it. I have applied for every available job, college
class, and early release program. No reply. But I have a lot of time. I
am clearly going to need to work on patience. If I try to make things
move faster than they do, I will become frustrated and I need to work
on letting others make my decisions for a while. See if that makes
me better. I hope it does. Twenty-eight days down, 1,472 to go. Yep,
I've got time.

Another Monday, another day without mail. Mail is the high point of
the day for any offender. Our link to the outside world. No matter.
Today, and two more times this week, I get to go to the ball
diamond. To elaborate, it's more than a ball diamond. The outdoor
rec area consists of the diamond, a football field, a soccer field, a
ropes course, two handball courts, two full length basketball courts,
and a perimeter track.

Turns out the ropes course is actually just a bunch of razor wire to
prevent escape. None of the guards laugh when I ask if I can try it
out. Oh, there's the standard goose-shit-filled pond too.

As it turns out, I'm not as limber, fast, strong, or accurate as I used
to be. However, I've always had a pretty easy time with
base/softball. Today I went 2 for 3 with two triples that went all the
way to the fence. I had four putouts, and recorded 1 throwing error.
I've done quite well in one way or another, every time I go out there.
Every time gaining strength and agility. I'll be in shape in no time.
Something has to burn off the 3,300 calories we get here. We won
13-12.

Best part of today. I was bored over at 3rd base. I looked down. And found an agate.

Agate hunting has been a part of my life for a long time now. It's what I spent my time doing the last few days of my freedom. That, and smoking meth. I tell you what, walking into a courtroom knowing you won't be leaving, knowing you may never see certain people, and knowing the Judge will look down on you and say you're going away for four years is tough. I knew after my court appearance on June 18, 2014 that all those things would happen 8 days later. Given another chance, I would have used those days more wisely. Instead I smoked more meth, and looked for agates.

The First Worst Day

-Anne-

I've found myself brooding about the day Vince declared he would drop out of high school. I asked myself, "Why am I thinking about this now?" I've always considered it the worst day of my life—and I've had some doozies—but it has been 20 years. After a few days it struck me that it was bound to come back around because it was a milestone that marked when "it" all began.

A few months before Vince's dropping out manifesto, I had been Absolutely Shocked to find out that he was drinking and smoking pot (and much more that, thankfully I didn't find out about until years later). Well, lots of kids experimented, right? I wasn't happy about it but it was sort of normal.

Dropping out? NOT Normal.

He was 16 though, so legally he could drop out. I marched him down to the Vice Principal's office at Central and announced to him, "My son wants to drop out! Talk to him!" I figured he would be best equipped with the facts on how much less high school drop outs earn over a lifetime, how they end up homeless or in prison or, even worse, how my son might end up living in a trailer home, wearing Zubas, and working as a short-order cook.

But the VP disinterestedly slid a form across his desk and said to Vince, "Sign here." It was a waiver of responsibility or some such form, formalizing his "withdrawal" from school and absolving them of responsibility. I'm not clear on what I did then. Probably cried, pleaded, accused the VP of being an accessory to failure, cursed myself for thinking anyone had my back as a single mom. But the guy said, "If they wanna drop out, we can't stop 'em."

Vince signed, and that was it. The school no longer had to deal with his truancy or factor in his failing grades into any reports to the school district or state. My son dropping out would improve their average scores, no doubt. He was no longer their problem.

****

We went home separately from the high school after his withdrawal/dropout was done, and stood wordless when we met. I had threatened him that, if he wasn't in school, he'd have to move out. Education was how I had gotten ahead and it would damn well be his ticket to doing better than me.

So I told him to leave. He could come home the minute he decided to go back to school. We could look at a different school, an alternative school, whatever. But he had to finish high school—that wasn't such an unrealistic expectation, was it?

He walked out the door with a pillow sack full of his clothes. I figured he'd be back in a couple of days, after he realized he couldn't make it on his own making minimum wage.

When I hadn't heard from him for three or four days, I went to the sub shop where he had a job as a dishwasher. They said he'd taken another job. Where? They didn't know.

I didn't see him again for a year.

21

I reported him missing to the police, who looked at me skeptically. "You kicked him out for dropping out," one of them said as though that was perfectly understandable. "But now you want him back?"

These are Vince's school portraits from 9th grade and about a year later, just before he dropped out:

I found the second one stashed in his room months after he'd left.

I talked to his friends in the neighborhood, but they said he had dropped them months before. They said he'd acquired some stoner friends whose last names or addresses they didn't know. They did give me one lead, a kid called Mike, and I knocked on the door of that house two or three times during the year but there was never an answer. My cousin, who lived a block away from their house, called me a couple times to say she thought she'd seen my son walking down the sidewalk but she'd been driving fast and wasn't sure...

But sure enough, that's where he was. Mike's parents were survivalists, homeschoolers, and pot heads. They felt sorry for Vince. What a buzzkill of a mom he had! So for a year, they all sat around and got high and drank and played video games like Grand Theft Auto. They had been home when I'd knocked.

Vince's using got so out of control that it was even too much for them, so they kicked him out and he showed up on my front porch, almost a year later, with his pillow sack.

****

-Vince-

Mike's parents were good people. I never had one drink at their home. They both worked full time and wouldn't let me live there if I did. Mike was never home schooled and he got his GED before his graduation day. I never smoked pot with his mom and only on occasion with his dad. They let us drink when we went up north to their land. But they made sure to keep an eye on us and always promoted responsibility. When I was arrested my first time Mike's dad told me that he wasn't kicking me out, but it was time to find another home. It was during my stay there that I worked as a security guard at Liberty State Bank, and overnights at a gas station off I-94. I don't want anybody to think Mike's parents ever did anything to negatively affect my life. Mike's dad accidentally shot himself in the stomach years later while making bullets. He was nearly paralyzed and hospitalized for months.

St. Cloud

-Anne-

I wonder where the city of St. Cloud, Minnesota got its name? That is where Vince is now ensconced: St. Cloud State Correctional Facility (SCF). It's about 2 hours' drive northwest of the Twin Cities of Minneapolis and St. Paul.

I love statistics so I felt a small thrill when I discovered the Daily Inmate Profile Report which, as its name implies, changes daily but probably not dramatically. The prison was built in 1898 on the site of an old granite quarry. On the day I looked, a "total of 1,098 adult offenders are under the Case Responsibility of Minnesota

Correctional Facility – St. Cloud with a total of 1,026 adult offenders currently on-site at this facility." Wow! I had no idea. Before he derailed, Vince had lived in a little town outside Rochester, called Fountain, which had a population of 410 people. SCF must feel like a big city to him. And it is only one of 10 correctional facilities in the state. And that doesn't include jails or workhouses.

Eighty-five percent of the prisoners are between the ages of 18 and 45. That's a lot of testosterone; I wonder if the drop off in the older population groups is related to men's lower testosterone levels as they age. Three hundred and seventeen are in for drug offenses, and the average sentence is 39 months (Vince got 50 months). The next category is domestic assault (232 inmates, serving an average of 23 months). Then there's just regular assault, with 194 inmates serving an average sentence of 37 months. I'm betting a lot of that was fueled by drugs and alcohol—not an excuse, a contributing factor. Then there are 52 guys in there for drunk driving, obviously involving alcohol, serving an average of 51 months. I'm guessing most of them must have committed multiple offenses.

Fifty-three percent of the inmates are white, compared with 85.5% of Minnesotans as a whole. Thirty-two percent are black and 11 percent are Native, compared with 5 and 1 percent overall in the state. Oh, those Asians, living up to their reputation of model minority! Three percent of those locked up and 4 percent of Minnesota's population. Latinos aren't separated out but there's a note that 59 prisoners counted in the groups above are Hispanic.

I scanned the religion column and saw that 52% were Christian, 7% Native, 3% Muslim, and a whopping 28% had no preference. Oh, and there was one Jew.

And oh, damn, there were my 20-year-old fears confirmed in black and white. Forty percent of the inmates had no high school diploma, compared with only 9 percent of Minnesotans overall.

Unraveling

-Vince-

February 2006

Almost five years into sobriety, things were unraveling in my life. Things assuredly appeared swell on the outside. But my desire for chaos prevailed when I decided to practice for an upcoming Caribbean cruise by having a couple of drinks with my girlfriend Sarah. I enjoyed a really good Italian beer, and a sip of her fancy woman drink that night.

The next night, sans girlfriend, I downed half a bottle of Jack Daniel's alone at a local pub. I woke up with the worst hangover I'd ever had. I vowed I would never drink again. And I didn't. Until the cruise the next week.
Viva la Mexico!

A few days after my relapse and before the cruise, Sarah, with whom I was going on the trip, broke up with me. I really didn't see it coming. We had gotten along so well. She was beautiful, smart, and funny. All the things everybody looks for. I took it pretty badly. Blamed myself, then her. Then me again. But we still went on the cruise.

If you have never been on a cruise, I have two pieces of advice for you. #1: Do it! #2: Bring all your money (don't forget your savings).

I spent most of the cruise on a pretty good buzz. We went from Miami to Costa Maya, to Grand Cayman, to Jamaica. I almost drowned in Grand Cayman after my snorkel filled with salt-water and I was in 7 feet of water. Until then I had never been in a body of water that had currents. I say I almost drowned because my lungs filled with burning water and I panicked. Until then I was unaware that the dog paddle was so useless in a current. In a lake, of which Minnesota has 10,000, you can float if you need to. Not true in the ocean.

Thankfully, the current brought me right to a floating dock after about a minute of breathing a mixture of air and water. I climbed up the ladder, threw up, and laid down until all the other assholes who knew how to swim were done snorkeling. Then I did an Olympic dive of the dock and the 100-meter breast stroke of a lifetime to the shore. Piece of cake. People looked at me as if I had been chased by a shark. Which was my motivation when I dove in. Fuck the ocean.

Sarah and I didn't speak much on the cruise, and I think only once after. After that I hit the ground running in Rochester. A couple days after I got back I picked up a nasty little meth habit. Lost my job after I found out I could get two days off paid if I said I was going to a family funeral. Suddenly, back to back weeks, both my grandparents suffered fatal heart attacks. I was so traumatized by the second that I never went back to work. But I got a huge check including severance. And I used that to fund my new drug-dealing business.

Worse Things

-Vince-

August 5, 2014
Today I received my official classification score and recommendation from the Minnesota Department of Corrections: 3 points, Level Two Minimum. It is about as not dangerous to society as a person can be, that's me. Sentenced to 50 months I would now like to present a list of things our state deems less dangerous than a person with 6 grams of meth in their hands.

Criminal Sexual Conduct 3rd Degree to include: sex trafficking, using a minor in a sexual performance in pornography.

Possession of said porn will get probation, but not prison.

You can solicit a child for sex and if you have done it before, you could face probation. Third time, you may receive up to 15 months in prison. That's just sex.

Here are some other things you can do and still avoid prison in Minnesota:

Financially exploit a vulnerable adult (up to $35,000)

Shoot a gun in a city bus, or at one

Run from a cop

Kidnap and release a person

Assault a person with bodily harm

Fail to affix tax stamp to heroin

Starve a retarded person

Negligently discharge an explosive

Shoot and kill a person while hunting

Kill somebody with your car

Kill an unborn baby

Stalk a person (UP TO 3 TIMES!)

Bribe

Assault a vulnerable adult

Bring a dangerous weapon on school property

Maliciously punish a child causing substantial bodily harm

Violate a restraining order

Bring a gun to court

Start a building on fire with people in it

Beat your husband or wife (but only twice)

My favorite: Illegal molestation of human remains. You can do that four times before you see 12 months of prison.

Now some of these have various ways of being explained and I put my little spin on some. But they are all on the Minnesota Sentencing Guidelines Grid and Offense Severity Table [2]. I am in 8-1 Severity 8, Criminal History Score 1. Bottom of the box sentence because I spoke to the judge at sentencing about life and what I wanted to do with it. She liked me and gave me over 4 years to think.

****

-Anne-

The day after Vince sent me this post (and I was feeling skeptical about what he'd written) I saw an article in the Star Trib about a chiropractor who had pleaded guilty to raping a patient, and would be sentenced to no more than 4 years in prison.

Boot Camp

-Anne-

After Vince does his time, he tells me, they'll send him to boot camp. "What is that?" I ask. "Just what it sounds like, mom. Just like boot camp if I were going into the army.

"But you're not going into the army."

"Well I don't know what the point is, but I'll do whatever they want me to do to get out of here."

Boot camp. Great preparation for army life, sure. But not for real life. An idea that sounds good, until you actually use your brain and think about it. Somebody's ill-conceived, half-baked plan to "whip those criminals into shape."

Boot camp seems to be the pat, knee-jerk answer to everything nowadays. Overweight? Sign up for booty-busting boot camp at your gym. Teenage son out of control? Send him to some boot camp-style ranch in South Dakota. What's next, meditation boot camp? Colicky baby boot camp? Alzheimer's patient boot camp?

I have never been through boot camp but my sister and one of my brothers have and I've seen all the movies and TV shows. My understanding is that every detail of your life, every waking moment of your day is tightly scheduled and controlled. All decisions are made for you. You have no choices except whether to stay or quit.

I have also heard the stories of young people discharged from the services, no longer with any routine or anyone telling them what to do, and they're bored and at loose ends and don't know how to

28

manage their time and that's where the drinking starts and then to your surprise they're re-enlisting.

I in no way mean to disparage armed services personnel by saying that prison life seems much the same as being in the military. Lights on at the same time every day, sharing your personal space with lots of other people of your gender, make your bunk, meals served to you, a time for exercise, a time to make phone calls, a time to shower, lights out at the same time. No bills to pay, some routine job if you're lucky.

Except ex-cons don't come out as heroes. There is no GI benefit, Michelle Obama isn't cheerleading for them, there's no VA medical system (let's hope a flawed VA system is better than nothing?).

Cho Mo

-Vince-

Today I was supposed to get my indigent canteen order. It didn't show. It would have contained necessary hygiene items and two envelopes. The weekly allotment. So for now I will continue to write, and stink. Oh Shit. It would also have contained the paper and pens with which I could have continued to write. So, I will do what I can. My roommate gave me some soap and toothpaste to get me by. But it is prison, so now I have to blow him. Ha, ha, ha! Just fuckin' with ya!

Yesterday there was a fire in the B Annex. That is the unit next to and slightly above the one I am in. It is much smaller and houses low risk offenders with jobs. Apparently it's true, if you don't clean out the lint trap in a dryer regularly, it will start a fire.

Because there was a lot of smoke, we were all hurried into the gym where we sat for about two hours enduring countless head counts and absolutely no air circulation. Hot. On the plus side we got to see a cho-mo beat down.

Cho-mo is the term we use to describe the soulless people who have raped, molested--or both--another human being. Because the State of Minnesota protects these people, because of their sexual preference, it is a hate crime to knowingly assault a child molester or rapist. Fortunately, we have people in here that don't give a fuck. I call them heroes, these 25-to-lifers aren't going anywhere soon, so they take it upon themselves to punish those people that society does not allow the victims to punish.

To all those out there, victims of torture, rape, molestation, child endangerment, elderly abuse, and worse, we have your back. Nobody makes it through here. A simple phone call to the outside with a name. The internet does the rest. They only have to use the MN DOC website.

Murderers, life-long dealers, thieves, animals. I live with them all. And to be truthful, almost everybody here is a decent person. When pushed to the edge, everybody can snap. But we all come together to deal with each cho-mo. Usually somebody is selected from the same race to administer punishment. And it's not just once. When they get to their permanent homes, C.S.C.s (Criminal Sexual Conducts) will be extorted, beaten, raped by men that are otherwise not gay, and in the worst cases, killed or crippled. So if any of you think the punishment by the law is too light, which it usually is, people here make sure they live here in constant fear. It seems that sex offenders do repeat a lot until they actually have to go to prison.

As an example, the first time I saw a beat down was on my third day. Two men came from behind me and launched an attack. One grabbed the cho mo's arms and held them while the other punched so hard over and over in the face that the cho mo coughed up blood and it came out through his cheek. The guards accidentally filled his face full of mace instead of the attackers. Oops!

Prayer for a Prisoner

-Anne-

30

I've only told a couple very close friends about Vince's new address. One of my neighbors slipped a poem by John O'Donohue [3] under my door, with a note apologizing if it was too sappy.

Too sappy? If she had given it to me the day before I might have thought so. My mood is fluctuating day by day. But today I cried as I read it. Not even so much because it was beautifully and realistically written, but because someone actually cared enough about prisoners to write it.

But if you Google "Prayer for a prisoner" you'll find a lot of hits, mostly from Catholic organizations. I make a mental note to check that out someday. Even though I'm not a believer, I found it really touching and comforting.

Coming to Terms with My Term

-Vince-

August 10, 2014
Excluding good time, and any other early release programs, my release date is July 25, 2017. If I am accepted into C.I.P. I will leave prison six months from the day I arrive in Willow River. The Challenge Incarceration Program there, otherwise known as boot camp, is designed to be as fast paced and rigorous as army boot camp, but also includes drug treatment, education, cognitive thinking skills classes, job training, and when that's over there's a 6 month intensive supervised release (ISR) program that they say is the real challenge. For 6 months: every day is the real challenge. For 6 months: everyday contact with an I.S.R. officer. Drug tests 4 times a week.

Must spend 8 hours a day actively seeking employment until you have a full time job. AA/NA involvement. Community service, 8 hours per week. I.S.R. officers can walk into your home at any time day or night with the key you have provided them. They can follow you. Their job is not to help you succeed. Their job is to make sure they are there to catch you slipping. They give you one fuck up. Then they put on an ankle bracelet. If you mess up again you go back to prison for your full term and they add on six months. I'd be out in 2019. Oh, and to not be a burden to society, they take your paycheck. Pay your bills, give you some small allowance and keep the rest. After that is parole for one year. Then I'm free. :-/

Believe it or not the success rate is quite high. Recidivism is low. And everybody comes out of boot camp in the best shape of his life. 5 miles rain or shine, daily workouts, healthy diet. Sounds like a challenge to me. I can't wait. Oooh but I will. My guess is that I'll get to go to boot camp in roughly 3 months. Until I leave St. Cloud, I'm locked in my cell for an average of 21 hours a day, 23 on weekends.

****

August 11
Thus far I have done the majority of my writing at night. I have Restless Legs Syndrome and cannot sleep. And it's nice and quiet. This week I will be starting my new medication, Mirapex.

Unbeknownst to me, the guards were doing an informal sleep study on me to prove that I was not faking symptoms to get drugs. The doctor said that the guards only found me asleep twice over the three nights of the study. They walk by every 30-40 minutes at night. So my medication was finally approved. When my pills actually arrive, well who knows.....

August 11, just after midnight
The biggest downfall of being sleepless is having no food. I have big hopes for the day ahead. I need a job. Working gets me out of my cell and puts a couple dollars a week in my account. If I get a good job like kitchen or cleaning crew, I would get paid up to $1 per hour after a while. We don't get all of that, but it's enough to buy necessaries.

August 16

32

So nice to have paper again, and college rule! College rule makes me write better than grade-school rule.

I've been on Mirapex now for 5 amazing, sleep-filled nights. When my Ma used the word "miracle" when describing it, she was spot on. RLS kiss my ass. I've been sleeping all the way through the night. Dreaming. And the doc says that my second nose should go away within a month. Ha! No side effects to speak of, actually. So that's my good news of the week.

****

-Anne-

RLS is a silly-sounding condition that runs in my family. I, my mother, my brothers, my sister, my cousin, we all have it to one degree or another. It causes an indescribable creeping sensation in the legs, and sometimes arms, as one is falling asleep, which makes you kick about in an effort to make it stop. It sounds silly, but try losing sleep night after night for your whole life, and it's not so much. RLS is another thing to worry about for Vince—a bunk mate would not appreciate him thrashing about and waking him up 10 times a night—what if he had a violent cellmate? What if Vince ended up having to sleep on the cement floor? What if, what if? I am impressed and a little surprised that they've addressed it so quickly.

Torture, Real Torture

-Anne-

As I wrote early on, I work for an international human rights organization. The main thing we do is treat survivors of torture. That is, people who were tortured by their own governments for protesting government corruption, or union organizing, belonging to a certain ethnic group or religion, or just being in the wrong place at the wrong time.

I'm not a clinician. I do research and I write a lot of grant proposals. I hope my blog posts don't sound like grant proposals.

We work in about a dozen countries and also with survivors in Minnesota, but the local rehabilitation takes place in a clinic separate from my office. So I rarely have face-to-face interaction with torture survivors. However, I review a lot of reports and find myself crying out in my heart, "Those poor people!" as I read about mass rapes used as a weapon to control populations and what goes on in the unbelievably-named Insein Prison in Burma.

Last week we had an event at which three survivors told their stories. I helped with rehearsing the program so I heard each story two or three times.

There was the man who had almost been burned alive, the young woman who, as a child, had witnessed her mother and father being beaten and dragged away to prison by police in the middle of the night, and the man who was blind in one eye from being beaten by the police in jail after distributing pro-democracy leaflets.

The one I can't get out of my head...I won't describe the details but it involved meat hooks. And this is not an HBO series—it's happening to real people all over the world, right now.

And so I always catch myself from saying things like, "Sitting through that meeting was torture!"

You may be wondering, "Why would anyone work for such a place!? Answer: I've been fascinated with everything international, and have felt a calling to help make the world a better place, for as long as I can remember. I'm no saint or hero. I find human rights issues intellectually challenging so I get a satisfying career out of it. I am paid relatively well to read, research, think, and write about torture and other human rights violations all day long. And sometimes they send me to exotic places.

You could say I should feel reassured that the US government doesn't torture prisoners. Oh wait, it does! Because solitary confinement, waterboarding, stress positions, and other things we do are considered torture and/or inhumane under international law.

Well, our gov doesn't torture low-level drug offenders like Vince. That's true, that's good. I can't imagine being the parent of a political prisoner in Cameroon or Syria or Russia.

One upside of working directly with torture survivors is that the therapists see the whole person and they see him or her recover. People are not just torture survivors. They want to get their studies or careers back on track. They make jokes, have hobbies, go to church, and they need to have fun and have friends like everyone else.

That Race Issue

-Vince-

Bad news of the week. I'm still in prison. And my roommate went to a different prison. My new cellie, well, he's been here 5 days and hasn't showered or cleaned his bunk area.

As I hope Ma would back up, I have no tolerance for racism, ignorance, or intolerance. At some point in life I've had friends I'll never forget of all colors and shapes. I was told before I arrived here that prison makes people racist. Although I can tell you with confidence that nothing is going to make me racist, I can see where they are coming from.

Please don't jump the gun. I'm not talking about any particular race, creed, religion....ok, I'm sorry, I lied. The hatred that spews from the mouths of the white people is awful. Of course I couldn't possibly mean all white people. I have found my crowd. But we steer clear of the "Brothers" aka Skins. No offense, to all good people of any race, but there are some truly useless, no good assholes inside, and outside, of these walls. And maybe because of who I am and where I have been, most of them seem to be white. Or maybe it is because I have not seen a rapist that wasn't white. But hey, that's just in prison. Or maybe it's me just focusing on anything that takes my thoughts away from my problems. I don't know.

OK, I'm putting the pen down for a bit. I have to help my cellie out with something that I will write about in just a bit. Pretty cool.

Later: So the Department of Corrections actually does provide a number of services that seem quite helpful. My favorite, even though it does not apply to me, allows an inmate to write to a hearing officer at the Department of Motor Vehicles to ask that all fines and fees be absolved as part of his sentence. This means that as soon as a prisoner is released, they are eligible to take whatever tests are necessary to get their license back, or just have a clean start. I'm sure some of you out there know how much of a burden it can be to be paying fines. Well, now a portion of our time is for that. And of course it does not apply to someone with a vehicle-related offense such as D.U.I or vehicular manslaughter. I say bravo.

I can hear some of you out there saying, "Prisoners are bad. Prisoners eat babies. Maybe everybody should get off the hook for their tickets." I invite you to spend one night here with me.

Never Just One Thing

-Anne-

Did I mention that my sister has Stage 4 colon cancer? It's never just one thing, is it. Notice that's not a question. When I write a grant proposal, it's called "providing the context." So the main event in my life is Vince being in prison. And on top of that, my sister has cancer.

Or, is the main event that my mom has totaled two cars within a span of a few months, causing multiple hairline fractures of her spine (thankfully not killing herself or injuring anyone else), which means she's in pain all the time and has to wear a brace and use a walker and can't drive anymore or do most of the things she used to enjoy, like go for a walk?

Or wait, is the predominant thing in my life that my sister's roof leaks, she can't work, and she's overwhelmed by bills, housework, two teenage kids, and an abusive ex-husband? That's on top of the radiation, surgery, having to wear an ostomy bag that keeps falling off, chemotherapy, more surgery, being told she's cured, being told it's back, more chemo, more surgery to come, then more chemo....

Or is it my own apartment, because the maintenance guy who came in to fix the slow kitchen drain punctured the pipe, causing a flood that necessitated the entire room be torn up for—no sink or dishwasher, floor and countertops gone—for seven weeks. A yellow tape across the door that said "Do Not Enter". A little comic relief: I complained to the building manager about having to wash dishes in the bathroom sink. His suggestion was that I put my dirty dishes in a shopping cart, take them via elevator to an empty apartment on another floor, wash them there, then take them back to my place. And this is a "luxury" apartment building.

To practice self-care, I went for a hike along the banks of the Mississippi. It was muddy and I thought, "It's slippery here—someone could fall!" And then the someone was me. Torn knee ligament. Crutches for a month. Here is where I will admit that I love an inanimate object–my car, my beloved turquoise Mini Cooper—which a manual transmission. I found a coworker who traded cars—her old tan sedan was an automatic. The battery died the next day. The engine light kept coming on. The plastic under sheath, which I had never even known existed on every car, came off while I was going 80 on the interstate. That'll make you feel you are really alive!

And so it seems that challenges just fan out and out and on and on. Going to work at a torture treatment center feels like going to a spa right now, although I sure am having a hard time concentrating. So then I worry I will lose my job, but I can't even focus on that for very long; my worry jumps back and forth from my mom to Vince to my sister and back and all over the place, like a ping pong ball in a clothes dryer.

Drug Sentences

-Vince-

The amount of time some people are sentenced to for drug problems is absurd. I've never spelled that word and I feel as though I've done so incorrectly. But…my neighbor here, with a wife and two kids, got caught with a little bit of coke—one gram—think one packet of sugar. And because of a drug charge 13 years before, he's gone for 64 months. Another, convicted of making meth a dozen years ago, caught with a thimble full 6 months ago: 88 months.

Used to be the court system forced people into treatment. They realized treatment didn't work, but for the wrong reason. Treatment worked for me, one time, for 4 years and 11 months, because I wanted it. I was done, at least for a bit. But people these days go straight to prison. Some people really do realize the gravity of their mistakes when they're arrested. They tell the judge, prosecutors and their lawyers that they want to go to treatment and they are shot down. Sad.

Laws are now written in such a way that, me personally, I never sold any drugs to anybody wearing a wire, nor did I sell any drugs to a cop or informant. But I was still charged with 1st Degree Sales. No drugs were on my person, or in my car. I never admitted to having or using any drugs. If I had gone to trial and been convicted, I would have received 98 months because they found an empty box that had contained a scale and more than 10 sugar-packet-sized baggies of meth in the hotel room.

I may come off as being bitter, because I am. Mostly because my actions are responsible for Katie being locked up. But I am happy that my drug use is over for now. I say that because I have not yet been sober for this entire day. And sobriety is one day at a time for now.

Do I want to stay sober after boot camp? Yes. Will I? No fucking clue. Sometimes the beast is stronger than I am. My problem is not one I can just hand over to Jesus or God and then ignore it. Mine is a work in progress. A learning experience, if you will. Tempt me with a minnow and I may bite. Try to help me and I may run. I'm just starting to figure myself out, and I can be a real mother fucker. And I'm going to write it all down for your pleasure.

****

-Anne-

Vince tells me he got a notice that he had received a letter from me and it was destroyed. My heart pounds with impotent anger. What had I said? He explains that it had probably been something physical about it that could have conceivably been used to smuggle drugs. Had I sent him a card that had layers glued together? Or something with stickers? Stickers. That was it. I had a running joke with a friend in England about grey vs. red squirrels, and she had sent me a packet of lovely red squirrel stickers as a joke. I had plastered them all over a letter to Vince, and they had shredded it and sent him a notice. Why not photocopy it and give him the copy? Why even tell him he was missing something? That was just plain cruel.

Visiting Rules

-Anne-

In order to visit a prisoner, you have to fill out a form and be approved. This can take "several weeks", whatever that means.

So I go to the website to get the form and it advises me to review the rules for visitors, which is seven pages long. There is a separate grid that lists the consequences of breaking various rules.

There is the obvious stuff like, I'm not allowed to bring him a birthday cake with a file baked into it. I'm not allowed to bring in drugs, tobacco, weapons or ammo or simulated weapons or escape paraphernalia. I guess that rules out that coil of rope I was going to give him for his birthday, ha ha.

Long list of clothing restrictions, including those related to gangs, like "no hoodies."

Once I'm in, I am not allowed to threaten or use abusive language … ooh, I can't use written abuse, either. I'm not allowed to bring anything in, not even my car keys or a Kleenex, so how would I write something abusive anyway?

My favorites: No masturbation, mutual masturbation, oral sex, or sexual intercourse in the visiting area. There is a whole nother set of rules for child visitors.

This is going to be a whole new world for me, I think, unenthusiastically. I assume many of these rules were written because someone did something that was "disturbing to others" to use their term. I fill out the form and mail it in. At least there's no charge for this, as there is for writing, calling, and emailing.

PS: I just found out I'll be going to Turkey, Jordan, Israel, and the Occupied Palestinian Territories for work over the next couple of months. I want to give the prison-visiting experience the full attention it deserves, so most of the posts for the next month will be Vince's, until I have time to dedicate to writing.

Happy Holidays

-Vince-

Happy Labor Day! Today is a special day for prisoners. We get two meals instead of three and no recreation time, and no showers. But the same number of guards, if not more, are on duty. Who wouldn't want to get time and a half?! Not even those of us on the cleaning crew get to leave our cells today. I am jealous of those lucky enough to have TVs. I would go steal one from the guy three cells down, here for sexual assault of his 16-year-old niece, but here they call that extortion. I would be punished rather than rewarded. I wonder if the COs tell people on the outside that they protect child molesters and rapists. Personally, I would be embarrassed.

I mentioned us only having two meals today. Well they are pretty big meals. Brunch consisted of one cup of cereal, 16 oz of milk, 8 oz of OJ, coffee (horrible), two English muffins, a cinnamon roll, two turkey-sausage patties, two slices of American "cheese", scrambled eggs and what I think may have been an attempt at a potato-less corned-beef hash with turkey instead of beef. I feel fatter having written that. I do not know what dinner has in store for me but I know it is just as much.

****

Food. How I miss being a cook. I have held many jobs over the years. Not all of them in some form of food service, but most of them. I have been in charge of kitchens that smoothly put out a thousand plates in a day, and some that couldn't find 100 people to sit down on a Saturday night. From The Boulevard in Palm Beach, FL to The Riverside on the Root in Lanesboro, MN, I have put out hundreds of thousands of plates, some pretty, some not so much. But as I recall, it all started because my Mother had chosen to become a vegetarian.

If you have never visited Lanesboro, do so before you die. I have had the privilege not only of living there, but working in the two busiest restaurants in town. Although the population is only 788, the summer tourists easily triple that number and on Buffalo Bill weekend, an estimated 10,000 people invade the town. And they all must be fed.

Commonly called terrorists by the locals, the tourists are a breed of horrible spandex-wearing monsters that kick puppies and drink lattes. Blood does not course through their veins, rather some thick, vomitous ooze that would otherwise be found greasing the wheels on some kind of horrible machine at a concentration camp. But much to my amazement, they still eat human food.

If you ever find yourself on a beautiful trail in the middle of the woods, slowly passing streams, bridges, cliffs, and all forms of beauty on your bicycle, do us all a favor. Before you stop in any

41

town, take a quick peek at what you're wearing. If in fact it is Spandex like I suspect, know this: we can all see your penis. Especially those of us sitting down to eat when you come in for free water and to take a dump in our restroom. It's not just an outline. It's your penis, covered only by a super thin flexible fabric, leaving nothing to the imagination. With that, I'm DONE with the subject. Shit, one last thing. Take your fucking helmets off when you go into a business!! Nobody is going to hurt you, as much as they may want to!

Without customers, of course, I wouldn't have had jobs. Losing many jobs over the years has always been my fault. A lot of them from stealing whatever I could. Some from pure laziness. Much like the restaurant industry, street-level pharmaceutical sales always has customers. And it has always been my back - up. I've always been good with people, even though I don't really like too many of them. Every time I was fired from a job I would go back to my street job. Not always successfully, and in the long run, of course, ultimately a failure. Was my last time my last time? I truly believe that I want to be done forever. Just like I did in 2001.

And we hop, skip, and jump to the next subject! I don't transition well.

Today is my first day on house crew with full privileges. Essentially, starting at 2:30, I don't have to be in my cell. I get to use the phone during all flag periods. I can shower any time, when there isn't a line of 80 people trying to get into five showers. Yesterday I showered alone for the first time in two months. The shower area is open and I can be seen by all guards and about half of the unit. But I wasn't surrounded by naked guys.

A quick note: Almost everybody drops the soap more than once per week. Fact is, soap is slippery. We all laugh and make jokes. That's as far as it goes.

Tick Tock Doc

-Vince-

Today I finally saw the Optometrist. I learned two things from him. One, that my astigmatism is what he called "rare," meaning it is very rare to come across such an oblong set of eyes. Must run in the family. And two, that I had actually been scheduled to see him twice but was removed from the list because I am supposedly leaving this facility soon.

It takes roughly two weeks to get glasses once you've seen the doc. So I'm excited to be able to see again. And I am also thrilled to get the insider tip about my departure. If I get my red box today, that would mean I am going to Moose Lake until I am approved for boot camp. (A red box is the basic items prisoners are transferred with— to be described when I actually get one.)

I have, however, learned to not get excited about anything here until it actually happens. Even eating. If I think we will be fed lunch at 11:30, it won't happen until 1. Since 2:30, my starting time for work, I have been in my cell all but 20 minutes. It's only 3:15 with the majority of the days' activities to come, but you see what good getting excited did me….4:00 and still in my cell…. And if I think I'm going to see the optometrist in July, it's September…and so on. So for now, I'll wait to shit my pants.

Tonight we get to go out to the big recreation area. That is where I get to let out all, if any aggression I have stored in me. Softball is by far my favorite activity here. Last week we were denied the opportunity because we were locked down. They never tell us why.

During a lockdown we are not allowed to leave our cells for any reason. No showers. No phones, nothing. Food is brought to us in traditional carry-out three-compartment Styrofoam containers, although I can assure you, you would never order the contents within.

Things can start to get stinky quickly without showers as there is no air flow and the temperature is usually 10-15 degrees warmer than it should be. People with money are lucky enough to buy fans for their rooms, while the rest of us enjoy the ability to take off our t-shirts, which still does not churn the air. Most days are worse than others but winter is on the way.

Justice and Jesus

-Vince-

I just got the most important letter of my life from Katie today. Because of my testimony and the fact that I took prison over probation she pled guilty to a 5th Degree Possession and received a sentence of time served! Because she had that Department of Corrections hold I wrote about in a previous post, she will still be locked up for six more months, but I am free. My soul is free. I'm crying I am so happy. I hope you people never know the burden I've had on me. But it's over! When I read her letter the first time, I felt as if my heart had beat for the first time since December. OK, now I'm focused on boot camp! Fuck I feel great. I mean, you know as great as I can feel in prison. But I finally feel that I'm here for the right reason, I mean the *just* reason.

Today is Day 2 of my rigorous training program. Yesterday I did like 40 pushups. Not bad for an out-of-shape 35 year old man who weighs 210 pounds. Progress, not perfection. I made what I estimate to be a 15-pound weight by filling a 3-gallon garbage bag half full of water, tying it up, and putting that in several more bags to protect from leaks. And then put that in a laundry bag so I can do curls. It doesn't weigh all that much but if I do enough of them…it hurts.

On Sunday I went to the chapel for a Christian Ministry service thing because the chapel has air conditioning and comfy seats. I figured I could get in a good nap. Negative. Apparently the pastor is half deaf and the AC must have been fucking with his hearing aid so he was yelling over nothing and kept telling what I could only assume were jokes about a resurrection, zombie Jesus, ghosts, and god—oh my!

I was the only one laughing. I don't think I'll go back. But I don't need to. Here's the best part. I said some prayers during his routine that he asked us to repeat along with him. Now my soul is saved and absolved and—don't go around telling people this because I feel a little bashful—but I have a reservation in heaven!

If I write the judge that sentenced me do you think that she will let me go since J.C. already did my time? Or do you think maybe it's all just a sham and won't actually apply in the real world? A lot of good questions....

I'm not one for organized religion, never have been. My official religion here is N/A.

Speaking of that other N.A., I have been attending weekly AA/NA meetings and for the first time last week, I was there for something other than the air con; I went for me. The meeting lasted two hours and when it was over I felt that feeling I used to get when I left meetings years ago. And although I couldn't go anywhere afterwards for late night coffee, I still felt better than I had in awhile.

****

-Anne-

A reader asked, after reading this post, if Vince was being released. No, When he says he is "free" he is only referring to his guilt being relieved because his plea agreement meant less time for Katie. His sentence remains the same.

Love on the Line

-Vince-

I occasionally notice certain things that seem unbelievable. Like I can't believe I have not heard one song in two months. No music at all. Or, when I was in Olmsted County Jail, I hadn't seen a tree for

45

over a month. Things people take for granted but to the extreme. I haven't seen a bear in years but most people could say the same. Music is such a part of life. It is in everything we do. Around us all the time. And now I hear only the music in my head. It's just not the same.

To clear up a couple things ma said in an earlier blog post: I was at no point looking at 11 years. Katie was, due to her criminal history. If I had taken my case to trial and lost, I could have received a maximum of 117 months (almost 10 years) but that would only be a worst-case scenario. Let's say the task force had spent a year investigating me, had several controlled buys on me, and had to dress up and use grenades to blow down the door to my meth lab and hooker hut and then found me with guns and the President's daughter doing a line off my dick. I still would have more likely seen about 86 months. That's about 54 months with good time. Eligible for boot camp in 48 months. More time, yes. But I'm glad I plead out.

Ma was spot on about one thing. For me, Florida was a state of mind. I never wanted to leave. I knew that if Minnesota made me stay in MN on probation, it would lead to an inevitable relapse. Florida is where I grew up. Where I first learned how to be a friend. And how to have friends.

Growing up I had a tough time keeping friends. We seemed to move around a lot. I think I spent my time trying to make new friends in new places more than trying to hang on to old friendships. Something I still do to this day. Some of the people I have been closest to in my life I can discard without feeling. Family, friends, it doesn't seem to matter. It's not what I would call a conscious decision. It just happens. I'm not going to blame it, or anything, on my upbringing. That would be cheap.

I'll say this: sometimes I wish I could take an ice cream scoop and remove the part of my brain that doesn't care about anything. But idiot doctors say that is far more complicated than it sounds. I lack the surgical tools to remove my scalp and skull and that gross gray layer to get to my brain, and cannot legally obtain the anesthetic necessary to do it.

Back to Florida. I was surrounded by support. Everybody I knew had a sober existence. To me, true sobriety meant I wasn't trying to be sober anymore; I was living sober. Meetings, sure. Softball in a sober league, fuck yeah!

My friends and I were part of an enormous network of like-minded individuals. By that I mean if we decided to stray, we would seek out our other comforts, our drugs of choice. But as a pack, nobody wanted to stray. I believe to this day I would still be sober if I had stayed put. But I am not ashamed of anything that has happened since my relapse either. I am constantly learning. Unfortunately, I seem to learn from the same mistake more than a few times. Or do I?

As much as I know I want to be sober when I get out, a part of me sits in here and reminisces about the very few good high times. I am going to need a strong support group again. Katie and I plan on being together when I get out. But if she's using then, as she knows, I will not be there. I have a pretty good feeling she wants sobriety too. We have been through a lot together over the last eight months, even though we have only actually seen each other a handful of times in passing at the county detention center.

While I was out on bail we spoke almost nightly for a while. Illegally of course, because we were co-defendants.

You see. Some criminals are smart. Technically, Katie received mail from my alter-ego, Damon Martinez. And when she called me, it was after midnight from her job in the jail laundry room. Those calls, to our knowledge, were not recorded. I thought it was funny that her code name was Katy, instead of Katie. I would hear the standard prison jail operator greeting say I had a call from Katy, and I would accept and yell at her and she would say, "Oh baby, it's a different spelling." And that's where we fell in love. On the phone. I was on the road dealing drugs all night, she was in jail and I was on bail. And we fell in love.

Sundays

-Vince-

Today begins with Styrofoam. Breakfast delivered is a good sign that once again we will have no outside recreation, no showers, no AA/NA, no fun at all. Oh shit, no library! These are the days I really look forward to getting mail. Which of course means there will be none. Ugh.

I don't know why we're locked down, of course. But I do know that it's not my fault. I'm soooo bored.

Sundays are alright for one reason only. Breakfast. Cornbread and syrup. A southern delight. I traded my fish-oil pills so I'm up early drinking coffee. They just called warning for chow over the speakers. Oooh baby I can almost taste it.

I will also likely get a good amount of writing done today. Not just because of the coffee, but because I'm not getting out of the cell until 13 hours from now, aside from the 15-minute meal times. Nobody counts the meals as out time because we are not allowed to do anything before, during, or after chow.

Seating is not up to us either. I have twice been sent back to the unit because I refused to sit at the cho-mo table. I don't think it's fair for the COs to face that situation, but like I've said before, MN protects child molesters and actually takes proactive steps to let them mingle with us. For example, they do not have to register as a predator within the prison system. I'm five cells down from a guy I was in jail with in Rochester for flying all the way from Texas to have sex with a 13-14 year old girl. Sadly for him, all he met was the host and camera crew of "How to Catch a Predator." Sentenced to seven years although he denies it because he never actually had sex with her. The fact (unsubstantiated but probable) that he had four felony points gives him the seven years. Had it been his first time....probation.

I just realized another reason I enjoy Sunday mornings. Quiet. Sooo quiet. On weekdays, announcements start at 8am. People going to work, school, to see the doctor, going various places. All of them called by name over the PA system. This unit houses 160 men. Roughly 70% have daily obligations. I get back from breakfast at 7:30. Just as I'm about to fall back asleep they start. I wouldn't care if I had something to do. But I just sit in my cell. All day. Listening to that and the unending chatter. The black people each fighting to be louder than the next one. The natives making astoundingly life-like bird calls (that can actually be pretty cool). People calling out chess moves to cells 100 feet away. The PA system telling people to be quiet. One hundred sixty simultaneous voices yelling, "Fuck you!" (Including me. Yeah, I'm a part of something!) And the noise of the fans joining all the ingredients together in a harmonious fruit cake recipe.

But not on Sunday. Today only the noise of the fans parts the silence. It is so consistent though it's as if it weren't there. Every 30 minutes a CO drones by paying attention only to walking straight and looking buff. I do not comment because it looks like he could easily pull me through the bars. Like Wylie Coyote, my body breaking into neat cubes and my eyeballs bouncing on top of the stack and blinking in astonishment. Yes, I'm simply more creative on coffee Sundays!

I also accomplish a lot of air guitar and air drums on Sundays. Right now, actually a minute ago I was playing the guitar solo to one of my favorite songs, the "Fletcher Memorial Home" by *Pink Floyd*. I don't have a radio or TV but one learns to hone the mind in prison. I can hear it note for note, even as I write. But now my mind skipped over the rest of that track and to the next CD, David and David's "Welcome to the Boomtown". Another favorite of mine. I need a radio. Sadly they cost $17.00 and I only have 11 cents. A 13" LCD TV in here costs $210. About $140 over retail, but about 50% of the inmates have them here.

49

Zorba the Greek

-Vince-

Yeah! Indigent canteen time. Add to inventory: one 1.5 ounce bar of Bob Barker soap, two #10 envelopes, one manuscript envelope, 35 sheets college-rule paper, two safety pens, and a single disposable razor.

Each week, indigent offenders are allowed to order one over-the-counter item such as aspirin (100-count for 97 cents). Melatonin, anti-dandruff shampoo, etc. This week I chose the 120-count Ultra EPA/DHA Fish Oil Supplements. These OTCs are what we poor people trade for what we really need. This bottle sells to a prisoner for $5.77. I trade away half of it for half price. I get an envelope, and a couple spoons full of coffee crystals. Next week I am getting the jackpot. A box of Prilosec, $14.77. Hopefully I can get deodorant and a few ramen noodles for that. Oh by the way, in prison, ramen is gold.

I should mention that St. Cloud is the only prison that has all day lock down. All others, people are essentially free to roam as they choose. You can spend four hours outside. Wherever I end up will not have any fences. Actually, whenever I get to boot camp, there will be no fences. All other facilities for men are enclosed. Did you know that the only female prison in MN, Shakopee, has no fences? Since it opened, only one person has escaped.

Of course the more severe offenders are not allowed outside at St. Cloud. There are indoor courtyards too, surrounded by high walls and some barbed wire. Anywho, like I was saying, St. Cloud is the intake prison for all males in MN. Once I leave for another facility, unless I am taken to a county jail for storage, I will have many more programs, opportunities, and…I don't really know what yet, available to me.

In my head, the song "Welcome to the Boom Town"…"Handsome Kevin got a little off track. Took a year off of college and he never went baaack. Now he smokes way too much, got a permanent haze...deals dope outta Denny's, keeps a table in the baaaack. He always listens to the ground. He always listens to the ground! So I say...welcome! Welcome to the boom town!"

That part kind of reminds me of...me. Although Perkins was a little more likely. Listen to that song once and you'll be hooked. And now I will write for you the ingredients of my ideal mixed tape. That song, plus "Keep on Smilin'" by *Wet Willie*, "Burning Sky", by *Bad Company*. "We are Young" by *F.U.N.* "Angel", by *Jimi*. "Son of a Preacher Man", not by *Janice*. Sorry hun, *Aretha* is better. "Cry Baby", by *Janice*. "Rubber Biscuit", by the *Blues Brothers*. "It's All Too Much", the *Beatles*. "Suck My Kiss", *Red Hot Chili Peppers*. "I Just Had Sex", by *the Lonely Island*. "One time One Night", by *Los Lobos*. And "Zorba the Greek", the *Herb Alpert* version from "Lock Stock and Two Smoking Barrels".

I'm not saying there aren't better songs out there. But all of those on one CD, I could listen to repeatedly. Alright, I have to write a couple letters to other folks now. So, until next time. Enjoy all of your freedoms. I hope you never have to learn how much they actually mean.

****

-Anne-

Zorba the Greek? How weird. Because my dad had the soundtrack to the movie and used to play the album over and over and over...while slowly getting sloshed. One night I couldn't sleep. I went downstairs and my dad sat me on his lap and we listened to Zorba together. And no, there was nothing creepy about it. The next night I did the same thing but he was already drunk and flew into a rage, calling me a god-damned fucking little shit and chasing me upstairs. I remember feeling very small and very alone, crying under my covers in the dark. Well, I was small—6 or 7 years old. I have no idea where my mother was, probably hiding under her bed.

Cellular Data

-Vince-

I complained enough to the house staff about my smelly cellie that I finally got a room all by myself! It's all the way up on the 4th tier, so it's really hot, but I'm okay with that. No longer will I wake up in the middle of the night and see someone pooping three feet away, and staring at me. Nor will I have to point out to him, daily, that showers do not bite. It is nice up here.

If I could draw, I would, but I can barely write (although the copy of "Eats, Shoots & Leaves: The Zero Tolerance Approach to Punctuation" that I found in my new room will surely help with punctuation).

I will try to describe my room and what I can see from my cell as I sit at my metal desk.

The bed starts directly behind me, and is six feet by two and a half feet and three inches thick. Directly in front of me, above the desk about one foot, is an electrical outlet with two plug-ins and a switch that leads to the light next to it. To the left of the desk and attached is a six-foot-tall steel locker. I keep all my hygiene stuff in there and hang my hand-washed clothes to dry on the hooks. To my left is the sink, that produces only extremely hot water or fairly warm water. It's what I drink because my choices are limited to that. And next to the sink, behind me and to the left, sits the porcelain god. No crown of course. Unfortunately too many people have been injured or killed in the past by toilet seats. So we sit on the cold white surface. The walls are all white-painted brick. High gloss. Probably 30-40 layers. And the small grey shelf above my bed houses my paperwork and my books.

Outside my cell I see seas of bars. Directly outside is the four-foot walkway with five horizontal bars and every eight feet a much thicker post that links them all. The railing is about four and a half feet tall to prevent people from easily being thrown over. Beyond that, everything is brick, and glass, barred windows with a view of the fenced-in area that serves as the recreation area for offenders in segregation, the narrow brick shell of the corridor to the mess hall, and juuuussst a little patch of grass along the wall. The ceiling is also brick but it is arched. It honestly looks like it should have fallen down years ago but the paint holds it together. And that's pretty much my view for 22 hours a day. Except on Saturdays and Sundays, then it's 23.

Rant to Rock

-Vince-

I just finished reading a strange but fascinating novel by Chuck Palahniuk called Rant. Give it a go if you haven't yet. But prepare yourself …especially if you have a weak stomach. I am now reading Be Cool by Elmore Leonard. By comparison, I read the Crichton novel Airframe, 431 pages, in one day. It has taken me the same amount of time to struggle through 150 pages of nothing but dialogue by Leonard. I think it's because all my brain does is imagine two people talking. Don't get me wrong. It's great dialogue, and a damn good movie, but the book….well. I'll finish it because I'm in prison. Tim Dorsey and Dean Koontz remain my favorite authors followed by Michael Crichton.

****

Tension is rising within the gangs. I have no idea what any of them are called, but two of the rival black gangs are feuding. I was about two feet away from a near fight between what I later found out were the prison leaders of their respective gangs. I would have been badly injured just being close to a large fight. The COs do not care who is involved. We lost all of our rights at sentencing. There are always plenty of staff available and they come out of nowhere. Tackle people, mace, and otherwise render senses useless.

I made it past the stare down and about halfway up the four flights of stairs to my galley when I heard elevated voices and the dee-doo-dee-doo-dee-doo noise that their communications devices make when a fight breaks out. I also later learned that it was just a little pushing and shoving. But the COs don't care. They came and took the two gang leaders to the hole. That will have little effect on the overall atmosphere. If there's going to be a gang fight, it's already planned.

(We got to go outside. Next subject: "How to send money to an inmate")

Of course anything that takes the COs' focus off of whatever they do inevitably means even more time stuck in our cells. We're already five minutes late for going out to the courtyard, where I play volleyball. With no sign—oops, here we go. Write later.

****

No matter where you are, who you are, or who you are sending money to in the Minnesota prison system, you will do it incorrectly. At least on the first try. I'm here to help. And I would like you all to try using my instructions.

No matter where in MN your prisoner lives, all money needs to be mailed to Moose Lake. If you send anything else to Moose Lake like a letter or a letter in the same envelope as the money, it will be denied and sent back to you. The address is PO Box 1000, Moose Lake, MN 55767.

Do not send cash or a personal check. It will be denied and sent back to you. Only send cashier's checks or money orders. The USPS sells money orders up to $500 for about $1.50. And you're at the post office. Perfect place to mail it out. The money order should be filled out with the abbreviation code of the prison; mine would be: MCF-SCL and made payable to the prisoner with his name followed by Offender ID number. If anything is wrong at all and there is no return address the money is kept as part of the cost of confinement, and the prisoner may not be notified. Place the properly-filled-out

54

money order or cashier's check and Nothing Else in the envelope and do your best to get it to Moose Lake by Thursdays. We only get to use our money once a week. But we appreciate any amount, any day.

****

My day was just made. I was coming back from getting my medication, and paused by my neighbor's door. He noticed, and I said, "Sorry, I haven't seen TV in so long, I just wanted to take it in." He laughed. Then he said, "You don't have anything?" I shook my head. And he gave me a radio! Complete with ear buds (no speakers allowed for any electronics here).

The first song on once I find 103.7 The Loon is something new and terrible by Robert Plant. Then a pause, then the "Immigrant Song". Rock n' roll, baby! I'm happy now. Music...oooh love hurts...

Hear Today, Gone Tomorrow

-Vince-

I got my last letter to Katie back in the mail today which means she is finally out of that horrible jail. I should find out soon if she's free or back in prison somewhere else to finish out her term on her last charges.

I'm excited for her. She's had a tough life. Yah, yah, yah, she's made some bad choices. They didn't affect you so keep it to yourself. She's a good girl. And I truly hope she's making good choices if she is out there.

I learned a lot in one hour on the radio. Tomorrow's forecast. Sale of the Century at every car dealership. Every day. My all-time favorite band is Pink Floyd. They haven't put out an album since the 1900s. I believe they are all in their 70s. And they have decided to put out a new album. I mean...that's pretty bold. If there's even one song about world hunger, poverty, or something in the world being broken, let's all get together and fix that, I'm gonna shit.

****

I have to complain about one thing. Although it is truly amazing to be able to drown out the sound of people yelling back and forth with music on my radio, the commercials are almost as bad. Carrier Air Conditioning uses professional baseball players, naturally from the MN Twins, to advertise for them. Comparing everything about Carrier to the sport. The service is a "home run," and they're going to "strike out" the old prices, and come meet the "rookie of the year" on the sales team! Get it? Do you get it? A home run is good. So the service must be good. But in all reality, and in comparison to it, a home run is actually very rare. A good season will yield 30, out of 600 at-bats. So what he's saying is, five percent of the times you buy air conditioners in your life, you'll get good service. Maybe that's just how I see it. But I only looked at the facts. Fact is, I'm in prison. I shouldn't complain, but I just did.

What I could say, and I will, is that the food here is a home run!

****

Fuck my life. I should have mentioned that it is against company policy to have a radio in your room if you didn't purchase one from the canteen, which I did not. When electronics arrive they are engraved with the OID number and the offender's last name. So my guess is my neighbor and I will be getting Loss of Privileges. I will find out soon. I went out only for five minutes to get my pill and I came back and it was gone. $17 that wasn't even mine. These guards are assholes. I know I'm supposed to follow the rules. But I think it's a little ridiculous. My neighbor has plenty of money. Wasn't using his radio. And I have none, and he went out of his way to help out a fellow inmate. Well I suppose the right thing to do is take all of the LOP if they let me. He shouldn't be punished for being kind.

The First Time

-Vince-

It was November or December of 1997. I was making a living selling weed, acid, and mushrooms. I had a side-job I liked equally—stealing high-end bicycles from local sporting goods stores in St. Paul. By high-end I mean $2,000-3,000 each. All fitted with the latest in gas shocks, hydraulic brake systems, Diore XP derailleurs, and of course the cheapest plastic banana seat possible.

I was doing pretty well. One cold morning I walked up to the Schwinn bike shop with the intention of riding away with a $1,000 profit. Sadly for me, there was a lot of traffic in the store. Employees and customers everywhere. But I wasn't going to let that stop me. The bike I wanted wasn't available so I decided to grab what I could. Bad move. I took it off the rack, wheeled it out the door, and off came the chain. I remember my legs spinning the pedals really, really fast. Then the employee came from behind. He gently stopped me and brought me back into the store. There was no point in running. He was bigger than me, and George the barber next door saw me and knew me.

So there I sat in the back of the store waiting for the police. One officer arrived and asked me a couple questions and that was it. I was arrested for Felony Theft of over $500 and taken to the St. Paul Police Dept. Today it remains the most disgusting place I have ever been.

No sheets, no pillow, just a blanket to protect me from years of detainees' sweaty bodies. The stainless steel toilet no longer reflected light. The floors sticky with unknown substances. I know this: It was not from food.

****

-Anne-

57

The jail must not be that disgusting. Six years earlier, when he was 13, he and an 11-year-old best-friend David burst into the house, shaking with fear because they'd been caught in the act of cutting a hood ornament off a caddy and the owner had slammed David's arm in the car door—hard. I conducted a search of Vince's room and found a box brimming with hood ornaments in his closet. David's mom and I took them to the St. Paul Police Dept, hoping they'd be "scared straight," as they say. The cops locked them up in an empty cell for about 10 minutes. They seemed scared, alright, and David's mom and I congratulated ourselves on our great tough love strategy and thought that would be the end of it.

Yeah, Yeah, Whatever

-Vince-

My neighbor and I got six days each for the radio. Loss of privileges is just that. No phone, no outdoor activities. Since those are literally the only privileges we have it may not sound so bad, but that brings our out-of-cell time per day to meals and medication. They cannot prevent me from going to religious services and, I believe, AA/NA. This'll really show us. I tried to take all 12 days but they said no. The neighbor shrugged it off. I'm glad about that.

I did sign up for the library last night and I hope we're allowed to go to that. Reading is my only option for in-cell entertainment. They can't take that away, can they? I tell ya. The service here is a home run!

****

Back to my first arrest. I sat in the cold, dark, disgusting holding pen of the SPPD only for a few hours until we were all chained together and driven to the nearby Ramsey County Adult Detention Center. They crammed us all in one room, which smelled like hot dogs and wet dogs, and left us for hours. Every now and then they would call people out. Bring more in. But not me. I stayed in there the whole

58

night. I dared not use the bathroom in fear of contracting a mixture of rabies and syphilis. I now know the reason they did not take me out. It was my first crime ever, and I was going to be released after arraignment in the morning.

After I was seen by the judge, I was released right from the courtroom. I don't believe they do that anymore. I walked from the jail to the place I was staying, a couple miles away, and sat on the toilet for a bit. That was a helluva walk with the internal waste containers full.

Eventually, through the legal system, I was sentenced to one year of Project Remand. Upon successful completion of said program, the charge would be dropped to a misdemeanor, and I would move on with my life, felony free.

Yeah. About that.

I wasn't really ever one for following orders or obeying the law.

The first thing they wanted me to do was go to in-patient drug treatment. Since I wasn't addicted to anything other than pot, I surely did not need treatment. And I was kicked out in under a week.

I immediately called my case worker and told her. I was not punished for that, simply told to follow all future directives. I think I lasted maybe a month and I started drinking for the first time in my life. Alcohol is the easiest thing to cheat with because it leaves the body quickly. What I didn't know was that alcohol leads to poor decision making. And I eventually started getting high again and not showing up for my meetings. Turns out they get all pissed off about that sort of thing and issue something called a warrant. The first of many throughout my life.

That first violation was a slap on the wrist. The second time, a few months later, the judge re-structured my sentence. He changed my stay of adjudication into a stay of imposition, and sent me to the work house for a few days. My new sentence gave me one year and one day in prison if I didn't complete three years of probation successfully, which I almost certainly did not. Stay tuned!

A Great Day

-Vince-

A couple great things happened today. Even though I was on LOP I got to go to my AA meeting and I listened to somebody that really had an impact on me. After the meeting I felt great. When I got back to my unit the Sargeant waved me over and offered me the swamper job! That's the house cleaning crew. Pretty much the job everybody hopes for. It pays 25 cents per hour at 80 hours every two weeks. I get half of that and the other half goes to pay my fines and court costs. So that's great news. And I walk up the four flights of stairs to my room and on my bed is a little slip of paper that tells me I finally got some money on my account! From two different people! Thank you both! So I ordered a radio!

What a day. I ordered a whole lot of other things, too. Real toothpaste and deodorant. Good razors. $15 in phone time. $5 in envelopes. Ear buds, so I can actually listen to my radio. Noodles and rice. And my favorite…a half pound bag of Folgers Crystals instant coffee.

It takes nine days to get an order once it has been placed. The price may be right. But fuck you, Bob Barker, your products are just not that great. Sure, technically, we could use our own feces to shave our faces. But we just don't. Much like we don't use your 3-in-1 shampoo, body wash, and shave soap. I heard real soap doesn't have to come with a disclaimer that says, "Made in a factory that also processes peanuts." Bob, you're a legend for one thing. Let's keep it that way.

I moved for the second time in five days. All the way from the top of the north side to the most desired floor—level four of the south side.

My shift doesn't start until 2:30 so I'm in my cell until then. But I am still excited to be here.

Tomorrow morning brings full privileges of the job. Out of my cell. I'm always excited for mail. Thursday I get my radio. And Saturday I get the headphones so I can actually listen to my radio! Like I've said before, the small, petty things are all we have to be excited for. What we all hope for is anything that helps the time fly. Jobs, TVs, radios. Two out of three ain't bad.

****

My first day on the job went well. I still have to serve my LOP so I don't reap the full benefits, but I was out of my cell more than I normally would be, even with the LOP. And I feel as if I got as much exercise as I would have if I had gone out to the ball diamond, what with all the stairs.

The person I replaced left because he got his acceptance letter from boot camp. It took nine weeks and two days to get his letter. He said he won't actually be going to boot camp until March, he's just leaving to be stored somewhere until an opening occurs. Any news is good news. My application was submitted five weeks ago. Reason dictates I should receive my acceptance letter in a month. We shall see.

A side note: Anybody that stays in a MN prison must attend school to get either their high school diploma or General Equivalency Degree (GED). Nobody can move from St. Cloud, including to boot camp, without one.

For me, boot camp will include six months of drug treatment. Four hours per day, six days a week. We also do work out in the community. Repair homes. Shovel entire neighborhoods free of snow by hand. Cut down trees, by hand. Use those trees to construct new homes and new barracks for future offenders. Learn to lead. Learn to follow. Look up the rate of recidivism. I'm sure it's pretty good.

****

-Anne-

When I googled "Minnesota recidivism rates" I found an article titled, "Minnesota Leads Nation in Recidivism." I hoped it meant we were the best at keeping people from returning to prison, but no. "…61 percent of prisoners released in 2004 were back behind bars within three years for committing new crimes or for violating terms of their release. The national average was 43 percent (based on 41 states reporting)…" Damn. But I'm sure Vince will be the exception.

50 Shades of Bored

-Vince-

I mentioned in a previous post that the tension was rising between the black gangs and there may be some gang activity sooner or later. Well that's over. Now, because one dumb-ass white person used the N word, there is racial tension.

The most annoying person on my side of the unit happens to be black; this will change every week or so as people cycle through. He never shuts up. No exaggeration. And a part of me definitely wanted to yell, "Shut the fuck up!" but I never would have inserted that extra word at the end. It's not my style. But I am white. So I am grouped in with the rest of them. So if he was loud before, it's amplified and now he throws in big words like Cracker and Honky. He implied that all of our mothers like N dick. To that I shrugged my shoulders. Go get 'em, ma!

For a Saturday night the unit is relatively calm. The day is almost done. The mellow methodical humming of the fans will become the lullaby that guides me to sleep. I will drift off into fantasies unknown and awake to the same day, every day, with only minor differences that simply appear to be noteworthy because of the setting. Only outside these walls does real life take place.

****

Sunday morning and the COs are doing cell searches. Including strip search. I wonder what they're looking for. My guess, they have nothing better to do. They have never found anything harmful since I've been here. So they will use their "power" and take away our extra towels, then go home and beat their wives. Then go to the bar and brag about being…oops. I was interrupted and searched. My room was destroyed after they read the part above.

When I came back to my cell the guy says, "I read your letter. I'm gonna go home now and beat my wife." And I blurted out, "I was right!" before he had a chance to retract. He was so pissed I could see his face change color. But there isn't a thing he can do.

Nothing was found in any of the 120 cells that stand tall in a giant cluster in the middle of the rectangular-shaped unit. But we are all aware that they are on the prowl. If any uprisings are planned, they have been thwarted for a least a couple days.

* The contents of this, and all previous ideas for blog posts, are entirely fictional. Any resemblance of characters or situations or prisons to those in the real world are coincidental. I do not condone or admit to any criminal activity herewithin.

Rain, Rain

-Vince-

Rain, rain, go away. You're fucking up my plans for the day. Today was going to be the first time I would be able to go to the ball diamond in over a week.

Last night we had another fire somewhere in the prison. They herded us into the cafeteria after taking away our flag time, yet again. They didn't count us, which leads me to believe it was just a drill. It seems like at least twice a week they find a reason to take away the little freedoms we have. One Sunday night they locked us in because of "severe weather." To all of us it looked like a standard light rain. To the COs it was necessary to tell us all to hide behind our mattresses. Of all the people I have spoken with, none so far have admitted to actually doing that.

Just now over the PA they said they are "conducting a B-level Switch In due to visibility." That means they are locking us in our cells because they can't see far outside. I can see outside. I guess I should have thought of all this before I came to prison, right?

****

Yay! I got my radio! I won't complain about commercials this time. I'm grateful to my neighbor for lending me his headphones for that. Headphones aren't engraved. I can't believe Pearl Jam is classic rock. I'm getting old.

****

One thing about the second career that I have chosen, the one that landed me in here, is that I have lost some, if only a few, good friends. Many of them I may see during my stay here. Some, unfortunately, are in Sherburne County, the federal holding facility for Minnesota. I sure am glad I didn't catch a federal case. They routinely hand out sentences of 20-30 years. And you do 90% of your time vs. 66% of MN time. Of course most of the larger sentences are from weapons charges. A lot of time is added to a sentence when a gun is used in the commission of a felony. I don't mean discharged. Just present. Not even on your person, anywhere. Believe it or not, cops lie all the time.

A gun is supposed to be within reach of a person to be chargeable. A gun can be moved from a trunk to a glove box with relative ease by a cop. And when only a suspect questions it, they lose their lives through time served.

In my case, the police moved my wallet with $500 in it. I was in the lobby of the hotel, 60 feet away, around the corner and through a door away from where they found the meth. But they took my wallet to "ID" me. Then they took pictures of my wallet next to the meth. That way they could seize the money. I'm in prison. I've already been convicted and can't be tried again. So I have no reason to lie, do I?

The fact is, police are terrible at their jobs. Not all of them. But if all police were honest and followed procedure, there would be a sharp drop in conviction rates. And we can't have that, can we?

Recidivism, Up Close

-Vince-

82 days since court, I think. I don't know how many days are in each month.

Four days have passed since I wrote the word month. I received several letters from a few of my friends in various jails in various counties so I spent some time writing back to them. If you know anybody in prison, write to them. I can't stress that enough. Even if you're mad at them, tell them you're mad! This is a place where we begin to fix things. We begin to feel again. And I can assure you we think about all the people that have been hurt along the way. But we may be afraid to write. We don't know what to say or how to say what needs to be said.

Katie is back in jail. She was unable to resist the temptation, she got high. That leaves me in prison for no reason. I could have been out on probation, working on my problems from the outside. Maybe I would have fucked up too. But I was not given the chance. I'm pissed. I'm sad. I'm hurt. Yet I am numb as I have always been, to one form of betrayal or another.

The Visit

-Anne-

I'm back from a trip to Istanbul and eager to write about my visit with Vince from a few weeks ago.

First, this photo is not Vince. It's a photo I plucked off the internet of some guy wearing "Instant Weirdo Glasses," a gag gift I have bought myself to give to nieces and nephews.

But it does look very much like Vince with his prison-issue glasses, and I laughed out loud at my first sight of him, thinking it was a joke, then realized they wouldn't sell Instant Weirdo Glasses in a prison commissary, caught myself and felt guilty.

Being taken aback by his appearance after not seeing him for a long time is kind of a pattern. I remember after his relapse after five years of being clean, when he had been MIA for months using meth somewhere, I found him in Lanesboro and was thoroughly alarmed by how black and bottomless his eyes were. Another time, I came home from Kenya to find he had lost his job and everything he owned, including his apartment and all his clothes, and he was wearing an old tattered snowmobile suit and boots with no socks or, presumably, underwear. At least the glasses were good for a laugh. At least he can see.

I had assumed I would cry all the way to St. Cloud, so I'd stolen a box of Kleenex from work and thrown it in the Mini. I left from work to save time, and yet it was still a six-hour undertaking. Two-hours up, a half-hour wait, two hours with Vince, then an hour and a half drive back home.

But it wasn't as bad as I'd thought it would be. I didn't cry at all. I choked up twice but I didn't cry.

The first choke up was when I caught my first look at the prison. Picture the grimmest, bleakest, most Dickensian-style prison you can imagine, and that's it. Granite is grey, after all. You see the wall first.

There are no signs telling you where to go but you can't miss the main building:

Yes, there are bars on all the windows. I had read and re-read the visiting instructions, so I left everything but 50 cents and my car key in the car, hoping my purse would be safe in a prison parking lot. The 50 cents was to pay for a locker in which I would put my car key, because I couldn't bring anything into the visiting room, not even a Kleenex. Although I'm sure other people smuggle all sorts of stuff in, I wasn't going to drive two hours and then get busted for trying to smuggle in a Kleenex.

I felt uncertain walking up to the foreboding main doors but with no signage it was my best guess. I was anxious that I wouldn't be let in, even though I'd been approved, according to Vince. Visitors don't get any notification from the prison saying they've been approved; they leave that up to the inmates. Not the most reliable communicators.

I climbed two flights of stairs and found the reception area. Before I could even think about what I needed to do next, another woman visitor asked me, "First time?" How did she know? She waved me over to a desk where I filled out a form, which I then slid into a drawer with my ID to an officer sitting in a glass booth. He did something on his computer. My anxiety spiked, thinking he'd turn to me and say, "We have no record of your visitor form being received." But he asked me to put my fist into the drawer so he could stamp it with something invisible. Why invisible ink? One of many "whys?" I will not bother to investigate. All that mattered was that I was in.

I'm Not One of You

-Anne-

The officer told me that Vince would have to eat and shower before being allowed to come to the visiting room. Eating and showering would take me at least an hour and a half, but I figured they didn't linger over such things here. I found the lockers and deposited my car key.

I exhaled and was finally able to take in my surroundings. The visiting room was "decorated" in 80s colors—oak furniture with teal and mauve upholstery and grey carpet. All very run down. Not skanky, quite, but shabby. I looked around for interesting details I could write about in the blog but there were none. The only reading material was a rack with brochures about support groups for children whose parents are incarcerated.

And there are plenty of them, if this waiting room was any indication. In the half hour I waited, five kids under the age of three or so waited with their mothers. Four of them were black. Was it good that they were too young to understand? Or by bringing them to visit daddy in prison at such a young age, where they being conditioned to think this was normal and acceptable?

There was an elderly couple. They looked like they were straight off a farm. I wondered who they were here to visit—their son, grandson? Their name was called and he had to clutch his pants to hold them up while they went through the metal detector, since he had to remove his suspenders and place them in a tray to the side.

I felt a strong urge to stand up and yell, "I'm not one of you!"

I know this about myself: One of my defenses when my life feels like a pressure cooker is to adopt a smug, superior attitude to everyone around me. But I keep it inside my head.

It was quitting time, and a stream of employees came out as I waited, scanning their badges, waiting as the bars slowly rolled open, then skirting the metal detector and vamoosing for the weekend. Five or six attractive women came out and I wondered what they did here and why they would work here.

There was a bank of security monitors along one wall. In black and white, hundreds of men inside streamed from point A to point B. The perspective was from above them, and tilted at an angle. It reminded me of leaf cutter ants I had seen in Costa Rica, marching along blindly, down one tree, across a path, and down a hill into a hole.

My last name—Vince's last name—was called over a loudspeaker, mispronounced as usual, and I shot up to walk through the metal detector. The wall of bars slid back and I was inside a sally port—a controlled entry way with glass guard booths on either side and sliding walls of bars on either end. The guard told me to put my hand under a black light so he could see the number stamped on my hand. He escorted me through two more doors of bars, then I was in.

When I'm 64

-Anne-

The visiting room was similar to the waiting room, a mash up of Victorian pillars, graceful arched doorways, bars and bars and more bars, and mauve and teal furniture. The best of the 1880s and 1980s. There was a raised platform with a guards' desk on it with a very bored, very fat guard, and a box of Kleenex.

Chairs were arranged in rows facing each other, about four feet apart. One side was for children, the other for everyone else. There was probably capacity for 100 pairs of prisoners/visitors.

Vince was already seated, and in addition to his new glasses he had narrow sideburns down to his chin. I eventually noticed that most of the guys in the room had facial hair that, well, you don't see every day on the outside. One result of them not having much else to do,

70

and those crappy Bob Barker razors. They were all wearing white T-shirts, faux jeans with elastic waists, and denim long-sleeved shirts. "We joke at breakfast, 'Hey, you wore the same outfit as me!'" Vince said.

This was his opener after we had our one allowable five-second hug and sat down.

The room wasn't full; we had the whole row to ourselves except for one other pair about five seats down. This was what caused me to choke up the second time. The visitor was an elderly lady who reminded me of my mom—well dressed, frail. Her son looked like any middle aged guy who works in your tech support office—balding, slightly paunchy, outdated (but not Instant Weirdo) glasses.

As I was gazing at them, wondering if she was my future, Vince was telling me how prisoners were strip searched before and after each visit. That got my attention and I noticed a line of guys going one-by-one into a room with a guard, who was wearing blue latex gloves.

"Strip searched?" I asked in shock. You mean ….

"No, mom, a strip search. You lift your balls, bend over and cough. It's not a body-cavity search"

He made it sound like a strip search was no big deal, while a body-cavity search was something only real losers had to put up with.

I looked down at the elderly lady again, then looked Vince in the eye. "Don't make me do that when I'm old," I said. He gave a kind of non-response and I knew it would be up to me to decide whether or not to visit him when I was elderly, if he landed in prison again.

I was really surprised, and then disappointed, that a photographer was available to take pictures of prisoners and their visitors, but I hadn't know that, and Vince was short 50 cents credit so we couldn't buy a ticket to have it done. He told me he wasn't allowed to communicate with other prisoners in the visiting room, otherwise he could easily borrow some credit. He asked the guard if he could do that, but the guy shook his head sympathetically, no. Apparently I could have bought credit out in the waiting area. It was all very confusing, and I have a master's degree. But maybe I'm not very street wise.

I could see a young couple across the room posing for photos. Vince told me there were four allowable poses. Three were non-contact and the fourth allowed people to hold hands, but they had to stand at least a foot apart.

Talking Points

-Anne-

What did Vince and I talk about during our visit?

I told him about my sister's cancer, my mom's frailty. We discussed whether drug dealing is a victimless crime or not. He detailed the timeline for being moved to another facility. He talked about chomos (child molesters)—is all the talk about them a way for him to not focus on himself? There was talk of Narcotics Anonymous vs. Alcoholics Anonymous. Vince feels that AA is useless to him since he's a drug addict, not an alcoholic. I felt that AA was better than nothing, and that addiction is addiction. Vince asked me to try to get whatever money was sitting in his unemployment account on a bank card he no longer had. We wondered if he really has bipolar disorder, as he had been diagnosed by Hazelden during his third round of chemical dependency treatment. We agreed he probably doesn't.

I updated him on news of the world, since he didn't get any news until he had his radio. I told him about the protests over the shooting death of Michael Brown by a police officer in Ferguson, Missouri and a viral video taken by a black man in St. Paul who was bullied by the police. "Maybe that explains why there's so much tension lately," he said.

It occurred to me to ask how prisoners with TVs get reception. I have to pay for cable because the government in its wisdom has decided to make it almost impossible for anyone to get broadcast TV, which has been free since television was invented. He thought they got cable, and that the prison was tapping into that illegally. I thought that sounded far-fetched but if you're reading this, Comcast, go get 'em.

I asked him what he thought the purpose of boot camp was, and he said, "punishment." And yet he spoke animatedly about it and was clearly looking forward to it.

****

It wasn't until I was driving to St. Cloud that I realized I hadn't seen Vince for a year and a half. It had been spring, and I went to see him because he'd lost yet another job. This one, cooking at a place called the Bent Wrench, had lasted for a couple years.

One thing I will say for Vince is, he will take responsibility and doesn't ask for anything from me when he's down and out. "I fucked up, again," was his explanation for losing the job. I drove to Lanesboro and rented a side-by-side tandem reclining bike. It was a beautiful spring day and I had brought a cooler with some Strong Bow cider. Vince and I biked along the paths to a rock quarry, then got out and hunted for agates and had a cider.

Then we pedalled back to town and I offered to splurge and get us dinner at the best restaurant, The Riverside. When we walked in, the owner asked Vince how things were, Vince said he was between jobs, and the owner offered him a cooking job on the spot, starting the next day. The guy had clearly had his eye on Vince but didn't want to poach him since it's a very small world down there. The Riverside had been Vince's dream place to work. We had a great meal and I thought, wasn't it great when things just worked out like that?

I had just a few texts from him over the ensuing summer and fall. He was super busy, he said, but loved the job. It wouldn't be good for me to come visit, because he was working so much that he couldn't spend time with me. Now, in prison, he told me he had been working six days a week at the Riverside, but he'd also been dealing drugs all night, every night.

God Help Us, Every One

-Anne-

Merry Christmas! If you're reading this , I'm guessing you're an addict, or you love an addict, or both. There's clearly a tension between the two "sides," especially during this festive season.

It's been a theme throughout my life.

My dad was considered a genius. He never went to college but he picked up computer skills in four years on an aircraft carrier in the Navy. He also had people skills—he could tell jokes, pick up foreign languages, play the guitar, and from all accounts was the life of the party and everyone loved him.

I was born in upstate New York, where he had his first job, at IBM. We moved to Florida, where he worked setting up mainframe computers at NASA. We moved to Minnesota, where he worked for 3M and traveled for them around the world—Australia, Japan, Italy, France, Germany, England. He was appointed as an instructor in the Graduate School of Business at the University of Wisconsin, Madison, on April 19, 1968.

On May 9, 1968 he died of an overdose of paraldehyde and alcohol in a Madison motel room. It was 12 hours from the time of ingestion of the paraldehyde until he essentially drowned in his own lung fluids. He was 32 years old.

I was eight. They said he had died of a stroke. I knew that wasn't true but also knew not to ask any questions.

I went on to become a rebellious teenager. I made a suicide attempt when I was 16, and while I was in the hospital my mother told me the true cause of my father's death. They released me two months later, and I promptly began smoking as much pot and drinking as much alcohol as humanly possible without overdosing. A year later I was pregnant by my drug-dealer boyfriend.

Thus Vince came into the world, and having someone to take care of turned my life around. He was also my insurance policy against trying to kill myself again. I would never do that to a kid.

I finished high school, went to college, got a 2-year degree. I got a job, worked full time, went to night school full time, got my bachelor's degree. I got a better job, then a better one, and then a better one. I bought a car, then a house. Then a better house. I went to grad school and earned a master's degree. I moved to England, came back, bought my Mini Cooper as a souvenir. I've been on an African safari, saw Iggy Pop in concert in the south of France, ate a club sandwich in a brothel in Dubai. I sold the grand house and rented a fantastic apartment with a view of the river and a driver and concierge and a pool and champagne happy hours every weeknight.

And yet I was swimming against the tides of addiction and mental illness—the legacy of my dad and the reality of my son.

How have I managed to live such a full life? First and foremost, I am not an addict. It's that simple. I love a stiff cherry gimlet in a dark bar, but I can stop at one or two. If I couldn't, I doubt I would be alive to write this. So if you're not an addict, count your blessings, every day. If you are, I love you.

I love you because I know how hard you struggle, and how easily you just say, "Fuck it" and crack open that beer. I know how funny and smart and tender you can be and what a selfish jerk you can be. I know how guilty you feel about how you've treated me and how pissed and resentful you feel toward me for my meddling, hinting, and guilting. I try to understand you, and I sulk because you don't seem to spend a minute thinking about me.

Relationships: the source of, and answer to, all of our problems.

Charles Dickens wrote, "A wonderful fact to reflect upon, that every human creature is constituted to be that profound secret and mystery to every other." This year, let's keep trying to understand and love one another.

To paraphrase Tiny Tim in Charles Dickens' "A Christmas Carol, "God help us, every one!

Fa La La La La

-Vince-

I haven't written any blog posts in nearly a week. My job keeps me busy, and I'll say that there is a little more effort involved in the actual writing vs. typing, from my point of view, anyway.

My co-blogger, aka Mom, came to visit me today. Like everybody else, she had a good laugh at my prison-issue glasses. But then we sat down and talked for two hours. We could have talked for two more and time would have flown by just as quickly. It was really nice to see a familiar face. We spoke on topics ranging from family health to sign-language-interpreting gorillas. It will probably be my only visit during my whole tenure as a prisoner, and it was a good one.

****

Last night I started reading Abraham Lincoln, Vampire Hunter. I only made it through 40 pages and I had to get to sleep but so far I'm interested. I'm sure once I leave prison I'll go back to reading zero books. My mind is impossible to control so I'm easily distracted. Sometimes I can't get through a page without daydreaming. I'll catch myself. And do it again minutes later. Brain. Bad brain.

****

I haven't been sick in years. Years! I am in the middle of a terrible cold, and I don't like it. I have been told several times over the years that, despite my claims, I am not a doctor. Even if I were, there's little I can do to suppress the effects of the virus. So I'll do the standard: rest, drink plenty of fluids, and complain.

****

I'm not at all religious but I went to a Christmas program for something to do, and I had a blast. There were six or seven musicians, all in their 70s or 80s, from some denomination whose name I cannot recall. Each played a different instrument ranging from accordion to piano to guitar. They had 50 grown men, drug dealers, pimps, and armed robbers, singing Twelve Days of Christmas and even doing the chicken dance. That was the best. We were all laughing. And we all needed that.

I think it may have been the first time in a while that some of the guys smiled. Which will usually, unfortunately, later, lead to crying. Quietly, so your cellmate doesn't hear. We will be thinking of our friends, families, and why we can't be with them this holiday season. I am one of the lucky ones. I won't be locked up next year. Some will. Some will be forever. And although they are here permanently for a reason, it will still hurt. They may not show it, but they will surely feel it.

Ice Cream Dreams

-Vince-

2006
I had just come back from my cruise and had begun drinking regularly. It was easy to get away with it because I was in Rochester, and my family had never come to visit me there. I could simply not answer my phone when I was drunk and call back when I wasn't. It was easy until I started using meth.

Less than a month after nearly a five-year period of sobriety, I started hitting the hard stuff. I skipped the usual, "only on weekends" routine and got myself into a good daily habit. My job at the ice cream plant paid well. I had thousands at my disposal, but I knew that wouldn't be enough. I made the decision to start selling.

When you are a dealer, the drug is always on hand. It has to be in order to have any level of success. I was able to be on the clock 24/7 with little naps here and there. For my own benefit I cannot get into detail about any specific sales.

During what would become my last weeks at the plant, I decided to take a week off for my birthday. I had been up for seven straight days when my birthday arrived. I had a sudden feeling that something was wrong. I looked around and everything was sterile-white and there was a huge pile-up on Line Two at the plant. I ran toward it and began removing smashed boxes of ice cream and throwing them on the floor, trying to get at the main problem which appeared to be a reflector covered in ice cream. Suddenly there was a horn, and the light shrunk down to two headlights staring me down in the night. It was 4am and I was out in the middle of 6th Avenue, across from Soldiers Field. I can only imagine the look on my face. I casually walked back to the sidewalk, and the car drove away. I decided it was time to sleep.

I slept through the entire weekend. I don't remember having any dreams.

****

I heard kind of a funny joke today from a CO, of all people. He stops me and says, "So, Jeffrey Dahmer asks his mother over for lunch, and she's eating and says, 'Jeffrey, I don't like your friends.'" And he says, "Well then, just eat the vegetables." Ha!

For two days I went without my meds for RLS and as it turns out, I need them. My prescription had expired and the doctor upped my dosage, but the new pills didn't get here in time. Now I'm on .25 mg and I finally slept. I had only been able to sleep in 40 minute increments for the last two nights. Just before REM sleep is when my legs start to go crazy.

It didn't help that they woke us up at 1:30am for a stand-up head count. We will never know the reason for that. The guards just do what they're told. Is it too cliché to say that the Nazis also did what they were told? I guess there's no comparison of the two. But it makes me feel better knowing that they will read this.

Prison is really nice as long as you close your eyes and imagine you're someplace else. There are many places I have been that will never be seen by most. Where the people care not for family or career or dignity but only their high. I've been there, and I've been them. Those. They. As I sit at my desk I try to think of those places, instead of where I want to be, where I should be. All of the things I should have accomplished by now. My wife and kids that don't exist. The home I don't own. Fuck. Either way it's depressing. It makes me want to get high.

Drugs: The cause of, and solution to, all of my problems.

January-ish, 2001
I don't know how long I had been drifting from curb to couch. Homeless in nearly every definition of the word. I didn't spend every night out in the cold. Most of the nights that I did, I stayed awake, looking for opportunity. There was one of the most desperate times of my life. I was addicted to crack, and I really didn't care about much else.

I resorted mostly to stealing things out of garages and pawning them to get what I needed. Stealing food was sometimes necessary but one of the benefits of smoking crack is that it's really not all that necessary to eat very often.

True story: One time I spent 15 minutes smoking $20 worth of crack, and the next 12 hours with a torch trying to get another hit out of a pipe I made out of a pop can. In the end I had actually smoked about 10% of the aluminum can itself.

"I have come to the conclusion that my subjective account of my own motivation is largely mythical on almost all occasions. I don't know why I do things." J.B.S. Haldane

Clarifications

-Vince-

I got a letter from my friend who essentially adopted my dog. He's doing just fine. From my mother I was under the impression that he was on his death bed. Sometimes I think she says things just to make me feel bad. And sometimes it works.

I would like to clear a couple things up for the record, since Mom mailed me copies of her blog posts. First, I have never in my life touched heroin. I don't know if it's because it is generally associated with needles and I'm deathly afraid of needles, or if it's because I just don't like downers, but I have never used it. Also I have not used cocaine for over a decade, so when my mom randomly accuses me of having been charged with four felonies of possessing all sorts of shit, I get a little annoyed.

I was only charged with one count of 1st degree–sale–10 grams or more–cocaine or heroin or meth. Mine was meth. I plead guilty to, and was convicted of, possession–6 grams or more–2nd degree– cocaine or heroin or meth. In the hotel, they found 52 grams @ 86% purity, of meth. For my first drug charge, realistically I was looking at 84 months. I do not know where her 11-year figure comes from.

Second: Yes, there was a bake sale. Prison industry consists of many things. They strive to educate us during our stay. From construction to baking. We have the opportunity every couple of months to buy homemade cookies. I mean giant cookies. All proceeds go to the cost of confinement. In fact, every penny we make, spend, and receive while we are locked up is "taxed" and the cost of our living, as a burden to society, is reduced.

Just in the last fiscal quarter, in this prison alone, the phone calls we made (not collect) contributed over $250,000 to our housing, meals, wages, and clothing. The guards are state employees, so the tax-payers foot that bill.

Mom, I love you dearly. If anybody else put you through what I have put you through, I would not hesitate to torture them…Dear God…twice now, a different person has stopped by my cell, stared at me until I looked back at them and I shit you not, they both said,

"What you doin'? Writin' letters?" and then they proceeded to do this little weasel laugh. You know like "heh, heh, heh." I didn't get the joke if there was one.

This is my last piece of paper. I will try to find more but it may be a few weeks until I can write again.

Happy New Life

-Anne-

I am tempted to rebut each of Vince's "clarifications" in his last post. But one of my favorite self-help slogans is: "How important is it?"

I'm glad to leave 2014 behind and am hopeful that 2015 will better, or at least not worse.

I spent Christmas Eve in an emergency room with my poor sister. She was feeling pressure in her chest. Apparently chemo can cause blood clots. They administered nitro by pill and patch, did an EKG to rule out a heart attack, and killed her pain with Dilaudid, which is seven times stronger than morphine.

Her worst fear is that she will die alone in the hospital. I stayed until they admitted her and she fell asleep, about seven hours later.

****

Three years ago, I hit bottom. I had lived with depression for as long as I could remember, but then I had to have a tooth pulled and boy, will that make you feel old. Then during a Christmas Day blizzard my car was towed and I spent four hours waiting in line outside at the impound lot to pay $300 to get it back. I drove straight from there to Fountain to visit Vince. The trailer he shared with his friend was full of guns, beer cans, and smoke. I figured what the heck, if you can't beat 'em, join 'em, so after he assured me that none of the guns was loaded, we posed for photos that became my holiday cards

82

to my friends in the UK, where they had a good laugh over us gun-crazy Americans.

Due to the blizzard I spent the night in Vince's friend's 5-year-old daughter's bedroom; she was at her mom's. Here's a tip for parents who smoke: Keeping your kid's door closed doesn't keep smoke out. I couldn't open the window and after tossing and turning until 5am I slipped out and drove home. On the way I started itching. Great—now I had bedbugs!

****

I contemplated suicide. I leaned my forehead against the screen of my 20th floor window. I had turned 50 the year before. Thinking about being depressed every day for another 30-40 years wasn't real appealing.

Here are the things I had tried to manage depression and anxiety:
Meditation
Medication
Prayer (including begging, pleading, and bargaining)
Acting normal
Abstaining from drinking
Cutting down on coffee
Self-help books
Alanon
Exercise
Getting outside every day
Appreciating beauty, be it fine art, nature, music, babies, or kittens
Gratitude lists
Avoiding negative people / avoiding unnaturally happy people
Running away to other countries
Denial
Journaling
Telling myself, "At least I'm not a refugee / amputee / blind / fill-in-the-blank."
Psychotherapy
Retail therapy
Sleeping, drinking, and movie binges
Reaching out to friends, even when that was the last thing I wanted to do

****

I thought that jumping out of my window would be exhilarating, until I hit the ground. I had some leftover pain-killers from the dentist, and my prescription for Restless Legs. I googled an overdose of the two and learned that they wouldn't kill me, but that I would likely need a liver transplant. I decided to keep living.

****

That spring, I visited Vince again and this time, made a reservation at a B&B. On the free-bookshelf there, I picked up a tattered copy of, "Feeling Good: the New Mood Therapy", by David Burns, MD. I read it and did what it told me to do, and I stopped being depressed. For good.

The book was about Cognitive Therapy. I had been instructed to use it at least twice in the past, but I'd been too stressed out to do it. Basically, you write down your negative thoughts and then argue with them rationally until you've de-fanged them. Writing it down is important; if you try to do it in your head you'll end up down a rabbit hole.

So was a lifetime of depression cured overnight by one book? No. I think it was all the other things I had tried over the years—the good things, anyway—and then I added this on top of them and together they all added up to a breakthrough.

I still feel sad sometimes–there's plenty to feel sad about–but I'm not depressed and I'm committed to living.

Sorry for the long post but, if you're struggling, I want to encourage you to keep an open mind, keep plugging away, and keep trying new things.

PS: I didn't have bedbugs after all. I think I was just itchy from the smoke and dry air. Living with addiction can turn you into a drama addict.

Happy Birthday

-Vince-

Today is the 36th anniversary of the most important day in the history of my life, my birth.

Although I have spent many holidays in lockup, this is my first birthday. Not at all surprising to me is that nobody here cares. I was excited yesterday, however, to discover that I had money on my account. Most likely from my dear Mother. Thank you, mom.

So far today, I have read 150 pages of Wild Fire, a novel by my most recent favorite author, Nelson DeMille. And my plan for the rest of the day is to continue reading until and after lunch, and until work at 2:30. It's just another day.

Little changes.

As house crew, I have developed a rapport with the guards. We share a few laughs. Some of them are going to be assholes for the rest of their lives but most of them seem to enjoy having my sense of humor added to their daily routine.

I remarked the other day when we were trying to figure out why certain cells have such a horrible odor to them, "Maybe it's because they hold the spray bottles sideways, and nothing comes out." This is in reference to the way modern black gangsters are known to hold their guns, and sadly, the way, more often than not, they either refuse to clean, or try to cover up odor, with air freshener. Anyhow, it got quite a laugh.

Also, I noticed that the names I hear over the PA are becoming less familiar, and the OID numbers are getting higher as people cycle in and out. Today I heard a number that is just under 1,000 over mine. This means that, since I arrived three months ago, nearly a thousand others have come and gone. Maybe a hundred would be women going to Shakopee, but still big numbers. And that does not include repeat offenders. I couldn't even estimate how many of them have come back, in ratio to newbies.

****

One thing many offenders have in common is that they spent too many years avoiding the dentist. I have one broken tooth, but that can be repaired when I get out. A good number of my fellow felons have no teeth at all. It is comical to me. And gross. They don't use any kind of mouth cleansing products. Dry, sticky, clicking mouths full of rancid breath all around while I eat. Their noses nearly touch their chins. And I have trouble keeping a straight face in the chow hall when they're mashing their mixed veggies in their gross mouths. I picture them in clown makeup. But I sit near them. Not all meals here belong to nursing homes, and every now and then I score something crunchy and delicious. Ahhh, what a birthday.

Land of 10,000 Prisoners

-Vince-

Four calendar months since I walked into court, knowing that I would not leave without handcuffs. There were a million reasons and excuses I could have made up so I wouldn't have to go. But I did it. Making the transition from absolute freedom to ultimate restriction in just a few minutes was tough. But I'm strong. Here's how it went down.

I woke up at 11am in Chatfield, Minnesota, 25 minutes away from the Rochester Courthouse. I had to check in by 12:55pm. All I really wanted was a good meal and to chain smoke cigarettes and meth until I got there. I was successful. I checked in, grabbed a seat just in time for the judge to make an entrance. I was playing Angry Birds on my cell phone so I didn't stand up, and the court officer yelled at me and I shot back with a nice, "Go fuck yourself." So I had to sit in the hallway and wait for my name to be called which was ok by me because the first part of Rochester court is all in Spanish. At 1:40pm they called my name.

This is a selfie I took just before the court date. I had been up for days, and was clearly unhealthy.

Since I already had the terms of my plea agreement in place, I was at the desk in front of the judge for less than three minutes. She pronounced my sentence and the court administrator told me I could stand up at which point I shook my lawyer's hand and was promptly handcuffed. There was no banging of the gavel.

From my chair, I was led through the door that I'm sure exists in every courtroom that nobody wants to go through. To my surprise, once the guard and I were through he took one cuff off and put my hands in front, and we walked down a long hallway to booking. After that was the standard pictures and fingerprints and waiting. I believe I have described the rest of the journey from there.

Right now I am listening to a Pink Floyd song that I have never heard before. It is amazing. Oh. "The Boy in the Forest" is actually by *Andy Jackson*. OK anyone would confuse that with *Floyd*. He was *Pink Floyd*'s producer for many albums.

****

If anybody out there happened to see the story on the news about the 125th anniversary of St. Cloud State Prison, you got to see my living unit, B House, and more importantly, my front door.

They shot the footage of the living unit from in front of cell 143 which is two doors down from me in 145. I, however, was actually inside the broom closet at the time because the camera crew caught us off guard and I had to hide. We were cleaning and I was just finishing up when they came in. The warden didn't want any offenders on tape. I had a half a mind to take off my pants and streak down the main drag but I thought better of it.

The camera should pan down from the beautiful arched ceiling and end up pointing down the flag (the main drag I wanted to run down) and look for cell 145. That's my apartment.

****

-Anne-

The story is actually about how Minnesota has the lowest imprisonment rate for drug offenders in the nation. Maine has the lowest rate. Still, there are nearly 10,000 people in prison in Minnesota, the Land of 10,000 Lakes, and we pay about a half billion $$ a year to feed and house them.

Happy Birthday, After All

-Vince-

Yesterday after I emptied all of the garbages, filled the water container for the pill line, and made my afternoon cup of coffee, I went back to my room to read. I'm in the middle of Relic by Preston Douglas and Lincoln Child. It's not bad. It sort of has two story lines. One is kind of boring and scientific. The other is exciting and gory.

Anyhow, I got into my room and there it was. Dated my birthday and with my name highlighted in bright yellow, was my acceptance letter to boot camp. Finally!

Here's how it breaks down. Phase one is a minimum of six months and contains a highly structured daily schedule and treatment-oriented program that includes: intensive instruction on military drill, ceremony, bearing and courtesy; physical training, on- and off-site work crews, cognitive skills training, chemical dependency programming, education programming, restorative justice programming, and reintegration planning.

Phase two is a highly supervised community phase under intense surveillance and lasts a minimum of six months. And the final phase, also six months, is community-supervised release, and depending on behavior in phases one and two, can be shorter than six months. After that is standard parole for the remainder of my sentence, until 7-15-2018.

If I screw up, depending on severity, they can choose to put a location monitoring device on my leg or send me back to prison and take away all my good time. So I would sit in prison until 2018. That's pretty good incentive.

So…now I wait. One of these nights they will call my name and I will get my red box. When your name is called, you go get a 1.5 x 4' red bin (or two if necessary). Do not ask the CO where you're going. They don't know. In fact, they don't tell us until we get on the bus. It's for our safety, or some nonsense. If I knew where I was going, I could tell my family (really, just my mom) and friends. I could adjust my canteen order so I could have money to spend if I do end up at a county jail, and so I don't end up with a bunch of envelopes and post cards purchased from the DOC that I can't use at a county facility even though it is a DOC holding facility. Oh my God that sounds so complicated. It is.

Sunny Day, Everything's A-OK

-Anne-

I visited Vince again, for his birthday. This time a friend went with me and we made a day trip out of it. Stefanie brought a couple big bags full of toys and books that her granddaughters had outgrown, and handed them out to the kids in the prison waiting room, which I thought was touching and brilliant. The kids couldn't bring toys into the visiting area, but they could play with them until they had to walk through the metal detector and the sea of bars.

Vince and I had a good visit, again, then Stefanie and I drove around, got turned around and lost a couple times, and discovered a nature preserve where we went for a long walk. It was a beautiful warmish day. I had brought a couple beers in the trunk and we hung out in a field and each drank one, and I smoked a cigar.

Below is a screen shot from the Minnesota Department of Corrections from their manual for families of incarcerated people. I just happened to find it about six months after Vince was locked up. I am listed as his next of kin / emergency contact or whatever in the DOC system. How hard would it have been for someone to send me a form email with a link to this?

Some of the information would have been really useful, like knowing there's an email system where I can send messages to Vince for 10 cents. Other tips, not so helpful, like the one about

91

buying a cell phone with the prison area code so calls are cheaper. A friend of mine, whose son was also imprisoned, did this and then they transferred him without notice to another state and she was stuck with a second cell phone and call time she could never use.

I'm a highly resourceful person with unlimited internet and phone access. I have time to figure things out. But what about the mom who is now raising three kids by herself and working full time? No more second income or child support once the man is inside. Maybe no health insurance, car, etc. Certainly no help from a partner, if the guy was any kind of decent partner before he was arrested. I read the whole manual, finding some encouragement in the fact that the DOC seems to get how significant imprisonment is to a family.

It's not just about locking up a bad guy, as they are so fond of saying in the media. It's about all the people affected by it. If you're interested, go google their Tip Sheet for Parents, the Tip Sheet for Incarcerated Parents, and believe it or not, the Sesame Street Handbook for Children Ages 3-8.

It would be funny if it didn't involve real children. As a child who was lied to about the whereabouts and cause of my dad's death, I appreciated the tip that encourages parents to talk openly about how the other parent is in prison, and to take the children to visit. This is because children will fill in any blanks with their imaginations, and what they imagine will be worse than the reality. I wouldn't go that far—the reality is pretty awful and our society wants it that way because it's punishment—but I am a big believer in being honest with children.

Now the section on Dating an Offender, that's hilarious. Unintentionally so, but still. I know, I know; if I was dating an offender it wouldn't be funny.

Dating an Offender
If you are dating someone in prison, it may be difficult to really get to know the inmate. You may be the offender's only connection to the outside world. The offender may lean on you more so than if you were dating on the outside. Therefore, your letters, visits, and

92

telephone communications become very important to the offender. The offender may also depend heavily on you to send gifts, money or to do things you don't really want or can't afford to do. Try not to let the offender put pressure on you. Don't focus only on the needs of the offender and don't feel pressured into taking care of only his or her needs. Be sure to find time for yourself and keep a proper focus on your own needs and feelings. When you communicate with each other, try to talk about your past and your goals and hopes for the future. A more balanced relationship will help you decide if you want to maintain it after the offender is released.

Prison, Prison Everywhere

-Anne-

There's this phenomenon where, if something's on your mind, it's what you see everywhere you go. That's how this prison thing has been for me. Why did I never notice before how the word "prison" comes up all the time, everywhere?

I open my little neighborhood newspaper and there's a story about a local guy, a recovering addict who spent time in prison, just published a book called "Sobriety: A Graphic Novel"(Hazelden Publishing). The next week, there's a story about a local woman who just published "A Mother Load of Addiction". When her children were young adults, people would ask what they were doing. "I would say that my daughter was at college at St. Thomas and my son was at St. Cloud." What she did not add was that her son was not at St. Cloud State University, but was serving time at the nearby state correctional facility for a drug-related holdup.

In my Sunday paper there's an article about an old law that requires drug dealers to buy a tax stamp from the Minnesota Department of Revenue. Inside, an editorial by a judge who writes about mass incarceration, "There's a problem, yes. Is it proof of racism? No. Are there solutions? Yes, but they shouldn't involve an end to punishment." The following week there's an article about prison phone reform. "They've got the monopoly, so they charge whatever they want," said one Minnesota mother, struggling to stay in touch with her imprisoned son." Not me, but it could have been. Today there was a question in the advice column from a woman worried about her mom's ex-con boyfriend being around her 18-month-old daughter. The columnist's advice? "When it comes to baby proofing your house, I would put access to ex-cons at the top of the list."

I turn on the radio in my car and it's Back to the 80s day with Grand Master Flash's White Lines (Don't, Don't Do It): "A street kid gets arrested, gonna do some time. He got out three years from now just to commit more crime. A business man is caught, with 24 kilos. He's out on bail and out of jail and that's the way it goes." It's a great tune, by the way.

I go to a party and everyone is laughing about the show Orange is the New Black. I've only seen the first season since I am old-school and still get Netflix DVDs. Hilarious! people say. Yes, it is funny, but not so much when you have an actual loved one behind bars. I didn't see the end of the last season coming…it was really upsetting.

A local university announces it has a law professor named Mark Osler who has been chosen to join a team of experts screening 18,000 prisoners who applied to have their sentences commuted through Obama's new drug clemency program.

I go to the Arrow Awards show. This is an hour and a half of British TV commercials and public service announcements that have won awards for creativity. Most of them are hilarious and I look forward to this bit of escapism every year. But then there is one where an ex offender is talking to a potential employer and you can hit the "skip" button to recreate how employers reject ex offender job applicants out of hand.

I pick up a pile of old New Yorker magazines in the business center of my building—I like to cut out the cartoons and mail them to Vince, although they don't always get through. In one, there's a very long but fascinating article about the "alternatives-to-incarceration" industry. This is where private companies get paid to hound people who've failed to pay their parking tickets, for instance, piling on more and more late fees and fines until they're on the verge of losing their homes.

These are just the prison references I come across in my home life. Work offers many more.

Moose Lake

Welcome to Moose Lake

-Vince-

It all happened so quickly: Monday night they called my name for a red box; Tuesday morning I packed up all my stuff; and by Wednesday afternoon I was way up north in Moose Lake State Prison.

I'm excited. I'm not being stored in a county jail. For a few days, however, I am being stored in a segregation unit, by myself, without any of my property, until there is an opening in general population. I don't really get why they took me from St. Cloud if they had no room here. But I'll accept the time in sec if it means they're giving me an early start to Boot Camp. All of the people that had been approved for Boot Camp and were being transferred with me were scheduled to enter Boot Camp two months from now. So I'm thinking, hopefully, that somehow I got bumped up.

****

I've been in seg 2 1/2 days now and I still haven't been able to make a phone call. It kind of pisses me off that they treat me like somebody that has gotten into a fight or has broken the major rules. Not the attitude I had when I arrived. Being in solitude has definitely changed my opinion. It makes no sense to me. Why am I here?

****

This really sucks. Friday night and at the very least I'll be stuck here for the weekend. I still have no idea when I will be able to use a phone. The schedule said today, but nobody ever came to let me know when.

****

96

When I was in Hazelden in 2001, I was diagnosed with Bipolar Disorder, although I think if I knew the correct responses to their questions, I could have been diagnosed with excessive flatulence and dementia. If it had a pill, it could be cured at Hazelden Center for Youth and Families.

Anyhow…my mother is the only one other than them to inquire of my mental stability; repeatedly. Looking back at just the first page I wrote since my arrival in Moose Lake, I can see some big mood swings. Naturally I can deduce that my emotional stability, or instability, is a product of my environment. Makes sense, since I have been in some pretty shitty places, the segregation unit of Moose Lake State Prison being one of them. If I were at Disneyland, I would not need pills. Here, I need pills, right?

****

-Anne-

In the Department of Corrections handbook, under "Prison Lingo", Segregation (solitary confinement) is defined as a "restricted living unit used to house offenders who have violated major rules." The United Nations Convention Against Torture considers solitary confinement and indefinite detention to be forms of cruel and unusual punishment, if not torture. The US is one of the big offenders, along with Iran, North Korea, and Saudi Arabia. Thing is, those countries are known for locking up political dissidents and throwing away the key—it kind of makes sense even if it's horribly wrong. Vince is a petty drug dealer.

As an introvert who loves spending time alone, I had to think through why solitary is considered a form of torture. It goes back to what I wrote in my Christmas Day post, about how human connections, while they can be challenging, are the ultimate source of meaning in life. While I enjoy being alone, I have a choice about it, and I can pick up the phone and call a friend or go hang out in a coffee shop whenever I want to end my isolation.

Prison, Prison Everywhere, Part II

-Anne-

I have to move. The apartment vacancy rate in the Twin Cities is so low that landlords have the upper hand, and mine is taking advantage of that to raise my rent $307 per month. "It's a business decision," they say. "We realize some people will be priced out of the building."

Some people. I'm one of those people.

My apartment has been my sanctuary for almost five years. But I work for a nonprofit, so I have to be realistic. I gave my notice and then started sifting through the over 16,000 apartment ads on Craigslist.

****

At work, I get emails about prison all the time. One of our funders, the Open Society Foundations, draws my attention to a federal report that reveals "near-unremitting abuse of juveniles held at New York's Rikers Island jail." Thank god Vince is 36 years old, big and tall, and he can look scary when he needs to. There was a second one from OSF about how the suicide rate for people held behind bars awaiting trial is 10 times that of the world outside. Delete.

There's another one from an organization called Empathy, about prisoners in Uganda. Okay, once again, I'm grateful Vince isn't in prison in Uganda. Yet another one from the National Academies Press announcing their new report, The Growth of Incarceration in the United States. And then there was this one, from Human Rights Watch, called The Human Rights Case for Drug Reform : How Drug Criminalization Destroys Lives, Feeds Abuses, and Subverts the Rule of Law.

I am researching a big foundation and find this article about one of the family members who was arrested on suspicion of possessing

Class A drugs. During a search of the house, police found the body of his wife in their bedroom–she had died two months earlier. A coroner said that her death was as a result of "dependent abuse" of drugs.

Then I find the Public Welfare Foundation which, among its criminal justice interests, aims to "Reduce jail populations through the use of diversion at the front end of the criminal justice system that connects individuals with substance abuse disorders and mental illness to the public health system." Well duh!

I stumble upon JustLeadershipUSA , an outfit with an "ambitious decarceration goal" because "Mass incarceration is the most significant domestic threat to the fabric of our democracy."

I wonder, if all the money spent on reports and task forces and glitzy websites and conferences and foundation executives' salaries was used to fund treatment for low-income prisoners … nah! What a crazy idea.

Lastly, there is Richard Branson, chairman of Virgin Atlantic Airlines and Virgin Records, of all people, writing a blog about ending the war on drugs. All I can think of is the time that a friend of mine who travels more than anyone I know let me use 125,000 of her air miles and I flew business class from London to Minneapolis-St. Paul. I waited for my flight in Virgin's " Upper Class " lounge, as they call it at Heathrow. The décor was fantastically posh and I discreetly gorged myself on smoked salmon and champagne, trying to act like I really belonged there.

Solitary

-Vince-

Boring! That's the only way to describe my time here so far. I got to choose a couple real winners from the seg book cart the other day. When I asked the Native man about a couple authors I was interested in, he stared at me with his mouth wide open. That's it; he just stared. Eventually I pointed to a red one and a blue one, and he responded to that. Unfortunately I only have 1,000 pages to last me until I get out of here. On the up-side, I read terrible books really slowly!

A CO went around and knocked on a few doors asking if people wanted to use the phone. I knocked on my side of the door and asked if I could use the phone. He said, "No, not your day." No shit.

I've heard that Moose Lake is an old psych hospital. At the very least, it is an old hospital. From what I saw of it four days ago, the outside is all red brick and barb wire. The inside is very sterile. White on white, all high-gloss, splatter-resistant walls. I can't wait to get out and explore.

In Moose Lake there is no controlled movement. Once I get down to general population, I can just sign out and go to the gym. And I can spend some extra time in the library once I get out of the hole. Of course, this is all just hearsay. I haven't actually seen any of it with my own eye, yet. Fuck. Did I ever even mention that I'm a cyclops? Don't tell anyone.

****

I wrote a kite to the staff about not getting a phone call and within 10 minutes of receiving it they brought down a phone and apologized for their oversight! I'm impressed. I wrote the kite in a respectful manner and in turn I was treated with respect. I think I like it this way. And to clarify for those out in the real world, a kite is a piece of paper on which we write our requests, suggestions, and complaints to the staff of the facility. They are rarely responded to, and almost never is the response in our favor; this was an exception, probably because even they knew that my rights had been violated up until this point.

****

I believe it's Sunday. I'm still in the hole. I haven't spent one second out of my cell since Thursday morning. A CO asked me if I wanted recreation. I said yes. Five minutes later, my door unlocked and I stepped out into the common area with my shower stuff, my mail, and a lot of questions. The common area is a room with one table, four seats. That is all. Nobody else. I didn't get to shower, send out my mail, or speak to another human. After an hour of sitting alone at the table an angry voice yelled, "Recreation is over! Stand by your door!" I did. And I have declined recreation ever since. Still no shower. I need one.

One Battle Won

-Anne-

As Vince has written , the tourist trade in Lanesboro dies off in winter, so he goes on seasonal unemployment. The State loads his weekly payment onto a debit card which is managed by Mega Bank, the name I will use so they don't sue me for libel or slander or whatever. When Vince was arrested, he was no longer eligible to receive additional payments; fair enough. However, he still had a balance in his account, which he couldn't access.

So I started calling Mega Bank. I will not bore you with the details of how much time I spent on hold, making copies, faxing and mailing and emailing the Power of Attorney form Vince had painstakingly found in the prison library, and doing it all over again because Mega Bank claimed they never received it, and so on. Months passed.

My friend Stefanie, who had come with me to visit Vince, works for a big consulting firm. I said to her, "I feel so cynical! I wonder if big corporations ignore people like me until we give up, and then they keep the money, and all those tiny accounts add up …." She laughed and said I wasn't being cynical at all, that that's exactly what they do. They wait you out. They do nothing. They make a nice profit.

But I am a fighter. Hearing Stephanie's take on it made me mad, which energized me. I called the Minnesota Attorney General's Office. When a real person answered the phone and asked me to describe my complaint, I was tongue tied for a moment. "I … I wasn't ready to talk … I'm not used to a government agency or company that actually answers the phone."

The AG sent a letter to the CEO of Mega Bank, asking him to respond within five business days. Mega Bank ignored the letter. I don't know what transpired after that but I received a check for $154.03 within a couple weeks. In particular, I'd like to recognize Joao Halab in the AG's office for pursuing this on my and Vince's behalf.

A hundred and fifty bucks may not sound like a lot of money, but it meant coffee and ramen and pens and paper to Vince. And to give Vince credit, he told me to keep $50 for my effort, which I did.

****

I've got other battles going as well. They are mostly internal ones; I am choosing not to expend my energy on them because I know I cannot win them.

I wrote that I have to move because I am being priced out of my apartment. I haven't found a new place yet. It seems there are either spacious penthouses with doormen and champagne happy hours for $2,000 a month, or dark cramped rat holes for $800 a month, and not much in between.

My landlord has started showing my apartment, which amps up the pressure. I called a friend who lives in the building and asked, "Should I make a point of being home when they come in with the potential renters, so I can make sarcastic remarks about how they're taking advantage of the economy to jack up rents?" She said NO without hesitation. I knew that was the right answer, but I needed to hear it.

But when I came home from seeing yet another "no-go" apartment, there were people in my living room. These potential new renters gushed about what a beautiful apartment I have. I kept my mouth shut.

The poor leasing agent is also being priced out of his apartment, which he's been receiving as a benefit of being an employee, so he's very sympathetic. He called me a couple hours later to say that a corporation that makes industrial cleaners had rented my apartment sight unseen but would be sending someone the next day just to verify the square footage. They'll be using it to house MBA interns.

This is me a couple years ago reveling in the view from my apartment:

****

My other internal battle is a February work trip to the Occupied Palestinian Territories. I can't say much except that it's complicated and adds additional pressure to find a new apartment by the time I leave, because I'll come back and need to move five days later.

Solitary, Still

-Vince-

It wasn't always the hard stuff.

Shortly after I lost my job at the ice cream plant, one of my close friends wore a wire into my apartment and attempted to buy some meth from me. Fortunately, I had been tipped off that his house had been raided not even an hour before he showed up. I slammed the door in his face, and started thinking. I had a standing offer to move to Fountain with an old friend and his girlfriend, and I took them up on it. The first night there I started back up with my heavy drinking, and I didn't stop until seven years later when I got into the hard stuff again. But it was a fun seven years!

After one very trying month living in a trailer in Fountain with a man that couldn't control his anger while drunk, which was all day every day, I moved a short distance to the town I was working in, Lanesboro **Pause** If you ever get a chance to get a copy of the book, Inadmissible Evidence by Phillip Friedman, do it. But before you read it, just go ahead and burn it. Or if you want to know what it's like in prison isolation, read it. Thank you for your time. **Play**

Lauren, Ralph Lauren

-Anne-

In some of Vince's posts it sounds like I abandoned him.

But during the seven "fun" years, as he calls them, when he was "only drinking," I did visit him every couple of months. Remember, it's a two-hour drive to Fountain / Lanesboro, so each visit meant a six- to eight-hour day or staying overnight. Mondays were his only days off, so a visit usually involved me taking a day off work, too.

104

I hope I don't sound defensive. It's just interesting, and very common in families, that our emotional impression of events is so different.

At first, right after his relapse, visiting him was so emotion-laden that I might weep in the car most of the way home. The first time I saw him after six months of not knowing where he was, after his meth bender, I was shocked by his appearance. Gaunt, hollow eyes—they even appeared to have changed color from brown to almost black. His clothes looked as though he had just survived a ship wreck—torn and filthy. He was 27 but he looked 10 years older. Someone passing by us asked him, "Hey Vince, who's your date?" He didn't like that.

I asked him if I could buy him a pair of jeans and he said, "Sure mom, but they have to be Lauren—Ralph Lauren."

It was always the same routine. He didn't use email or Facebook or talk on the phone; communications was solely by text. So I would text and ask if such-and-such a weekend would be good for me to come visit. Half the time he wouldn't reply. Then I would text again a few days later, and a few days later, until finally I'd get a text back from him saying he'd dropped his phone in the river but he would love to see me.

When I arrived in town it was always awkward. He was usually working so I would have a burger and a beer. I always had the impression that he wished he could escape from me—to go use? I don't know. He didn't want money from me; he never asked for money and, after all, he was working full-time. When he lost his job I might take him shopping for clothes or buy him a contact lenses refill so he could see, but I never gave him money.

We would go agate hunting. He would show me the homemade raft
he and his friend had built out of empty industrial-sized ketchup tubs
and duct tape. We'd go to the Amish market and make fun of their
eye glasses, which were all the same steel-rimmed, round, and
always smeary. We camped with his group of friends. Vince would
toss a ball for his dog, Willie, or play catch with one of his friends.
One time someone won a meat raffle and Vince roasted it all over
the campfire and I gorged myself.

I would show up in my Mini with my Emporio Armani bags and my
Murano glass beer bottle opener I'd bought in Venice. These were
almost like protective shields, as if they declared (again), "I'm not

one of you hillbillies!" (A friend in London works at Armani and is my source for these sturdy plastic bags which are great for camping. I am way too cheap to actually buy anything there.).

Vince's best friend talked to me nonstop, but Vince would say barely 20 words. There was never any animosity, just an elusiveness. Who was he? What did he want in life? Was this it? Did he ever date? Did he wish he had kids? Would he ever go back and finish his degree? Did he ever think about buying a house?

If I couldn't contain myself and asked one of these questions, he would deflect it with a joke. When I left, he would hug me and say, "I love you mom."

It got easier as time went by. And, I have to admit, once I gave up my vow to never drink in front of him, we all loosened up a bit. Alcohol, such a time-honored stress reliever.

I came to feel proud of Vince. He worked, paid his bills, paid taxes, had friends, had fun. He seemed to have overcome the drug demons and was only drinking moderately. Well, moderately for him. For the umpteenth time, I was lulled into thinking it would stay this way forever.

Ashamed of Ashamed

-Anne-

Did you know it's possible to feel ashamed of feeling ashamed?

Well it is. A couple times, Vince and his friends came to St. Paul for the weekend and stayed with me. They brought everything one needs for an overnight:

And since I live in a nonsmoking building, they smoked out in front of the building, or took their home-rolled cigarettes and a cooler full of beer up to the roof and played poker up there. I would bring up a platter of food—hard boiled eggs, olive tapenade, crackers, some fruit—but they wouldn't touch it. Once I bought four kinds of sausages at Whole Foods, figuring they were meat eaters, but they wouldn't touch them–too froo froo.

Vince took his shoes off inside my door, as he had been trained to do from childhood:

This is where the shame came in. Here I was, living in what was billed as a "luxury" apartment building, and my son wore shoes like this. And then I felt ashamed of feeling ashamed. Of being such a snob.

Whoa! Time for an adorable kitten photo!

(Did I mention I do kitten fostering for the humane society?)

Anyway, another time we all went for sushi—Vince's and my all-time favorite food. And he couldn't eat it. He had to leave the table to be sick, and then I noticed that his abdomen was distended and my bubble of denial that he was "just drinking" was burst.

I had attended the family program at Hazelden, I knew the medical symptoms of chronic alcoholism, including liver disease.

****

A number of people have said to me that it must be kind of a relief that Vince is in prison. At least I know where he is, he can't drink or smoke, yatta yatta. Yeah, these things are true and they are good, although drugs and alcohol can be had, even in prison.

All I can do is keep my focus on myself—examining my embarrassment, and guilt over that embarrassment, forgiving myself for being human, for having feelings, for having mixed feelings.

Sprung!

-Vince-

I made it! Right after breakfast they changed me out of solitary and took me downstairs to Unit 10, the best unit according to word of mouth.

Already I've heard good news. People are going to Boot Camp early! One guy said his letter told him April, and he's locked in for February!

This place is massive. Until I get a job, I'm only allowed out of my cell until noon, after my first day. Once I have a job, I'm free to spend my day training or reading or really doing anything I choose.

111

So far I have chosen to take a really long shower, with all my own hygiene items. And that was exactly what I needed.

Next step, figure out my schedule, then develop a routine. I know sooner than later I have to get to the P90X workout. Cardio is huge at Boot Camp, along with five miles per day, the P90X is used in winter. Five miles in rain or snow or shine. I'm a little nervous about getting started. I know I can do it, it's just a matter of keeping focused. I have trouble keeping my thoughts on one activity for very long.

Or on one subject, for that matter. Next subject. Actually, I'll continue on Lanesboro.

I have mentioned the town in previous posts, about working in a couple of the restaurants there. Well that's not all I did.

****

OK, sorry, I'll have to get back to Lanesboro. I did my first real cardio exercise in quite a while. To qualify for Boot Camp, you have to be able to walk or run a mile in 14 minutes. I failed, but not by too much. I will try every day and I will improve. I also played four games of volleyball. So I kept my heart rate up for about an hour, and it felt pretty good.

I watched about five minutes of people doing the P90X thing. All I have to say to the person that invented that is Fuck You. Fuckin asshole.

****

Lanesboro is a town of 788. It has been named the B&B Capital of America or some such shit. So in the summer, the town can swell into the thousands. 10,000 or more for Buffalo Bill Days. In the winter, however, almost everything closes down … except for the bars.

That's where I learned that it's okay to have six beers before breakfast, skip breakfast, and go straight to the bar to start getting a good buzz on.

Usually by noon I could be near blackout, eat a small lunch, then go home and take a nap. That way I could go out and get drunk with the evening crowd too.

Even on my work days I could show up fairly hammered as long as I could function. I could even pull beers off the tap during the slow days of winter to keep a nice, even buzz.

Pause … Good news: It's not the P90X that we have to do and practice. It's the Reebok Step video. My apologies to the creator of the P90X workout. I'm sure it's a fine program. For insane people. My verbal assault was out of line.

We Are Who We Are

-Vince-

My brain is so easily distracted. My mom emailed some of my older blog posts and I saw my list for a perfect mixed tape. Well, I simply must make another … "Tangerine", *Led Zeppelin*; "Blinded by Rainbows", *Rolling Stones*; "One More Cup of Coffee", *Bob Dylan*.

One particular song reminds me of me and some parts of my relationship with my mother: "Headlights", by *Eminem*.

The Creep

-Anne-

Ouch. That *Eminem* song … so many ways I could go with that.

****

113

When I was in Istanbul in November, there was a guy from the Philippines in my meetings. His name was John Rockefeller. No, Rockefeller is not a Filipino name. His father had changed the family name in hopes that it would bring prosperity. It didn't.

I happened to be seated next to John on a dinner cruise the first night. I thought, "Oh no, trapped on a boat for three hours next to this guy—what could we possibly have in common?"

But then we started talking and by the end of the cruise I was calling him "son" and he was calling me "mom."

John's father was an alcoholic who had left the family when he was small. John was pimped out at the age of 10, sold to strangers for sex until he was too old and no longer desirable—19 or 20—and he began pimping out younger kids in order to make a living and survive.

By the time I met him, John was Vince's age, had recovered long ago, and ran a recovery program for street kids. Here we are, talking about his "River of Life" program. To prostituted young men, John has become their idol, big brother, and mentor. Everybody, including notorious gang leaders, listens intently to John and follows every word he says.

John and another sex worker had a son together. He was a teenager now, and John was doing his best to keep tabs on him, though the mother was an addict and moved around a lot.

I asked John if he thought that kids being raised by single mothers was the biggest reason that kids got in to trouble. He looked squarely at me and wagged his finger. "No. It is not the mothers. It's the fathers." Alcoholic fathers. Abusive fathers. Fathers who gamble away their paychecks. Fathers who leave.

****

On Vince's first birthday I called to invite his father to have cake with us, and he said he was too busy with "business." A drug deal, in other words. I never saw him again, except briefly in a crowd.

From time to time I would ask Vince if it bothered him that he didn't have a father. "Let's just call him The Creep," he said once, and we laughed and I never really got an answer, if he had one to give.

Vince never asked about The Creep. The Creep's dad had been a barge worker and his mother was a telephone operator who had grown up on a reservation. They lived in a dilapidated farm house in Rush City filled with cigarette smoke and no heat and large bowls of bite-sized Snickers and a big-screen TV. The Creep and I visited his grandmother once, on the rez. She lived in a tar paper shack without indoor plumbing or electricity.

I never mentioned to Vince that the Creep had been a drug dealer from a small town who didn't have a car or a phone, a high-school dropout who worked as a clerk in a gas station. A guy who aspired to nothing more than hanging out with his friends, drinking and smoking pot, laughing and telling stories about drinking and smoking pot. I never mentioned any of these things because I didn't want Vince to be influenced by them, if he harbored some unconscious admiration for The Creep.

The Creep had had a son with another woman before I met him, and went on to father four more children. I got $103 in child support once, but that was it.

****

I'm not trying to shift blame; after all I must have had a far stronger influence on Vince since I was there 24/7 for 16 years, right? I don't spend all day analyzing and angsting over why Vince is who he is. But for every Vince, there are 10,000 more like him in prison, in Minnesota alone. I'm sure they all derailed for a different mix of complicated reasons, just as I succeeded despite a complicated mix of factors that should have kept me down. If someone could figure it all out, they would deserve to win the Nobel Peace Prize.

Beginnings

-Vince-

I am very happy to be out of St. Cloud. That was a horrible place. Nobody seemed to be running it. Or, to put it another way, 100 people seemed to be running it in their own different ways. So if we were told to do something by one guard, we could actually get in trouble if another guard did not like it. But then that same guard would back up the other guard. I can't even explain it properly.

Mom may notice my writing become sloppier than usual. I am back down to a 4" flexible Bob Barker pen. I ordered some real pens for next week.

****

Back to the future. OK. So since I was about 16 years old, I have been keeping track of how many miles I have run total. Over the last two days, I have run a total of 3/4 mile, bringing my total over the last 20 years to 3/4 of a mile. Ahhh. I'm funny.

Today, I did about eight minutes of the Reebok Step program. I just did the footwork, sort of trying to get the timing down. It's tougher than it looks. I went two total miles on the treadmill, alternating between walking and running. I was able to run 1/4 mile at a time. But my muscles just aren't used to that much activity. Even outside of the drug-dealing, at my real jobs, all I really did was stand in one spot for 8-12 hours per day.

A little farther every day. Without trying to overdo it, I think I'll be good to go by the time I go. I need to stretch first, too. If I am injured while at Boot Camp, that is considered a program failure. And I would have to sit the remainder of my time in prison. Just over two more years. I can't fail. Rather, I do not want to fail.

Christella Clear

-Anne-

My sister's request for visitor status was denied. She hadn't actually signed her name, she had typed it in a fancy script. I can understand that.

****

My uncle died. He and my aunt lived three doors down from my family growing up. You might expect me to say he was like a father to me, since my dad had died, but he was an uncle, which is even better. He was kind and loving and innocent and curmudgeonly at the same time. He was a professor of English at a local private university and it was his life's mission to teach proper punctuation and grammar and an appreciation of reading English Lit.

When my cousin and I were sorting through his belongings, I came across a hand-written thank you note that Vince had sent him for some little favor. It was so cute, so I mailed it to Vince, along with the funeral notice.

There was a postage stamp on the envelope of the thank you letter, so the prison blocked it. Vince got a cryptic notice that something had been mailed by someone and that it had been denied. Did he want to file a complaint, or give them permission to destroy it? After several phone calls we figured out what it was and Vince said he wanted to go to the mat to get it back. He filled out a request form to have the materials sent back to me. The prison accidentally mailed the form to me. I mailed it back to Vince. By then he had filed a second form. Three weeks have passed without a response. I think they destroyed it and are hoping we'll forget it.

****

My niece's request for visitor status was denied. She moved a few weeks ago, so the address on her application form didn't match the one associated with her driver's license number. An honest mistake.

****

I sent Vince a photo of my sister with her new chemo 'do:

He and my sister used to be very close. Life intervened, they hadn't had much contact for years, but now prison and cancer had brought them back together.

I don't know how it all transpired but a prison mate of Vince did a sketch from the photo, and Vince started asking if I had received a package. This went on for weeks. And more weeks.

Finally I did receive a very large, flat package. Inside it was a sketch:

The return address was in Chicago, and there was a note on letterhead adorned with butterflies:

Dear Anne:

My name is Christella, I am the sister of an inmate that is a Moose Land Correctional Facilitees with your son Zinnce (I hope I got the name right). My brother was asked by your son to draw this picture, but they cannot give each other items so my brother mailed it to me and ask me to send it to you. Please send the enclose picture of the drawing to your son so he can see what Mark did.

I hope you like the drawing. Mark (my brother) told me the person in the photo was ill. I don't know her name but I will keep her in my prayers, along with Mark and your son.

God Bless,
Christella

A Job with Benefits

-Vince-

I am currently in a six-man pod, sort of what I think a dorm room might be like. Right now, I am the only person in it. I feel like any moment, a tumble weed will roll on by, just passing through, like all my roommates thus far.

This is the only six-man pod in the unit. It is where everybody goes their first day. People move or SRD (Supervised Release Date) all the time, so there is quite a turnover in this room. No, not the pastry. I happen to be next in line to move, and there are five people on the way here from Brainerd, but for now, I'm all alone. I will be moved to a two-man room as soon as one becomes available, probably tomorrow.

****

Ouch! The ladders on the bunks are on what was the foot side of the bed at St. Cloud. I hit my head on the sharp steel foot step.

Song list, continued: "Rastaman Chant", *Busta Rhymes*; "End of the Line", *Traveling Willburys*; "Love, Reign Over Me", *the Who*; "Don't Call Us, We'll Call You", *Sugarloaf*; "Flash", *Queen*; and "Flower", by *Moby*. That's the song from the opening credits of "Gone in 60 Seconds". I don't know any other *Moby* songs, just to let the ladies know.

****

For about three years, my routine in Lanesboro rarely changed. I would occasionally leave town and go as far as Fountain, about eight miles, to hang out with my good friend Seth. We had known each other since I moved to Fountain three years earlier. We were non-gay soulmates.

I took my excessive drinking farther than anybody in my friend group. Start early, go late, every penny of my disposable income went to drinking, weed, cigarettes, and gambling. I had a perfectly good driver's license but thankfully, no car. So that was it for that three years, then I got fired from the restaurant, lost my apartment, and pretty much everything like my mom wrote, and eventually had

121

to move in with Seth in Fountain, where I was able to secure jobs at the two restaurants in the town.

I moved out of Seth's after about a year and got my own place again, right across the street from work. After a while I was full time at the Bent Wrench, where I was allowed to have a tab. Oops.

****

-Anne-

My organization played a role in the release of what's referred to as "the torture report" on the CIA's interrogation activities post 9/11, in which they water boarded people, left them soaking wet in cold cells, suspended by shackles, or given "rectal feedings", which are really just a medieval torture, according to a medical doctor on our board of directors who has literally written the book on physicians' complicity in torture.

Why do I mention this? Because 50% of the American public still thinks torture was necessary and acceptable. So why would they give a shit about someone like Vince? If they think it's okay to water board some guy in Gitmo, why would they care one iota about Vince—a self-confessed druggie—rotting in solitary, or being denied family visits, or other minor but repeated indignities?

It seems to me that Conservatives love their families and friends and forgive them anything, but are harshly judgmental of strangers, while Liberals love strangers but can be indifferent to their family and friends.

Rodney King had it right when he asked, during the LA riots following the acquittal of the LAPD officers who had beaten him, "Can't we all just get along?"

Personal Hygiene

-Vince-

Today I was moved out of the six-man room into a more traditional two-man. We call it rolling the dice: Who will I get as a roommate? Well I did alright. My cellie is roughly 55, retired, and has a few too many DUIs. He will be my roommate for the duration of my stay in Moose Lake.

He's clean, quiet, smart, and he has coffee!

We spend an hour or so getting acquainted and it becomes obvious that we're going to get along. Another big step. I am now comfortable. Tomorrow morning I finally attend the orientation to Moose Lake. The future looks promising.

Once I get a job, the time will fly by. I have put in applications for every available position in every department. And although I have heard that anywhere in the kitchen/diningroom is the worst possible place to work, I believe it is where I will be most valuable. Unfortunately, they will probably not want my opinions or advice. I do hold a food safety certificate from the Minnesota Department of Health through 2015 , so I may be eligible for something better than "general worker."

****

-Anne-

Three years ago, despite all his food safety training, Vince got Salmonella. He was violently ill for a couple weeks and couldn't work. He didn't want me to visit him until the worst was over. His friend Seth tended to him; I'll leave it to Vince whether he wants to provide any of the gory details. When I finally saw him, the skin on his hands was bright red and hard from the prolonged dehydration.

He didn't have health insurance so he racked up some substantial medical bills. Since Salmonella is a potentially fatal communicable disease, the Minnesota Department of Health conducted an investigation but couldn't determine the source of the infection. Was it from Vince's work as a cook? Did he get it on his friend's farm— or while hunting? Any contact with animals, dead or alive, or their feces, could have done it. So his medical costs weren't covered by Workers' Compensation, and his employer didn't pay sick time, so he was just (sorry) shit out of luck.

Whenever things like this happen to my son, I hear the voices of condemnation and judgment in my head. They say it was his fault that all this happened—he didn't finish college so he wasn't at a safe desk job with health benefits and paid sick leave. He didn't have any savings. Maybe he was high or drunk and didn't take the right precautions ….

This is something we are particularly good at in America; we blame the poor for their plights and we hold on to the illusion that if they just worked harder and kept it up for another five or 10 years, they could become successful—in fact, they could make it big!

I am grateful for Obama Care. It's not perfect, but at least once Vince is out he'll have health insurance.

Moose Lake and the Dozen Dwarfs

-Anne-

I visited Vince at Moose Lake. It was "not too bad," as we say in Minnesota to mean, "it was awful."

The guard who accompanied me through the clanging locked doors was friendly; too much so. After all, I had seen Orange is the New Black and I wondered if he would go home and think about me. That's a nice way of putting it.

The waiting room was "decorated" in grey and teal, with paintings depicting bucks that would be a hunter's wet dream, Bald Eagles, and a log cabin in the woods with an American flag flying in its front yard.

Could it be even grimmer than St. Cloud? Yes, because it was built as the State Hospital for the Insane in 1936, during the Great Depression, so austerity was the guiding principle in its design.

I was directed by a CO sitting on a dais to greet Vince on the "hug rug", which was pretty much what it sounds like—a two-by-four foot rug where inmates and visitors were allowed their brief hug in front of a CO.

Vince knew it had been an old mental hospital. I explained how Ronald Reagan had emptied out all the mental hospitals in the 80s, under the cover of "helping people live in the community rather than institutions." Community turned out to mean mentally ill people huddled under bridges and in homeless shelters, because the community programs were so underfunded. .

"Reagan must have forgotten a few mentally ill guys here, mom. There's this guy who must have an IQ under 70 who sucks his thumb and tries to hide it by covering it with his sleeve."

And a guy in the cell next to his had breast implants. His cellie, his lover, had been transferred and Vince could hear him whimpering at night.

He talked about how Moose Lake was the repository for sex offenders, who he referred to as men who are "that way." He glanced around each time he said this; apparently bad mouthing sex offenders was an offense in itself. Vince claimed there were no statistics posted online for Moose Lake because 75% of the offenders there were chomos. .

Vince leaned forward and looked around the room to see if anyone was listening. "Mom, when you get home, do some research and find out why there are so many dwarfs in here.

"What?" I asked.

"Yeah. There're at least a dozen. And one midget."

He moved on to the next topic, how the inmates here had so little privacy that they defecated in the showers, and how he and his two buddies were playing a game of who would find a hair in their food at each meal, because there was always hair in the food.

He asked me to research something about "two-thirds, first offense" legislation, but since neither of us was allowed to have a pen or paper, I couldn't recall what it was when I got home. Some great advocate I am!

"The AA group is just a bunch of old timers telling war stories, so my buddies and I started our own group. We're all above-average intelligence," Vince informed me. I walked him through Cognitive Behavioral Therapy and he seemed to pay close attention.

We talked about his health. "They took me off Mirapex to save money, and put me on a new drug, so I was kicking all night with my Restless Legs—you know how it is." Indeed I do. "They finally told me they'd had me on a child's dose."

We did get to have our photo taken. This was pose #2, I believe.

Progress

-Vince-

I saw the doctor today. They told me they have to switch my medication because insurance won't cover it. I'll be going on something called Cinnamon, or Sinamet, or some such shit. I was really happy with my Mirapex: no side effects and it did the job. But it would appear as if it is not my choice.

Orientation was boring, but not as boring as sitting in my cell doing nothing. We got to watch the PREA (Prison Rape Elimination Act) video again, which I still find hilarious. I'm sure if ever there was one thing that would completely eliminate prison rape, it would be a half hour video tape from the late 80s, in which men with mustaches talk about blowing their cellies for candy bars. Have some dignity, guys. Hold out for a bag of coffee or something.

In the 10 days that I've been in general population, I have learned everything that they spoke on in the orientation. And anything that wasn't covered could be found in the handbook we received the night before the orientation. So for nine days, we had questions that needed answers. We found answers, in one way or another, to questions that all could have been avoided by giving us the God-damned .... Sorry, mounting frustrations.

It would appear that this prison, like St. Cloud, is run by 200 people in 300 different departments. And none of them seem to want to deal with prisoners.

Today I found out I got the one open industry job in the garments factory. Or, garments building, I don't know. I'll be making the clothing for inmates in all Minnesota prisons. I'm excited not only because I got the best and highest-paying job out there, but because I will no longer be on room restriction as of Monday. Until now, I've been stuck in my room after noon every day. I couldn't go to the gym except for on weekends. Now I can really begin my training.

I haven't been able to get on the treadmill since Sunday. So I'm sure when I get back on it Saturday it'll be just like the first time.

****

Am I just lazy? Mybae. Smotemies I relaly dn't want to erxecise. I have gnoe to the gym ticwe in the past two dyas, walkeld one mlie, then lfet. I couldn't even stay for an hour. Ugh.

****

Today, I said I would do it.
Today, I said I would not give up.
Today, I succeeded.
I ran a whole mile. In 10 min, 36 secs. Not bad.

Moose Lake Stats

-Anne-

As I wrote before, Moose Lake is the former State Hospital for the Insane, built in 1936. "Early treatments used there included insulin and electroshock, hydrotherapy, and physiotherapy. In the 1950s lobotomies were used on some patients." As you can probably tell from the stilted writing here, this is taken off a historical document; I always assume things were at least twice as worse as described in historical documents.

"When the Sandstone State Hospital closed in 1959, its program for inebriates [Inebriates! I love it.] was transferred to Moose Lake. By 1961, treatment of alcoholism was a specialization of Moose Lake. In 1966 a program for adolescents was begun, in which some of the participants attended public school and gained high school credits. Also in 1966 all of the hospital's medical/surgical wards were closed.

"The hospital closed as a psychiatric facility in 1995. It has since been owned and operated by the Minnesota Department of Corrections. The facility maintains a small treatment unit for drug/alcohol problems, as well as a sex offender treatment program."

The name was nice-ified to Moose Lake Regional Treatment Center at that time.

A "total of 1,060 adult offenders are under the Case Responsibility of Minnesota Correctional Facility – Moose Lake with a total of 1,044 adult offenders currently on-site at this facility."

I won't throw all the numbers at you; you can look at them yourself if you have nothing better to do. Moose Lake has a slightly older population than St. Cloud, maybe because it's where they house a lot of sex offenders who are locked up for life.

At St. Cloud, 126 inmates were in for Criminal Sexual Conduct (let's just call it what it usually is: rape), average sentence: 106 months. It's more than double that number at Moose Lake, 271 rapists with an average sentence of 137 months. In case your math isn't any good, that's over 11 years.

425 men are in Moose Lake for drug offenses, and the average sentence is 64 months. That's Vince.

The next category is domestic assault (120 inmates serving an average of 24 months). Then there's just regular assault, with 73 inmates serving an average sentence of 54 months.

Other crimes with interesting nomenclature include Crimes against Government, Escape/Fugitive, Counterfeiting/Fraud, and Harassment/Stalking/Bias.

While there was only one murderer at St. Cloud, there are 70 at Moose Lake. So yeah, it's a bit more of a serious place.

St. Cloud is somewhat more white and Latino, and with fewer Natives and African Americans. Whatever that means, if anything.

I scanned the religion column and saw that 58% were Christian, 3% Muslim, and a third had no preference. There are 10 pagans, 7 who called themselves "Eastern," 4 Atheists, and again, as in St. Cloud, one Jew. That must be scary, given what Vince has told me about the Skinheads and the Nation of Islam members talking about how they'd like to kill them some Jews.

Nothing about dwarfs.

Rules are Rules

-Vince-

Well, Mother. I hope you're proud of me at the peak. I have finally become what I always wanted to be when I grew up. For $2 a day, I sew the crotch flap on the front of men's briefs for the Minnesota Department of Corrections. I finally made the big time!

Actually, it's not all that bad. And I'm learning how to do something new. And as far as prison wages are concerned, I'm in a job where I can make $2 per hour if I bust my ass. In comparison, nearly every prison job starts at 25₵ per hour, and peaks at $1 per hour after a year. I started at 50₵.

I should mention that all prison wages are docked 50% to pay fines, fees, and restitution. So I actually get 25₵ per hour on my check, and I'm slowly paying my fine of $135 off. After that's paid, they will still take out 50% and put it in my gate fee account, which I get upon my release.

This week's book selections: Michael Crichton, Andromeda Strain; Nelson DeMille, Gold Coast; and Preston Douglas, Blasphemy. I started with Blasphemy. It's really good thus far. Look it up, maybe you'll agree.

****

I've been a busy boy. Mostly with work. And a fair amount of gym time. I've started playing something called pickle ball. It is a lot like tennis but indoor, with a wiffle ball and an oversized ping-pong paddle. It keeps my heart rate up for a good 1½ hours. It's way more fun than running. I really need to find a way to make running interesting. I can't stand it. I get bored after a mile and quit.

Tomorrow I get to see my caseworker to find out the actual date for boot camp. And I will explore other early-release options. In all reality, I have no desire to go to boot camp. If I have to sit a couple more months to be released in another way, I will probably go that route. But I'll go to boot camp, just to get out of my current SRD (Supervised Release Date, or parole) of March 1, 2017.

****

All right. I saw my caseworker. We went through my options. My boot camp date has been moved up. If I can make it through the six month program, I'll be a free man. That was my best option.

For most of the week at work I have been cutting, then sewing together, the elastic waist-bands that will eventually be sewn to the top of all the other completed parts to finish the 5XL briefs. Twelve hundred in all. Everybody else, however, had to take all 1,200 apart to replace one faulty piece of cover tape that was missed upon inspection. It looked like a horrible job. I even had to re-serge a few flys. But another week has passed.

Ten months from now, I'll be free. If I follow the rules. Participate actively in drug treatment, and keep my mouth shut. I'll be alright. I will keep in mind I'm saving 18 months of my life by doing this. I look forward to the challenge.

I was talking to a friend just now in the hallway and over the loudspeaker the CO yelled, "Close the door in the north!" Referring to my friend and me. I was halfway in my room, he was outside. For whatever reason, he came into the room to continue our conversation. What we didn't realize is that we could have both lost our boot camp eligibility for it. Because there are no cameras in the rooms, only the people that reside in a room are allowed in it. Because of rape and fighting they are strict about it.

****

I could have been taken to the hole. If you go to the hole for any reason, boot camp goes away. Fortunately, neither of us has had any disciplinary problems (in prison) and we were given written warnings. But now you can see how easy it could be to have to do that 1½ years in prison.

110% Solution

-Vince-

Today I was given a pass down to health services for my range of motion test. I had to move my limbs this way and that. I was pulled and pushed, but not prodded and poked. They save that for the physical. It was just another in a series of tests we must pass before we can go to Willow River, where Boot Camp is. I passed.

Without the occasional boost in our spending accounts, it would be really tough to keep up on hygiene supplies, phone time, stationery and envelopes, etc. You see … as I've said before, I make 50₵ an hour. I get half of that now, and the other half upon my release. So every two weeks I net roughly $20 for my 80 hours.

The things we buy from canteen here are substantially higher in price than you would find even in a small town grocery store. Here are some examples:

Ramen noodles, 37₵
Tide (16 loads) $6 (and we have to do laundry more than once a week, because they only allow us a certain amount of clothing)
Paper (150 count) $2.25
Briefs (that we make for 50₵ an hour) $3.35 each

So, we are grateful for any extra money because we can spend a little on ourselves. This time I spent $15 on a clip-on reading light and bulb. Probably retail $3 at Walmart. Now I can spend what I would have earned working 60 hours on phone time, envelopes and soap. Enough of that.

Today was great overall. Work was work. But in the gym, I did the tape, of which I can follow along the first eight or nine minutes. That leaves 11 or 12 minutes for me to go. But I'm trying. Then I lifted weights. And I ran/walked. Only a mile combined, but I'm building stamina.

Every day I feel myself changing. Little by little I move away from what I once was, more than once. And I can see that I can be both good and bad. And I want the good. But it's fucking tough. It's hard for me to want to be good. Some days I don't even want to try to better myself. I think it would be easier to sit another 18 months instead of doing boot camp. But more days than not, I walk down to the gym and make myself do the things that make me feel good about going. I make progress. I try to take today into tomorrow, when I won't want to do anything. I will. I will. I will.

I will write about it tomorrow.

Tomorrow: Well, I lifted weights and walked for half an hour. That's all I willed myself to do. I failed on all of boot camp's philosophies, which are:

I have free choice and free will.
I am accountable for my thoughts, feelings, and actions.
Today I commit myself to positive change.
I will give 110% of myself, 100% of the time.
If I do my best, I will succeed.

I'm not sure those are actually philosophies, but that's what they say they are in the handbook.

Outed

-Anne-

In a previous post I mentioned that Richard Branson, the British airline and media tycoon, has taken on US prison reform as a pet cause. He (one of his PR people, I'm sure) has a blog about it, so I posted a comment thanking him and pointing him to Vince's and my blog in case he wanted a firsthand account of what prison life is like.

I happened to go to Linked In about 15 minutes later, and there was my comment to Richard Branson, complete with the photo of me with my jailbird son! Linked In, not exactly the social network I would choose to share such a thing with! I zapped the post.

Little did I know that, during those 15 minutes, a coworker had seen the post and not only shared it on her Linked In page but also on Facebook. She is a super outgoing person; one of those people who has exceeded her maximum number of connections on Linked In. I'm not Facebook friends with coworkers, so I don't know how many Facebook friends she has, but I think it's a safe bet that they number in the thousands.

And she is Facebook friends with coworkers. So at work on Monday, coworkers started emailing me and stopping by my cube to say they'd read the blog—including my boss.

All of their feedback has been positive and supportive, and several have confided that they have a brother or son or someone in prison, too.

I figure that for every person who has talked to me about it, there are 2-3 others out there who have seen the blog and for one reason or other are not going to let on that they've read it.

I checked the blog stats for the first time ever, and saw a gigantic spike over the weekend. Vince and I had been building a steady readership in the dozens, and suddenly —Kaboom!—there were thousands. And because my coworker and I work for an international organization, Vince and I now have double digit readership in Armenia, the UK, Australia, Senegal, and Kenya.

I loved knowing that strangers in Armenia were reading the blog, but it turned my stomach to think about certain family members reading it.

I talked to a friend whose son has also been in prison. She reminded me that the whole point of the blog is to fight the shame and silence around imprisonment and addiction.

I kept getting overwhelmingly positive feedback. I talked it over with Vince, and he said, "Go for it, Mom. Post it on my Facebook page." I was okay with that. Then he said, "But you have to post it on yours, too."

Gulp. It felt like the right thing to do, but also scary. I called my mom to tell her she would see a photo of Vince and me on Facebook, and that the blog it led to contained swear words and unpleasant things. I don't think she really understood what it was all about but at least she wouldn't be taken by surprise. My sister already knew Vince and I were blogging because I'd shown her the first post where I mention she has cancer and had asked her if it was ok to publish. I called my cousin and my brother, who both said, "Just go for it."

I unfriended some people who weren't really friends, then hit the plunger.

Vince and I don't have that many FB friends but my niece, for instance, has nearly a thousand and she shared the link immediately, as did a few other people. When I got up the next morning, there were dozens of comments and also texts, emails, and phone messages. The most common themes have been: 1) this is courageous; 2) it's refreshing to read someone being "real" online; 3) you have important stories to tell; and 4) you made me cry and you made me laugh out loud.

Mission accomplished! Now all we need is a corporate sponsor so I can quit my job and work on this full time. I have a feeling it's not gonna be Bob Barker, Inc.

Hot Dog!

-Vince-

Dear Blog:

I decided to take a "mental health" day away from work. Although I have weekends off, everybody else was off too, so I can't accomplish much. Today is my chance to catch up on laundry, sleep, reading, and yes, writing.

I do not recall where I left off as I have sent everything I have written since my arrival in Moose Lake to my Mother for print.

Not much has changed. I haven't been running because it's been too cold for the outside track to be open, and there are only two working treadmills for over 1,000 prisoners. I have been doing the tape more often. And as impossible as I thought it was going to be, I am actually getting better at it.

I'm also active in volleyball and pickleball. A friend and I were in the pickleball tournament this past weekend. We lost all four games and were eliminated on the first day. But we tried.

I also try to lift weights when I can. I don't even bother most days, as the workout room is full, and I am not the type of person that fits in with that crowd. I will just leave it at that.

I submitted a list of ten puns into a contest for the prison newspaper to see if one of them could win me a little money. Unfortunately, no pun in ten did.

****

Hot dogs. To quote myself, "All of our meals are hot dogs. It's just a matter of what shape they're in today." Prison food is far worse than any institutional food. I see so much waste. I see huge wastes of your money, our time, and our "food." Simple things like giving us single-serve packets like ketchup and dressings vs. making a large batch of dressing then paying somebody 25 cents per hour to put individual portions on a tray. Over 1,000 trays, three times a day. That saves a lot of money over time. And that's just one idea.

This is Your Brain on Frozen Hash Browns

-Vince-

Sunday brunch: "Egg bake." Made with frozen hash browns (not made by a 25 cents per hour employee, shredding whole potatoes), grey ham, and overcooked eggs. Inedible. A packaged blueberry muffin, even though the facility has all equipment necessary for a fully functioning bakery.

Hell, they could even teach people how to bake. Then they could use that knowledge on the outside to be a productive member of society.

Canned "tropical" fruit. A bowl of water (aka oatmeal), a small container of apple juice that was still frozen, and milk. On the container of milk there is a slogan. We use it a lot around here. "You can taste the difference." It's true.

****

Please do not buy a "Pillow King " [another modified company name] pillow from the commercial you may have seen on TV. Just so you know, they are made here in our prison, by people making roughly $1 an hour. I suppose some could say that's better than outsourcing ... but is it? They pay for slave labor. We get no stock options. The prison gets the money. Money they don't have to use to pay our cost of confinement. Nope, you are all still paying that. Ugh. I'm sure my information is wrong. I'm done on the subject.

****

Every day getting closer to boot camp scares me. Every day I feel as if I do not want to go. True, it will save me 18 months of prison time. But I don't think I can make it through all of the physical activity. I've not come close to running over a mile. I've only run a mile two times in a month and a half. I haven't done one push up since I arrived. And I have absolutely no desire to do the tape. None.

I also think I'm afraid of what will happen when I'm released. I don't have a home, a car, any money, no clothes. Nothing. It's all provided for me here. I hate my brain. I sometimes doubt its decision making.

****

-Anne-

I checked into Pillow King, and they have a deal going where you pay only $115 for two pillows. A hundred and fifteen dollars for two pillows? Are they stuffed with down from the golden goose or what?

Visit Denied

-Anne-

I took the day off work to visit Vince before I left for the Middle East, but I never saw him. I was denied a visit because my shirt was too "low cut." Here I am out in the parking lot after I was ejected, showing off my slutty, low-cut shirt.

The correctional officer, a guy I'll call Power McTripper, told me I would have to go home and change my shirt.

Go home? I live two hours away. Then he suggested I drive into Moose Lake and buy a T-shirt. I protested that my shirt was not low cut; what was the definition of low cut? If there was one he didn't know what it was. I pointed out that I was not showing cleavage; in

140

fact I was physically incapable of doing so.... I said several times, "I can't believe I have to say these things to a strange man in a prison. I'm a 55-year-old woman here to visit my son. I am not wearing a low-cut top!" I felt so shamed. Did I look slutty? I doubted my own judgment.

That's when he said, "Well ma'am, it's for your own protection. See, if you bent over, then they could see ..."

That's when I blew it—I kind of called him a pervert. OKAY I did call him a pervert. Visit Denied.

I asked to talk to his supervisor. He said she was not working that day. I asked to talk to any supervisor. He said there were none working that day. I laughed, incredulous, "So you are running the whole prison?" I asked for his supervisor's name and phone number. He said, "You can look it up on the website, lady."

I started bawling and stumbled out the doors. A female CO was coming in and asked me if I was alright. I managed to blubber out my story and then said, "I think it was all a big power trip!" Of course she couldn't say anything but the look of complicit agreement on her face was clear.

I asked some visitors coming into the prison to snap a picture of me. I called my sister from my car. A group of officers came up, surrounded my car, and yelled, "You have to leave! You can not sit here in the parking lot." I rolled down my window, not understanding what could possibly be the problem. "You have to leave right now!" the closest one barked.

I drove out of the facility and called my sister again from the parking lot of the Dollar Store. "McTripper's brother-in-law probably owns the Dollar Store, conveniently located right outside the prison and handily ready to sell overpriced T-shirts!" I bawled.

"Well I don't know about that," she said, "but he sure was on a power trip. Now drive safely; you've got another two-hour drive ahead of you—don't make things worse by veering off the Interstate."

Vince called just as I was about to enter the freeway, and I pulled over to take his call. He had been sitting in the visiting room when he was called to the desk and told he would not have a visit due to a "clothing issue."

"I couldn't imagine what the hell that would be—my mom?"

"I feel so ashamed! I'm so sorry! I was so looking forward to seeing you!" I kept repeating. It really felt like it was my fault, like I had been trying to sneak in with my low-cut blouse to show all the inmates.

"Mom, this is what we have to put up with every day. If I had called a C.O. a pervert, I'd be back in solitary right now. We have to suck it up all the time. I'm proud of you, mom!"

I wondered, as I drove home, had the guard picked me out at random? Or did he have a big blue-collar chip on his shoulder toward well-dressed yuppies? Or did he sincerely think like a pervert, because after all, one out of four inmates at Moose Lake is there for sexual assault? Is it his job to see every bit of exposed skin as a potential incident?

Request Denied

-Vince-

My roommate is old. He has a TV, and we were watching FOX news. I should mention that I couldn't hear anything and the subtitles weren't on, so I was really just reading the ticker at the bottom. Anywho ... the ticker said, "Judge allows gays to get marriage licenses immediately in Miami Dade ...." The roommate says, "More queers getting married."

I said, "Does that bother you?" And he replies, "I just think it's gross and I don't like to think about it." I said, "Well don't. I never think about it. And it doesn't seem to bother me." He didn't like that.

****

I ran a mile today in 10:10. That's 3:50 better than the requirement for passing the fitness test. Still nowhere near the required 4.3 miles they run every other day at boot camp, but I hear they let you work up to it. Progress.

****

Get back to where you once belonged....

In 2002, after a year of successful aftercare in a half-way house in Palm Beach Gardens, Florida, I made the decision to return to Minnesota to take care of my court obligations, with the intent of returning to live a sober life with my network in Florida.

Vince during his 5 sober years

I had felony warrants in Hennepin and Ramsey counties that were about two years old. I ran from them to enter Hazelden in April

2001, because I wanted real change in my life and in my opinion, being forced into treatment doesn't work. (I should say in my experience, not in my opinion.)

In the month before my return to Minnesota, I gathered evidence of my actions and whereabouts over the previous 15 months or so, along with some letters from my family, counselors, peers, etc. regarding my behavior and recovery program.

My hope was that the documentation would influence the judges' opinions and sway their decision toward one that would keep me out of prison and let me get back to Florida.

Well, it went 50/50.

Because of my efforts in going to treatment, staying sober, and passing a urinalysis test when I got back to Minnesota, the Ramsey County judge basically kicked me out of jail and smiled at me right after she sent a pregnant woman to prison for four years. And I never even saw the judge in Hennepin. She let me out the day after I got there.

Now the hard part. The judges have no influence on the decision to let me move out of state. The State of Florida makes that call. And even with approval of both probation officers in Minnesota, and my Declaration of Domicile in Florida, they still didn't want any more know felons in their state. Request Denied.

I blame nothing but poor decision making on my part for my incarceration. There is a lot I could have done differently, but I always look back on that period of my life when I wanted to get back to where I once belonged, inevitably relapsed, and snowballed.

Theft: Full Circle

-Vince-

Why don't kleptomaniacs like puns?
Because they're always taking things, literally.

I mentioned once that in my younger years I made a living as a thief, stealing expensive mountain bikes from stores and taking the occasional piece of equipment from unlocked garages subsidized my drug habit for a while, and of course made me a felon at 18.

Who would have known, years later, I would make a much better and more honest living protecting the assets of Spencer Gifts. Spencer Gifts—purveyor of fine lava lamps, Halloween costumes, and gag gifts. Although I was only ever the assistant manager, I made over 100 citizen arrests of shoplifters over a one and a half year period. I even made the news for catching somebody trying to pass a fake $20 bill. This was all shortly after I moved from St. Paul to Rochester. About six months (I think) after I came back from Florida.

When a job opening became available for a regional loss prevention director, I applied, and that's when they found out I was a felon and was "not fired" but I decided to go work for the ice cream factory instead.

Two years later, after another brief drug delivery stint, I was in Lanesboro working at a busy corner café where I was fired for stealing. I really didn't feel bad about it then because I was a huge piece of shit and I felt as if they owed me more than they paid me. Or however I was able to justify it to myself, friends, and family. Probably a variety of excuses and explanations.

When sober, I haven't stolen anything since I was a kid. But I've resorted to theft in some form under the influence of every drug I've ever done. And there's another great reason for me to stop this train-wreck of a life. (Oh, I don't mean suicide. I mean I want to quit drugs.)

****

-Anne-

145

After Vince went off the rails I cleaned out a storage locker where a landlord had moved all his stuff. I pride myself on not having a storage locker. If you ever want to do something really depressing, clean out someone else's storage that's been left abandoned. I came across a couple dozen lapel pins Vince had received from Spencer Gifts in recognition of his shoplifter-catching abilities. Some were gold-tone, some were silver, and one was platinum with a diamond chip. I don't know what ever happened to them.

Sprinting Toward Freedom

-Vince-

Tuesday: They cancelled my medication again. This time they said it was an accident, but they can't do anything about it. I cannot sleep without medication because of Restless Legs Syndrome. I was awake until 4:30am. Got up at 5:15. It'll be the same tonight.

Wednesday: It was.

Yesterday, I ran a mile in under 10 minutes. 9:40, to be exact. Today, I went to the first of three boot camp orientation classes. In this one, one of the athletic trainers said that by the time we enter boot camp, he would like us to be able to run miles in under 7 minutes, and at least 3 miles in distance.

I looked around the room and saw some comforting expressions on some bewildered faces. The 350 pound rhino in front of me, still out of breath from raising his hand, asked if he should start walking now to get his heart rate good, which made little sense. I was happy to see that most people are far less prepared than myself.

I will say this, it may prove difficult for many guys in other ways. For example, we are required to speak proper English and refrain from using profanity. For the seven black guys in the group of 45

146

men in the class today, none were able to string together a real sentence. They will be doing a lot of pushups.

Work/Life Sameness

-Anne-

Greetings from Amman, Jordan. I am just back from a week in the Occupied Palestinian Territories and Israel (OPTI , as we say in our biz, which is rife with acronyms), where my colleagues and I had meetings with about 30 human rights activists and also held a training on how they can work more strategically.

Yesterday my American colleague and I rushed back over the Allenby Bridge from Jerusalem to Amman because a historical snowstorm was predicted. Our Palestinian coworker had to stay behind because the border staff is on strike, and they can process tourists (me) but not Palestinians. A good example of something we heard over and over about the situation in OPTI—"it's complicated."

Another thing that came up again and again was prisoners' rights, and torture, and torture in prisons ... there was as much blame on the Palestinian Authority as the Israelis, so the Palestinians are getting screwed by both sides but of course the Occupation is what has to change ... I could write a whole separate blog on this trip.

So now we've had about 4 inches of snow and everything is shut down, and I get to read some of the light literature I picked up in our meetings:

Before I left Minnesota, I called Moose Lake and talked with a guy there about my visit being denied. It was a very cordial, respectful conversation. I felt listened to. He explained that the dress policies had changed and that they had been trying to communicate this to visitors. I suggested they collect visitors' email addresses and send mass emails about rule changes, and he thought that would be a great idea and asked me to email it to him.

I feel better about "the incident" now, but will McTripper be at the front desk when I get there next time? I'm nervous about that, mostly because I feel I owe him an apology for calling him a pervert. Then a second later I think, " Wait —he owes me an apology!" I suppose both are true.

The weekend after I get home, I will move to a new apartment. Then I will have to visit Vince the following weekend because he moves to Boot Camp a few days later and he won't be allowed any visitors for two months. It's not the greatest timing—coming back from a long, intense work trip, moving, then having to do all that driving to Moose Lake, but I have missed hearing Vince's voice, and after being estranged from him, off and on, for many years I am so grateful that we can talk to and see each other regularly now.

Coffee Monster

-Vince-

Every now and then, I hear a story worth sharing. One of my main friends here told a story the first day I met him of an incident in St. Cloud that I still laugh about every time I think of it. He is a tutor here, and has new funny stories every day which I may or may not share at some point. But this one, not involving education, stands alone.

****

I had the same celly for a few months. He was totally insane, but a great celly because he was OCD. He cleaned all day every day. It was awesome. He washed his face over 100 times a day to the point where it was red and raw. Like I said, insane, but the cell was spotless.

He got moved to a single cell and I was stuck with a stinky little non-showering guy. There are a lot of "no-shower" guys in prison, but this one stuck out. He smelled like dead fish. He hung out in nothing but his tighty whities, complete with skid marks. I lived with him for a month before he got transferred. I was excited to get rid of him, but then I went through three more cellys in the next four days.

One morning, they moved my latest idiot celly. They usually replace people the same morning, very quickly. By about 10am, I figured I am gonna have the 8×10-foot cell to myself for one day at least. That was very exciting since I'd had no privacy for over six months. As it neared noon, I figured I was safe to take my first semi-private shit in way too long. I dropped my pants and the glorious private shit was not even fully out of my ass, when the cell door clicked open.

As I was sitting on the toilet, there was no way I could have prepared for or comprehended what bumbled into my cell. It was … the Coffee Monster!

A huge man with a long white beard labored into the cell with his belongings jammed in a sack over his shoulder. Just climbing the stairs to the unit had made him out of breath and dripping wet.

He looked like Santa from hell. He even had little snowflakes all over his clothes, hair, and beard but for some reason the snow was brown! It turns out that his giant container of instant coffee crystals had burst in his sack and completely covered his clothing, bedding, hair, shoulders, shirt, pants, arms … everything …. He left a trail of coffee that had mixed with his dripping sweat and made brown mushy footprints and piles.

When he slung the bag off his shoulder and shook out his shirt, it polka dotted the whole room, including my bed and sheets, with coffee. He looked at me like he didn't know what to do next. He asked how much longer I'd be on the toilet. Turns out he's Russian and speaks very broken English. All I could yell was, "Let me wipe my ass!"

150

At that moment they delivered lunch to us; the lunch room was being used for another purpose that day. So, instead of starting to clean up, coffee monster sat down and started to eat his cold fish sandwich, one foot away from me as I am cleaning my ass.

I finally got clean, but I couldn't really move because he was so fat, you can't get around him in the cell. I didn't want to get near him anyway because he was totally brown and wet. It's in his eyebrows for feck sake. I just stood there watching him eat then asked, "Are you gonna try cleaning this up?!" He pretended not to understand and said, "I think I do clean it up."

"No, no, you didn't clean it the fuck up! There's coffee hand prints on the walls! There's piles of coffee mush on the floor. My bed is covered in coffee!"

He took some toilet paper and made one swipe across the floor, still holding his half-eaten fish sandwich. A CO walked by and I told him we needed a mop. He said he'd get us one. He didn't. We sat there with the tension rising while the coffee and sweat dried all over the room and him.

Probably an hour passes. I'm stuck. I couldn't sit on my bed or touch anything. He kept trying to make conversation like nothing was out of the ordinary. I kept saying, "just shut up." Eventually a swamper came by and gave us a mop and new bedding. It took the rest of the day to clean.

Coffee Monster was 400 pounds and they gave him the top bunk. So every time he got into his bed, it was a big sweaty, moaning, breathing, flapping mess.

So he decided to spend most of the day sitting at our desk, which when you're as fat as him, puts you 1.5 inches away from me at all times. I eventually had to hang a towel from the top bunk between our faces just to escape him. I sat on my bed, pissed off, a towel hanging 6 inches from my face, with his fat head 6 inches on the other side of the towel doing nothing. Literally just sitting there all day unable to see my TV, unable to read English books. He just sat there looking at a towel with an angry dude behind it. About a week later, he got moved to a different unit. One without stairs, and he got a bottom bunk.

Banned

-Anne-

After three weeks of long-haul flights, sleeping in five different beds, crossing borders and checkpoints where soldiers armed with Uzis scrutinized our passports, where I was the scribe in meeting after meeting where everyone chain smoked and kept switching from English to Arabic, I arrived home.

It was a great trip. I love to travel and I love coming home. In this case, "home' was my apartment for five more days. My 16-year-old niece had come in while I was gone and packed for a couple hours, which was super helpful except she'd packed all my coffee mugs and drinking glasses. Oh well. I'd figure something out.

I savored going through my bags and re-discovering the few little baubles of ethno-bling I had bought along the way, like the camel made out of nails. I'd traded for it with a Bedouin woman in Petra; she now had my umbrella that says **World Bank** on it.

I turned to my pile of mail. I always enjoyed this part of coming home, even though there's rarely anything interesting in the mail anymore. Vince had told me before I left that he had a lot of blog material that would be waiting for me when I got home. I always looked forward to his letters, but there was nothing from him.

There was, however, an envelope with a Minnesota Department of Corrections return address. That was odd … Vince's letters had his own name on them … and here is what it was:

I was banned from visiting Vince until August. The nice guy I had spoken with on the phone had not mentioned the possibility of me being banned. I had told him I'd be leaving the country the next day for three weeks. The letter was postmarked the very day I left. He must have sprinted down the hall to get it printed and mailed to ensure I wouldn't be able to appeal within the 10-day appeals period.

My post-trip afterglow was blown. Many choice words flew out of my mouth. I won't repeat all of them here because, based on what has transpired since this day, I am concerned that the DOC is onto the blog and not happy about it.

A battle cry, "This is war !" came first, followed by a profound sense of physical, mental, and emotional exhaustion. I felt furious, overwhelmed, helpless. For the first time since Vince's incarceration, I felt like giving up. Just not fighting the ban. But I've always been wired to pursue justice. Sounds grandiose, maybe, but I simply cannot walk away from a fight when something is just wrong. I wish I could.

Now, I just wanted to get a good night's sleep so I could write my trip report, pack everything that remained to be packed, and deal with changing my address with my bank, the post office, Comcast, my credit card company, the electric company, the DMV, my health insurer, my employer, my magazines and newspapers, and on and on. Oh—right—and I would have to re-apply for visiting privileges with the DOC too, since my address would change.

Fear of Freedom

-Vince-

For the third time since my imprisonment—just in Moose Lake—I am trying out a new medication as per doctor's orders. This time it's Artane, and so far so good. Better than Sinamet. I still miss Mirapex. I am sleeping soundly through the night which is the desired outcome.

Today I ran a mile in 9m 17s. I can't seem to get over a mile though. Every time I'm done running, I know that I'm going to die. I don't actually die, but I do feel completely exhausted.

But … something happened today that is a first. I actually wanted to run. I looked forward to it. I knew in advance that I could do better than I had. And I know … that I can, and will, do better tomorrow.

My strategy is actually to run at a slower pace, and go 1½ miles. And alternate daily between going for distance and going for time.

OK it's not actually my strategy. The athletic trainer for boot camp told me it was a good way to build stamina. I'll take his advice.

One of my few good friends here left for boot camp three days ago. He was nervous. Not because he couldn't handle getting yelled at, or couldn't handle the physical training, but because he was a step closer to freedom.

A lot of guys are afraid of their release date because they've spent their whole lives screwing up and don't think much will change.

In my experience, prison is a horrible place. People talk a lot about repeating mistakes they made out there because it's all they know. I know how to make meth. I learned how, here in Moose Lake. I probably will not do it, although now it's an option. I have phone numbers of people that will be doing what I used to do when they get out. So I have those options too. Actually I threw those numbers away today.

The longer I stay in prison, the more I'm going to want to go back to the shit life. That's why I really want to get to boot camp, so I can be surrounded by people looking for a positive change. I haven't made too many good decisions in my lifetime, I need all the help I can get.

Kermit the Rapist

-Vince-

Other than running and doing the tape and playing various indoor competitive sports, I haven't done any real workout in a month. I went to the gym today with no real intention of doing anything at all, but the weight room was nearly empty so a friend and I went in.

Much to my surprise, my stamina has increased tenfold. I was like the Energizer Bunny. And when I was done, I felt ... high. It was an adrenaline rush I think. I probably could have kept going but I didn't want to burn myself out.

By the time I get to boot camp I have to be able to routinely do sets of 20 pushups. Good ones. Every time we fall out of line, do something out of formation, or screw up in any way, including talking back, we get dropped down. I plan on behaving myself, but it's good to be prepared.

I may have mentioned before that we have dogs in our unit. The Ruff Start program allows offenders to train rescue dogs for service as companions to the elderly and disabled out in the community.

Last week two of the dog trainers were taken to the hole for blowing each other in their room. I find it odd that they would let sex offenders keep a living animal in a room overnight with them. I'm not implying that there's any dog fucking going on here ... but they sure are given the opportunity.

One of the new dog trainers, I call him Kermit the rapist, has a first degree Criminal Sexual Assault. But just like the rest of the sex offenders, he says it was all just a misunderstanding. Oh, I gave him that name because he has a really high throaty voice, and much like a puppet, his lips never stop flapping. And also he's a convicted rapist.

****

-Anne-

In the international development world, we don't use the word "rape" even though it is used systematically to terrorize and intimidate entire communities. We call it Sexual and Gender-Based Violence, or SGBV. I realize that people are subjected to other acts of sexual violence, like having their breasts cut off. I realize men and boys are violated as well as women and girls. I know that various genders are violated in various ways by various other genders for gender-based motivations. But wasn't that a boring sentence you just read? I think that by trying to cover all possible bases by using the term SGBV, the whole issue becomes meaningless. The word rape gives me chills. SGBV? Yawn. But maybe that's just me.

The Buzz

-Vince-

Drugs are my drug of choice. My most recent favorite was meth. And since most of you have never used it, I will try my best to describe what it does.

Meth is unique in that it can be ingested several ways, each giving a different sensation, along with the standard benefit of increased brain activity and being able to stay up for days at a time.

You can put it in your veins, in your lungs, up your ass, in your nose, in your stomach, and ... well that about covers it.

I've never used needles; personal phobia. The rest I've done at least once.

When you snort it, it takes a few minutes to kick in, but it lasts a while. I preferred smoking it over a glass bubble. At head shops they call them incense burners, but I've never seen one used for that purpose. A bubble is a short (4-11") hollow glass tube with a globe at one end, with a small hole in it. It is lit from the bottom, not through the hole (meth is explosive) and when it melts it produces sort of a steam-smoke which is of course inhaled.

The high is almost immediate. Sadly, toward the end of my run, I pretty much had to have the bubble in my hand if I was awake.

My favorite part was when the effects of sleep deprivation kicked in. Some people couldn't handle it and they went crazy. I enjoyed the hallucinations and irrational thoughts. They would start at around day five.

Of course, after some time, your brain would sort of shut down and sleep would become necessary. More than a few times this happened while I was driving.

I have woken up airborne, backwards, and upside down while crashing four different cars, none of which I owned. Fortunately, I never injured anybody other than myself.

Looking back, they should have been some of the scariest moments of my life, but I was in such a daze at the time I just played it cool and worked with what I could. Three of the four cars were just fine. I returned them to their owners, gave them some "payment," and went about my business.

Yes, I should have been injured. One time I woke up going backward at 70 miles per hour in the oncoming lane on a corner of Highway 52 during a snowstorm. Somehow, all I hit was snow, which slowed me down much slower than ... say, a car. I had to come back the next day and I noticed the car was about three feet up in the air, snow packed in and around it. It took six people shoveling and two sets of chains but I drove it out.

Focus Schmocus

-Vince-

I'm sitting in my room, watching but not listening to the football game. I don't have a TV so I get to read subtitles because we don't share ear buds.

I've been in a funk since Friday, when my Mother was denied a visit to me because of the outfit she was wearing. This blog is a bit delayed so you may have read about the ordeal already. In fact I can't really write too much about it because there isn't much to write about. She came wearing a shirt they deemed too low cut. I think she could have gone to Walmart to get a shirt but she may have called the CO a pervert (smile) at which point they probably told her to leave.

She left the country a few days later so I may not get to see her for a while. No visits are allowed the first two months in boot camp.

****

Oddities:

On more than one occasion, I have seen people reaching into toilets between their legs … I really have no idea why.

There are no doors on the stalls for the toilets out where I work, so when I walk by there's a chance I will get to see something strange—to wit, yesterday I saw a man without pants or underpants on (not uncommon for men, apparently) standing up to wipe his behind. But then … he sat back down, smelled the TP, then put it in the toilet from the front, definitely completing the link of genitals and feces. And that's not even the strangest thing I saw yesterday. Ugh.

****

33 days to go.

Nothing new has happened in the last week.

Three days from now, two of my very few friends are heading to boot camp themselves. As I've said before, I don't associate with too many people in here. And after Wednesday, my small group will be down to two, including me.

In my last month here I need to focus on training anyhow. I'm really good at the tape now, but I still have no desire—ever—to run. Fortunately for me, they don't take excuses like that at boot camp. So I need to figure that out quickly.

The Church of Freeman

-Vince-

27 days to go.

What's the difference between an epiphany and a revelation? Well I had one of them I think.

I was watching the movie Evan Almighty the other day, and during a speech by Morgan Freeman he explains how He (God) answers prayers not by giving people what they ask for, but by the opportunity to earn it. I personally don't believe in any god, but every time Morgan Freeman speaks it's like the first time I heard the Beatles: Magical.

Anywho, I got to thinking. I have changed a lot in many ways in the last 7½ months. As of now, I do not want to be part of the drug world anymore. I no longer have any contact with people who use meth. And the longer I have no contact with them, the closer I can get to repairing the relationships with my family, and starting new friendships in the sober community.

But what about a career? What about continuing education? I have a plan, I just don't know how to implement it yet.

I have spent a lot of my years in kitchens of all shapes and sizes. I would really like to continue with that. Something that I've always wanted and would, quite frankly, look good on a resume, is a degree in culinary arts. I have a lot of college credit. I hated every class. But I love creating and learning about food. I have strong kitchen skills, but there is so much more to learn.

My only realistic option upon release from boot camp is to move in with a family member in The Cities. Option 2: a halfway house in Rochester. In Rochester, I know a hundred different ways to get meth in five minutes. Of course there is meth in The Cities but it will be farther from my mind if my family is around instead of druggies.

Unfortunately, I already owe so much on my defaulted student loans, there's no way I could pay for more college. That, you see, is the problem. Rob a bank?

Maybe not an epiphany or a revelation, but knowing what I want to do is certainly a step in the right direction. And certainly a better idea than dealing meth!

****

I haven't mentioned my ex co-defendant for some time. Well, that's because she hasn't been behaving herself. When I took the prison time it was in hope that she would use this chance to sober up. Tougher than it sounds. I know from experience.

Yesterday I found out that she's in jail again on another drug charge. This time it's only for hash, very minor in our state, but with her history, she may get a lengthy term.

I haven't spoken to anybody on the bad side of the law for over a month. Nothing good can come of it.

For the second time in my life, I'm excited about sobriety. I find myself thinking about getting out and finding a couple people I know who are currently in boot camp and sitting around laughing about prison over coffee. They are both from St. Paul.

I'm setting myself up for success, and it's going to be a lot of work. The second hardest part starts in 18 days. Six months after that, the real test: freedom.

Free Will

-Anne-

Vince has written about how he doesn't believe in any god. I used to. For 50 years I never doubted God's existence; I guess that's called faith.

I was a seeker. I didn't assume that, because I was born into a Catholic family, attended Catholic schools, and lived in a Catholic neighborhood, I would always be Catholic.

I spent my teens investigating other faiths and converted to one when I was 18. I'm not trying to be coy by not naming it. Once Vince is out it'll be no big deal. I belonged to a congregation, went to services every week, and put Vince through religious school, much to his displeasure. I wasn't a happy clappy bible banger. My congregation is as liberal as they get. Yes, I'm still a member, even though I don't believe in a god.

Since my dad had died young, I had no problem believing in an invisible father figure who would always be there for me.

Problem was, He wasn't there for me. For 50 years, I prayed. I tried the begging, pleading prayers and the grateful, worshipping ones. I tried shutting up and listening, aka meditating. But I never heard anything. I never got any answers and never felt comforted. People said, "you have to be patient," and "maybe God's answer is 'no'." I was well aware of how we contort our logic to make sense of God. For instance, how athletes thank God when they win but blame themselves when they lose.

Then one day, when I was 50, my belief in God just went poof! and disappeared. It was like a light switch had been flipped off. What a relief! I no longer had to try to shake answers or love out of a being I couldn't see or hear. I was free to pursue or not pursue whatever I wanted. I didn't have to wait around for a sign from God. If it didn't work out, I could analyze what went wrong, figure out my part, if any, and do it different next time.

Soon after my faith evaporated, I read the old classic novel Of Human Bondage, by W. Somerset Maugham, which is about an abusive relationship. This passage jumped out at me and summarized how I felt: "He was responsible only to himself for the things he did. Freedom! He was his own master at last. From old habit, unconsciously he thanked god he no longer believed in him."

I wouldn't go so far as to say everything is due to my effort, like in the old *Rush* song, "Free Will". It's easy to be smug when you're a millionaire rock star. The fact is, we live in a world with constraints like race, class, intellectual and physical abilities, bad timing, good luck, etc.

Another great mind, former professional wrestler, Navy Seal, and Minnesota Governor Jesse "The Body" Ventura, got into hot water for saying "Religion is a crutch for weak minded people." I wasn't weak minded all those years. I'm a very intelligent person. I just think I needed a father figure and I had been steeped in the Catholic life up until age 18, where questioning God's existence just wasn't done.

This new development did throw a wrench in the works for me in my Alanon meetings. Alanon is for families and friends of alcoholics and addicts. I attended weekly meetings and "worked the program," as they say. Alanon, like AA and the other 12-step groups, uses the term higher power interchangeably with god—and everything depends on believing in one. In my group, people only used the word God, and spoke of God, personally, like he was kindly uncle. I kept going for a year but it finally bugged me so much that I quit.

I've written in previous posts about believing that human connections are the key to spiritual growth and inner peace and a feeling of belonging and all that jazz. Vince is counting on his sober friends to keep him sober, and I think he's on the right track.

Ban Battle

-Anne-

Below is the email I wrote in response to my ban notice. As you may imagine, the many early versions of it were not nearly so neutral. I have edited out the typos I made. It's unusual for me to make typos but I was shaking with anger and frustration as I wrote and re-wrote it.

Dear Mr. ___:

I spoke with you on the phone February 3 about an incident in which I was denied a visit with my son, Vince. I thought that you and I had a respectful conversation in which I came to understand some of the changes to the clothing restrictions at Moose Lake. You seemed to listen to my perception that I was disrespected by Mr. McTripper and bullied by the gang of guards who yelled at me to leave the parking lot immediately when I was crying in my car after leaving the building.

I suggested that the DOC might collect visitor emails and send mass notices about changes in visiting rules, so that people like me, who have to take a day off work and drive two hours to get to Moose Lake, aren't caught by surprise. You said you thought that was a great idea and you gave me your email address so I could send it to you in writing. I told you I was leaving town the next day and would be out of the country for almost a month, so that I might not be able to follow up for a while. Again, I thought it was a respectful, constructive conversation.

You didn't mention anything about the possibility of me being banned from seeing my son.

So I was very surprised to find a BAN NOTICE, signed by you, upon my return home, postmarked the day after we spoke. It says I can appeal this within 10 days. Since I was in the Occupied Palestinian Territories (meeting with human rights attorneys about violations in prisons, ironically) until this past Monday night, I was unable to check my mail. I would like to appeal this ban, and I would be happy to show you my flight stubs to prove I was out of the country.

Will you please let me know the name of the warden and how to contact him/her for appeal? Or, just be honest and tell me that it doesn't matter that I was out of the country, I missed the window and there's no use appealing. If that is the case, then I would like to know how to file a formal complaint.

I have attached a photo of myself that day, wearing the "low cut" (quote) top that Mr. McTripper found so provocative, that made him so concerned I might "bend over" (quote).

Thank you,

Anne M.

Moose vs. Marertz

-Anne-

I think there's nothing more boring than trying to follow another person's story about fighting some big company or bureaucracy, but here is the correspondence so far between Moose Lake and me.

Good afternoon Ms. Marertz, [He spelled my name so wrong that I don't need to anonymize it]

I do recall our conversation and agree it was respectful communication by both of us. Thank You again for the phone call.

I have proceeded to look into your suggestion (visitor signing up to get email alerts for changes) and see if it is a viable application for the department. This may take some time, but the communication I have had with the departments IT department as well as other supervisors/managers they like the concept. I will continue working on this project.

My recollection of the conversation regarding a ban notification was that I did state the possibility of you receiving a ban notification as you had taken a photo outside the facility and would not erase the photo as well as arguing with staff. I said if you would have stated your concern, went out and changed your blouse, you would have been able to visit, but due to the escalation of the situation and the photo taken outside the facility, you may receive a ban. I apologize if I was not clear enough on the ban notice, but my recollection is you acknowledged this possibilty and we ended the conversation appropriately.

I do recall you stated you would be out of the country for some time after we spoke, I believe that to be the case and would not request flight stubs for verification and would see this sufficient enough to

165

review your appeal outside the 15 day period. If you would like to appeal please submit your appeal prior to [13 days from the date of this email].

You may appeal to the Warden (Becky Dooley) by sending the appeal by mail to the facility addressed to the her, or you may email her at ____.

Again thank you for your suggestion

Respectfully,

Lt. Mike ____

The photo? The photo had not come up until I emailed it to him. The guards who surrounded my car hadn't said anything about the photo. No one had asked me to erase it. So he was making stuff up as he went along. And yet I decided it would be best to eat crow in my appeal, which I submitted 10 days later. I took out the biting sarcasm but couldn't resist drizzling a little on top.

Dear Ms. Dooley:

I am writing to appeal my six-month visitor ban. I am not aware of any guidelines or a form for this process, so I will just write this as a letter.

As you will see from our correspondence below, Mr. ____ and I have different recollections of our phone conversation. He recalls informing me that I will be banned, while I have no memory of that. He also seems to be saying that it is against the rules for me to have taken a photo of myself (attached)–the photo I took to show how I was dressed and that I was not wearing a low-cut top. If it is indeed against the rules for one to take a photo of oneself in the parking lot of a MN Correctional Facility, mea culpa, I honestly did not know.

As for the original incident, I take responsibility for my part in the conversation escalating and it would be great if Mr. McTripper

166

would do the same. I recognize that prison visits are tough for everyone. It's just a rotten situation all around.

When I spoke to Mr. ___, I told him I would be leaving the next day and be out of the country for work for three weeks. He sent the ban notice the next day–ensuring I would miss the appeal window. He has kindly consented to me having some extra time. Because I moved right after I got home, I wouldn't have been able to visit Vince until this weekend–and now I am banned–and on Tuesday he will be transferred to boot camp where he is not allowed to have visitors for 2 months. I am his only visitor, so if the ban stays in effect, he will have no visitors for 7 months.

I would be happy to discuss what happened over the phone. My number is ___.

Thank you,
Anne M

Pickled

-Vince-

Looking back I often wonder how my brain still functions.

I first smoked pot at a birthday party in middle school. Liike many people their first time, I didn't actually get high, so I faked it. Sitting in the back of a van at a drive-in movie, staring out at the big screen, pretending to be high like I had seen in the movies.

Just a couple short years later I had a huge tolerance and was trying out some different things.

I worked more than a few shifts at Burger King on heavy doses of Beavis and Butthead and Black Pyramid acid. Holy … shit. I was the drive-through order taker and I remember seeing the speaker melting off the wall as an order was being given to me. I was laughing hysterically and drooling but my boss wouldn't fire me because he got his weed from me. I was always able to get through my shifts uninjured, which annoyed me and my friends.

During the last year that I attended high school, I put myself into sort of a last chance program called OJT (on the job training).

At 17 years old I was given a badge, a taser, and a billy club and became one of three security guards at Liberty State Bank.

During the first half of my shift, I sorted mail in the mailroom in the basement, then I would go upstairs and direct traffic in the parking lot if it was busy or sit in the guard shack and smoke cigarettes and weed and sell mushrooms and weed. I could monitor all radio traffic so I knew they never suspected a thing.

I lost that job when they found out I dropped out of school. They even offered to buy me a computer so I could get my diploma online. I said no.

****

It's Monday morning. Last night I got my pass to take the fitness test, the last step in the process of being officially okayed for boot camp.

Unfortunately, on Saturday night I was injured while playing pickle ball.

I wasn't even overdoing it. I actually thought somebody had hit me in the leg, but when I looked behind me, nobody was there, and I limped away.

When I got back to the unit, I asked the CO for a bag of ice. He asked why and I told him. And then he "pushed the button," as we call it. *Dee doo dee doo dee doo!* People came running from every direction. And then came the wheelchair. Fuck! How embarrassing.

They wheeled me about ¼ mile to Health Services where they stood me up, felt my leg, and told me to walk back to the unit, on my bad leg. Fuck!

I iced it down, slept, then took a hot shower in the morning. I was in some pain, had a little trouble walking but I was pretty sure I could make it through the test.

And I did.

Here's what I had to do: 20 pushups, 20 crunches, run a mile, do about 10 minutes of the tape, to show you'd been practicing, and some light weight lifting. Eight months ago, I would have dropped dead from that much physical activity. But I passed and I felt pretty good. Really good.

Eleven days until boot camp. I am no longer nervous. Only excited. Excited to change my life.

The Send Off

-Vince-

There are so many bad choices I've made in my life. But I am ready to break free of my old habits. Nine days until I commit myself to positive change, 189 days 'til freedom.

****

My second to last court appearance in June last year was a contested omnibus hearing where I finally decided to just make a deal. I was sick of my life and ready to go to prison. It happened a little faster than I thought it would, as I've written before.

I left the courtroom knowing that I had eight days left of freedom. Instead of using that time productively I went about my usual routine. Little did I know there was a plan in the works to leave me broke and broken.

Three days before my sentencing, I was robbed at knife point by three people that I thought I knew. They cornered me in a room and told me to empty my pockets, waving around a very short and wide knife.

You may not think of that as too much of a threat. But a person wielding a one-inch knife is ready to use it more quickly than a six-inch knife because it wouldn't likely produce a fatal wound.

So I emptied my pockets and the one with the knife sucker punched me in the eye. As I turned around he punched me again, in the same spot. That really hurt.

They all called me some names and then left. Their goal was to steal my truck and leave me stranded but fortunately the ignition was broken, and they could not figure out my homemade tweaker [meth user] ignition featuring a light switch for toggle and a doorbell button for the starter switch.

I got up. In a daze I walked to the bathroom. I had a huge black eye. My nose was bleeding and my ego was shot.

They took about $1,000 combined money and drugs from me. It was all I had. But even that didn't stop me. Nothing ever really did. I knew then that I needed to be locked up, in prison or chained to a radiator, it didn't matter. I knew I wanted to stop, but I couldn't. My name is Vince and I'm an addict.

****

-Anne-

I received a postcard from Vince. Between it and him writing, "I'm an addict," I felt hope for him for the first time in 10 years.

Hola,

One week away! I'm looking forward to a new life. Again.

Thank you so much for all your support, and hard work. It must be tough at times. I love you very much and I'm happy we have become so close.

Love,
Vince

But was it real? There's an old joke:
Q: How do you tell when an alcoholic is lying?
A: His lips are moving.

Vince writes about how many days till boot camp ... how many days till he's free ... then he can start to change his life. I'm a firm believer that you can change your life now , regardless of your circumstances. That work can only be done inside your head, using cognitive behavior therapy, meditation, and other techniques. If you don't know how to do it, as I didn't for many years, you're stuck. Physical fitness and self discipline are great, but I really hope this boot camp thing helps Vince figure out how to rewire his "stinking thinking," as they call it in AA.

Thank You

-Vince-

My leg finally feels better. I haven't done anything to risk re-injuring it and I kind of feel like a bum. Tomorrow I will go back to the gym and get back to my routine, although I won't be playing any more competitive sports. Too risky for me at this point.

15 meals and a wake up. One of several ways we measure time here. Five days left of prison. Soon there will be no more bars, no more yelling (by prisoners), and no more sex offenders. There are no fences at boot camp. Of course there would still be escape charges if

one were to leave without permission, but people seem to want to stay over there.

Sometime during our second week there, I've been told, we will be out in the community doing volunteer work. It's going to be quite the change.

****

Ten meals and a wake up. I suppose the real wake up starts at boot camp. I have been in contact with a couple like-minded people who left one and two months before me. Both said they have really enjoyed the change. These two, like me, are going for the right reason: to positively change their lives. And they both live in St. Paul, so I will have some friends in recovery when I get out. Very important.

That's what I lost when I left Florida. My group. My allies. The people I grew up with as an adult. I never got it back and I slowly let that become my excuse for using again.

****

Six meals and a wake up. It's Sunday night and I've been having sort of a tough time coming up with things to write about. So I decided to take this time to thank all of you who have been following this journey. My mom and I knew from the get go that this was going to be powerful stuff, and it takes a fair amount of courage to write it down knowing it can be seen by the masses.

Thank you for letting me let it all out. It has helped me transform into a new man. Six months ago I really wasn't too sure about this boot camp idea. Even after two months of sobriety I still wanted to be part of "the game." I was still writing to and talking to all the old characters, setting myself up for disaster. Now I haven't written or called anybody other than family and a couple guys that are in boot camp right now, for the right reason.

172

See You on the Other Side

-Vince-

Three days until freedom, 183 days until my release.

I will not be able to write as frequently from boot camp but I will when I can and I think it will be even more powerful than ever. The following story will be the last thing that I write from Moose Lake.

In the last 10 years, I have spent three + years on meth, six + years as a drunk, and eight months in prison.

By far, being a drunk took the worst toll on me. It didn't land me in the clink, but I lost so much of myself that it's really hard for me to look back on it and be honest about it.

My mother has written about it from her perspective and I've always just kind of brushed it off, not wanting to deal with the truth.

Truth is, I was a mess. Every day. Drunk. I held jobs through most of it. But in every other aspect of life I failed.

Every cent I had went to booze. No room for food or clothing. I guess I paid my rent most of the time. No, sometimes.

I had three days off per week. So starting right when I woke up, I would drink my breakfast, say 7am. Drink beers and smoke cigarettes until the bar opened at 11am, then drink into oblivion until I blacked out. Waking up somehow back in my apartment, or somebody else's.

I've woken up on pool tables. In the middle of the street surrounded by police. Under water, naked, having just tipped my best friend's canoe, losing it forever. And once I woke up and I realized I was clutching a fully loaded shotgun, with my finger on the trigger guard, safety off. I'm not saying I was suicidal, but I did question my motivation. Then laughed it off.

Every day, for years, I woke up with no food in the fridge. I worked in restaurants, but I still only really ever ate one meal a day, four days a week. I was not healthy.

****

It's Tuesday morning. 7:50am. In 24 hours I will be leaving this terrible place, in search of the tools that will make it so I never have to re-visit the places I have just described.

I had a picture of me taken one week before boot camp which my mother will somehow put near this last post, and we will put up a new picture in six months, just to show the physical improvement gained through the program. I weigh 200 pounds here. We'll hopefully see a transformation. Again, I will keep writing, just not so much.

Alright, it's time to go get my life back. Wish me luck.

Here I go.

Little Brother

The Dilemma

-Anne-

Vince has mentioned that he would like to write about his brother, so I should probably get out ahead of that. It's one of the episodes in our lives that I wonder about—did it cause or contribute in a big way to the way his life unfolded?

***

It was 1979. Nine-month-old Vince and I lived on the 18th floor of Skyline Towers, a subsidized high rise overlooking Interstate 94:

I had just started my second year of college. In the spring I would earn my two-year Occupational Therapy degree. I would be able to get a job and get off welfare, maybe even move out of public housing into a quaint little brick four-plex with wood floors and a stained glass window. That was my dream.

Here was my routine:

5:30am: Get up, shower, feed baby Vince

6:00am: Strap Vince into the collapsible stroller, put on the old beaver fur coat I had found at the Salvation Army and the moon boots I bought new after saving all summer. Sling my backpack full of text books over my shoulders, and head down the hall to the elevators.

6:15am: Exit the front door into the winter morning darkness. Cross the parking lot, then the pedestrian bridge over I94 where the wind was always biting. Push the stroller across the athletic field on the other side of the freeway (extra hard if there was fresh snow on the ground), walk two blocks to drop Vince off at daycare.

6:30am: Pry Vince off me, ignoring his crying and screaming. Ignore the guilt. I had to do this to get ahead, to better our lives. Walk two blocks to the bus stop.

6:45am: Catch the 21A to Minneapolis. This is a slow bus that stops at every corner.

7:30am: Catch a second bus that drops me off a block from school.

8:00am: First class. Study and go to classes all day. Pathology, Anatomy and Physiology, Abnormal Psychology, Medical Terminology, and Fundamentals of Occupational Therapy.

4:00pm: Repeat above, only backwards. Sometimes necessary to stop at the grocery, which slowed things down considerably because I had to haul the stroller and one of those little-old-lady shopping carts.

6:30pm: Arrive home, make dinner, feed Vince, clean, pay bills, make phone calls, etc.

7:30pm: Put baby to bed. Thank god he is such a good baby and loves to sleep. But I still like our routine of reading books, singing songs, and rocking.

8:0 pm: Study for a couple hours, in bed by 10.

***

Then I found out I was pregnant again. I had been using birth control and breast feeding. Taken together, these were supposed to protect me against getting pregnant. Lucky me, I was one of the one out of a hundred or whatever who did.

***

I've written about the guy Vince and I call The Creep. Why had I let The Creep anywhere near me after Vince was born? Because I felt obligated. He was Vince's father, after all, and my boyfriend. Even though he was terrible at both, I was a doormat. I can hardly believe this was me—it feels like it happened to another person.

***

I loved being a mother. But how could I keep up my schooling with two babies?
I loved babies. But how could I be a good mother to two of them?
I loved college—I was the star pupil in my class. But how could I keep it up with two kids?

***

I told The Creep. He looked like a badger caught in a snare.

"I spose we have ta get married then, huh?" was his response.

I don't know what I had wanted from him, but it wasn't that.

I told my mom. She was furious.

"This will kill your grandma," she said, and she wasn't exaggerating. My grandmother had run into the bathroom and thrown up when I'd told her I was pregnant the first time.

I told the head of my school program. She looked so disappointed.

"What are you going to do?" she asked, not expecting that I'd have any answer.

The Choice

I was unmarried and pregnant with a one-year-old baby, on welfare, living in public housing. I was 19.

I had just started to feel better about myself and the future. The first pregnancy had been due to carelessness. This time it was due to birth control failure. It was painful knowing people thought I was stupid.

I had just gotten rid of my pet rat, Smiley, because I couldn't afford to feed him. If I couldn't afford to feed a rat, how could I afford to feed another kid?

***

I had gone to a doctor because I was exhausted. His name was Charlie Brown, believe it or not.

I figured he would say I was anemic.

He laughed a yucky laugh when he saw the look on my face.

"That's what happens to girls like you."

"What?" I was confused.

"Girls who sleep around shouldn't be surprised when this happens."

"But it's the same father."

He glanced at Vince as though he was a cockroach.

"So the father is white?" He lowered his voice. "I know some people who would pay handsomely to adopt your baby."

If a doctor named Charlie Brown said this to me today, I would punch him in the face, then sue him. Instead, I thanked him mechanically and never returned.

179

***

In spring semester I would take Statistics, English Literature, and part two of Pathology, Anatomy and Physiology, and Abnormal Psychology. My favorite class was Pathology. The Hennepin County medical examiner taught it; his name was Vincent which I took as a good sign. It was basically one long gruesome slide show—or should I say, side show. There was the guy who had been decapitated when his snowmobile ran into a barbed wire fence, a baby born without a brain, and a glistening, five-foot-long tapeworm with eye-like markings. I loved it. I didn't want to drop out.

***

I went to see a social worker at Catholic Charities. Her name was Judy.

"You could give the gift of life to a childless couple!" she exclaimed. I had an image of her as a Tyrannosaurus Rex, drooling and flapping her little claws over this baby. This white baby.

I didn't care about helping some rich couple who probably lived in the burbs and had a foosball table in their basement.

"I don't want Vincent to be an only child," I said. My siblings and I didn't always get along, but I imagined being an only child as very lonely.

"You can always have more children," said Judy, "when you're married. You're certainly fertile!"

***

My psych instructor gave a lecture on "high risk youth," the new buzz phrase. There were certain early experiences, like being beaten, locked in a basement, or put up for adoption, that caused youth to become drug addicts, criminals, and psychotic.

"Statistics show our prisons are full of men who were abused, neglected, or abandoned by their parents—usually single mothers on welfare."

My best friend from high school was adopted. I thought about the times I had seen her mother belittling her. "You're so fat! Are you going to wear that ?" What if I gave this baby up for adoption, which I now understood was an act of abandonment, and his new parents abused him?

***

I told some of my classmates and they urged me to have an abortion. "At this stage it's just a clump of cells," they reasoned. This was true, but I couldn't have an abortion so soon after giving birth. I couldn't explain it. I just couldn't do it.

"Don't be a tool of the pro-lifers!" the one male student in my class said. That was a valid concern too, but I had to set it aside. Choice meant choice, right?

My mother didn't tell me what to do. "But if you go through with adoption," she said, I don't want you anywhere near the family. It's got to be our secret."

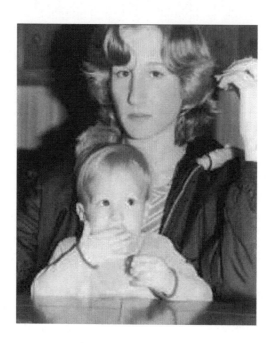

The Slog

If you started reading this blog for the prison theme you may be wondering, what does any of this have to do with Vince going to prison? I don't know if it does—you tell me.

***

And so I informed people of my decision, which I had known from the moment I'd found out I was pregnant again: I would give the baby up for adoption.

I told Judy, the Catholic Charities social worker, and her eyes lit up. "I do have a few reservations," I told her about what I had learned about adopted people in my Abnormal Psychology class. Judy laughed lightly and handed me a clipboard with forms. While I was signing them she said, "We have to trust that God knows what's best for us. Even if it's painful—especially if it's painful, we just have to put ourselves in God's loving hands." I thought this was muddled but made a mental note to try to pray in my spare time.

I told my college advisor. "My due date is right before finals but I promise there won't be any interruptions in my attendance." She looked a little stunned and said, "We'll understand if you need to take some time off."

"No, no—that won't be necessary," I cut her off. I didn't want them to cut me any slack. I would graduate on time. The whole point of this plan was to do what was best for all three of us, so I needed to graduate and get a job.

**

The other point of the plan was to keep it all hush-hush. I would stay away from the family, my friends, and the whole neighborhood where they all lived. If my grandma called and asked if she could visit me, I would make an excuse to keep her away. It would only be for six months, right? It wasn't as extreme as the case of Margie, a girl I knew in high school, who went through her whole pregnancy and adoption while living in her family's house. None of them ever talked about it. Now that was weird.

**

So there Vince and I sat, alone, on his first birthday. I had called The Creep and invited him but he had "some really important business" to take care of. In other words, a drug deal. He never laid eyes on Vince again.

I did what you're supposed to do for a baby's first birthday. I made a cake with one candle and let him eat it with his fingers and smear it all over the place. And I cried.

Then I stiffened myself and plunged my feelings way down into the deep freeze and didn't feel anything again for a year. That's the thing about avoiding negative feelings—it makes you unable to experience positive ones, either.

***

Life went on as before. I trudged through the snow to the daycare, studied furiously, and cleaned the house as though I was in boot camp. As happened during my first pregnancy, perverts tried to pick me up at the bus stop, in stores, in the elevator of my building.

The student who had pressured me to have an abortion was disappointed when I told him I was going the adoption route. "That's …I'm sorry, but that's just selfish," he said. "That poor kid," he said, staring at my belly.

Sometimes students I didn't know would try to strike up a conversation.

"When's your baby due?" they would ask brightly.

"April," I would respond flatly, giving them fair warning that proceeding with the conversation would be a mistake.

"Do you want a boy or a girl?"

"I don't really care, since I'm giving it up for adoption."

This would result in sputtering and something like, "You're so brave—good luck!" as they backed their way out of the room as fast as possible. I hated that line—"You're so brave."

Now that I had set my course I didn't second guess it, but if you had asked me I might have said I was just being practical.

Muggers

In March I was mugged.

My teenage sister babysat Vince while I went to get groceries. She adored Vince and couldn't be kept away, so she was in on the Big Secret but we never discussed it.

It was the first of the month; everyone had cashed their AFDC checks and was flush. I was walking home, a bag in each arm, when a guy asked me the time. I said I didn't have a watch. Seconds later he tackled me from behind. I did a belly flop onto the sidewalk. The groceries flew. I saw the eggs popping open. The milk bounced but didn't break, then spun around on the ice and harpooned a snowbank 20 feet away. The guy ran off with my purse.

It all seemed to happen in slow motion. My wrists and palms and one cheek were bleeding. I scrambled onto my hands and knees and looked behind me. He was running down the hill, laughing. The joke was on him, since I had just spent all my money.

I leaped to my feet and screamed impotently, "Fucker!"

I gathered up what was salvageable of my groceries. Then it hit me that I hadn't given a thought to the baby and how hitting the sidewalk might have hurt it; I had thought only of the groceries. I reasoned that any shock would have been cushioned by amniotic fluid, but I felt no connection to this baby like I had with Vince.

Could the baby feel the lack of love? Would it cause him to neglect his own children, or be an alcoholic, or become criminally insane? I jerked my mind away from these thoughts and any rising doubts or feelings that welled up.

Feeling wouldn't be a good idea. It might make me change my mind. This was like a prison sentence, I thought. I have to wait out my term, separated from my friends and family. Once I was released, I would keep it a secret from everyone, forever, including Vince. That was the point. That was to avoid the shame.

***

My grandmother dropped in on me on New Year's Day. My mother had told her I was missing from the family Christmas gathering because I had taken it into my head to start my own family traditions.

I was five and a half months pregnant and wearing a baggy sweatshirt. I wanted to fling myself on her, tell her the truth, beg her forgiveness, and tell her it was all going to be fine after April. But instead I acted cold. I could tell she was bewildered and hurt but she didn't ask any questions and she didn't stay long.

***

Time flew. I was like a serious machine whose job it was to keep moving, always moving. Read papers, churn out papers. Interact

186

with fellow students as if I was one of them. Transport Vince from home to daycare to home again. Feed him, clothe him, clean him. Clean the apartment so everything looked normal.

I was on a fiscal austerity plan, thanks to Ronald Reagan. I now washed all my laundry by hand in the bathtub, including the cloth diapers, and hung everything around the apartment to dry.

I had received a $2,500 tuition bill and gone running to the financial aid office in a panic.

"Don't you watch the news?" the financial aid lady asked. "About the big welfare reforms? Your programs got axed."

One of the programs in question was social security survivor benefits for widows and orphans. Since my dad had died when I was eight, I received a few hundred dollars a month. This was supposed to last until I was 22. I broke the no-contact rule and called my brother, who was also in college. "Yeah, that bastard Reagan pushed a reform package through Congress that lowered the maximum age to 20. I'll get cut off next year."

"That fucker," was all I could say.

The job training benefit that was covering my tuition had also been cut. I was forced to take out a student loan to pay my tuition, another reason I had to graduate and get a job—so I could make the loan payments.

It's a Boy!

I was 20 years old and eight months pregnant with my second child, who I planned to place for adoption. This plan included avoiding my family and friends so that it could be kept a secret.

But in early April I ran into my aunt and cousin Mary, who was 14, at the grocery. My aunt chatted about the weather, not dropping her gaze below my neck. Mary gawped at my belly but didn't ask any questions.

***

The pains came early in the morning. I woke up and tears came, silently, so as not to wake Vince. I had been able to freeze my emotions for six months but now, on the precipice of saying good-bye, they came.

I flung myself out of bed and called my mother, who dropped my sister off to stay with Vince and drove me to the hospital. The pains continued, fast and strong. As I laid writhing on a gurney a doctor I'd never seen loomed over me and said, "Good morning, I'm doctor O'Brien, and I'll be with you during your labor and delivery."

I had an absurd urge to reply, "Top o' the mornin' to you!" in a fake Irish accent but the labor was going fast and painful. My mother sat by the bed while I panted. They wheeled me into the delivery room and Dr. O appeared again. "You don't mind if a couple of residents observe, do you?" she asked—more of a statement than a question. I consented with a grunt, not really caring or understanding.

A line of residents in gowns and masks filed into the room and stood against the wall—there must have been eight or 10 of them. "Do you want a girl or a boy?" asked Dr. O, showing off her patient rapport-building skills to the residents. "I don't care!" I groaned, "I'm giving it up for adoption!" She recoiled. A nurse leaned in and whispered something to her, maybe my instructions that I didn't want the baby handed to me. I couldn't hold it or I might change my mind.

"It's a boy!" Dr. G exclaimed, holding him up for the residents to see. She stepped forward and held him up to show me. I saw that he had all his fingers and toes and looked healthy. She handed him to the nurse, who took him out of the room.

Dr. Brown's name made it onto the birth card, even though I hadn't seen him or any doctor since early pregnancy.

Baby: MAERTZ
Mother: Ann
Date of birth: 4/27/80
Room:
Room:
Time: 7:08
Weight: 7-13   Length: 21½
Head: 13½   Chest: 13
Baby's Doctor: Brown
Mother's Doctor: Brown

I'm a BOY!

***

They wheeled me down to the geriatric ward. It was for my own good, the orderly said. This way I wouldn't be surrounded by happy mothers and fathers with their babies, or tempted to go find him in the nursery.

My roommate was an old woman who kept croaking, "The pain!"

It couldn't have been more than an hour after the birth that Judy, the Catholic Charities social worker, showed up. Had they called her? She didn't ask how I felt or if I had any second thoughts, but thrust a clipboard toward me and started flipping forms and pointing to where I should sign.

Just then my sister walked in, carrying the baby. "He's so beautiful!" she said. "Just hold him once!"

Judy looked horrified.

"Take him away," I pleaded. She moved forward an inch, hesitated, then turned and left the room.

***

Judy laughed when she saw the name I had put on the form. "Isaac?"

189

I tried to explain that, in the bible, Isaac was sacrificed, and that was how I saw what I was doing.

I thought it was odd I had to explain this to someone from Catholic Charities.

"I should have told you not to give him a name. His parents will change it. You have to admit that Isaac is kind of a *weird* name."

I said I'd be happy to write and explain why I'd chosen the name, how meaningful it was.

"That wouldn't be a good idea. They want to know as little about you as possible. A clean start, you know. It's for the best."
I signed the forms. I watched my hand moving across the paper. It was like a mannequin hand.

After Judy left I got dressed, walked out, and caught the bus home.

Unfrozen

1980. I was 20 years old. My second son was in foster care until his adoption was finalized. I had kept the pregnancy and birth Top Secret except from my mother and sister.

Now I moved forward with my life as if nothing had ever happened, and I never gave it a second thought.

Haha! Just kidding! That was never going to happen.

***

Six weeks had to pass before the adoption would be finalized. I suppose that was to ensure I wouldn't change my mind. I didn't. I gave birth on a Sunday and walked out of the hospital that afternoon. Finals started the following week, so I was back in school studying for and taking exams the next day.

Once I finished exams I had to study for the big test that would make me a Certified Occupational Therapy Assistant. There were lots of other distractions to keep me busy and keep my mind off of Isaac. I would think of him as "Isaac" for the next 20 years.

I got the highest scores in my class, so I won an all-expenses paid trip to the National Occupational Therapy Association convention in San Antonio, Texas. This was a big deal for someone who lived in public housing, took the bus everywhere, and washed laundry by hand in the bathtub.

***

Six weeks passed. I went to the courthouse. In the courtroom it was just me, The Creep, the judge, and about 50 strangers who were there for other cases. The Creep and I didn't speak. This would be the last time we would ever see each other. He was pleased, I was sure, that he'd be off the hook for child support—not that he paid any for Vince.

***

There's a psychological phenomenon called dissociation in which you seem to separate from your own body because you are under so much stress. This must be what happened to me, because it was like I was a spectator to myself. It was like I was sitting in the jury box, watching the judge lean forward and ask, "Do you know what you're doing, miss?"

"Yes," I replied.

Again, like when I signed the papers in the hospital, it was as if I was watching a mannequin hand sign my name at the bottom of the forms.

It was over in 10 minutes. I stumbled, dazed, out of the courtroom with the official-looking order that said **Termination of Parental Rights** at the top and my signature at the bottom.

***

I went to San Antonio, which was my introduction to the concept of "open bars" at conventions. Free drinks! I drank all night, then slept by the pool all day until the bar opened again. What a great professional opportunity!

I came home and kept drinking. School was over so I had all the time in the world to spend with Vince. Except that my relationship with him had changed. I had gone from doting, passionately-engaged mother to detached, emotionally-absent caretaker. I escaped by cleaning the bathroom, applying for jobs, reading thick novels, scouring the kitchen sink, making lists of things, and drinking.

I kept busy, in part, to blot out the fact that I kept hearing the sounds and smelling the smells of a hospital delivery room. I knew from psych classes that sometimes the mind reacted like this under severe stress—I wasn't psychotic—but it worried me. What next—would Dr. O and her residents show up in my bedside?

Vince had never been needy before but now he started whining and hanging on me and it really got on my nerves. He was 18 months old; was this some kind of annoying phase? I tried to gently put him off but that only seemed to make him want more attention. Finally, I lost it. I shoved him and screamed, "Get away from me!" He tumbled to the floor, whimpering.

I was horrified and rushed to comfort him, pulled him onto my lap and rocking him. Was this the future I had sacrificed everything for?

Labeled

What I have described in this series of posts is a closed adoption. Once parental rights are terminated, the birth parent has no rights, period. Ironically, there was a massive change in adoption laws the year after Isaac was born which made open adoption the norm. This is where the birth mother can choose to maintain some level of contact with the child—everything from photos once a year to monthly visits—worked out in cooperation with the adoptive parents. But that didn't help me.

***

As my emotions thawed after terminating my parental rights, my predominant feeling was rage. True, no one had forced me to place Isaac for adoption, but I hadn't felt I had any other option. All the forces of society had been arrayed against me keeping him.

I thought about Charlie Brown, the doctor who had offered to find me a baby buyer; about Judy, the Catholic Charities social worker who had made light of my concerns; the perverts who had hit on me—a pregnant girl at the bus stop with a baby in a stroller; the mugger who assaulted me; Ronald Reagan, who ensured I would start my career with student loan debt; Dr. O, who invited a dozen strangers to observe me go through one of the most excruciating moments of my life; and the judge, who had asked me pityingly if I understood what I was doing.

I wasn't angry with The Creep; he would soon go on to father more children. Vince and I have joked that they could form their own support group, "Adult Children of The Creep." The guy had dug himself into such a deep hole that I figured the rest of his life would be his punishment.

***

A few weeks after I signed the final papers, it occurred to me that I should have a photo of Isaac. I told myself this was for Vince—if I told him some day. I called Judy and there was a long pause after I said my name, as though she had already forgotten who I was.

"Why didn't you ask for a photo before the papers were signed?" she asked.

"I don't know," I stammered, feeling stupid and ashamed. I hated her but knew I was at her mercy. "I would really, really appreciate it if you would ask the parents."

She told me I would have to put my request in writing, which I did. Six weeks later she called to say that the parents had denied my request.

"Since you didn't request a photo before you signed the papers, they're under no legal obligation to give you one now. They're concerned you might see the baby in a shopping mall or something ... they wouldn't want any scenes. It's for the best.

"They want you to know that they love him very much and they gave him a beautiful name. Of course, I can't tell you what it is."

Wow, she was really enjoying herself. I added Isaac's adoptive parents to my hate list.

***

I had lost control with Vince, screamed at him, and shoved him to the floor. I called the county and asked to speak with a child protection worker. She asked a bunch of questions then pronounced, "Based on your family history and your recent drinking behavior, I think it's clear that you're an alcoholic." She recommended I place Vince in foster care so I could go to rehab. "You can say no, but there may be repercussions," she said ominously.

I didn't think I was an alcoholic but I placed Vince in foster care and got ready to go to treatment. The next day my mother demanded that I sign Vince over to her, so I did. It was only temporary, right?

From AA to LA to Homeless

Vince went to live with my mother, and I attended outpatient chemical dependency treatment. If you are in the "helping professions"—social work, psychotherapy—or if you even just have common sense and empathy, you won't be surprised to learn that I wasn't an alcoholic.

The expectation had been that I would go through pregnancy, birth, and adoption without any support, then go on as though nothing had happened. People seemed surprised that I was filled with rage and despair. They squirmed when I talked about it.

"You signed the papers; it's over—why keep bringing it up? Just don't think about it."

Alcohol is a time-honored stress reliever in such dissonant situations.

***

But I stopped drinking anyway. Sobriety—and a break from being a full-time mother and student—helped clear my head and face my emotions. I spent the month working the Twelve Steps of Alcoholics Anonymous and reading piles of self help books, and doing all the other things people do to get back on track.

After a month Vince came home. You were expecting some big drama? Sorry. In Minnesota we don't like drama. In fact we are all about avoidance of discomfort, or as I call it, "reality."

I didn't drink for a couple years. I went to AA, where the members often listened to my story and said, "I don't think you're an alcoholic." I should have been referred to Alanon, which is for family members and friends of alcoholics. People impacted by alcoholic behavior act just as crazy as their alcoholics, but there's no rehab for them. In fact I can recall my mother complaining that my dad got to go to "that country club"—Hazelden, a rehab center nestled on a lake with a pool, wooded walking trails, and tennis courts—while she stayed home with the four kids, the house, and the bills.

***

I got a job, moved out of the hi-rise, and started paying back my student loans. Vince began school and, while his grades were never great, he was popular with teachers and students. I made sure he brushed his teeth and washed behind his ears. I took him to baseball practice, religious school, and family functions. We watched Dr. Who together and went on little road trips to Lake Superior to hunt agates. You know, normal life.

***

Every spring I would find myself feeling blue and wonder what was wrong with me. Then it would hit me: Ah ha! Isaac's birthday is coming up. Every couple of years I would send a letter to be placed in his file, knowing it would probably never be read. When my mother talked about how many grandchildren she had, she didn't count Isaac. Intellectually, I knew this was the whole point—that it remain forever a secret—but to me he was always out there, somewhere.

***

Eight years later, when Vince was 10, I got entangled with an abusive rich guy. Vince and I almost moved to LA but instead we ended up losing our home and I lost my job. Three times in one year, we had to move and Vince had to change schools. I chose this time to tell him about Isaac. I thought it would comfort him to know he had a brother out there somewhere, assuming he was alive. Clearly I am not a psychotherapist, or I would have known this would backfire. Vince was devastated—it was a loss on top of losses.

He met his brother, eventually, and some day one or both of us will write about that.

***

Did these events have a permanent effect on Vince? They deeply affected me, so why not him, since he was so much younger and couldn't understand what was happening? If they did affect him, it's his job now to delve into them and resolve whatever leftover effects may be holding him back, which is what he seems to be doing.

Willow River

Doctor Wonderful

-Anne-

People have asked how Vince can write so well, considering he dropped out of school at 16. First, I read and talked to him from Day One. Second, I got a full scholarship to send him to a Montessori preschool. Then, even though I am such a city person that I break into hives when I pass outside the city limits, I moved to a suburb in order to send him to the highest-ranked public school system in Minnesota.

Vince was 10 when I finally finished my college degree. That enabled me to get a new job that paid $20,000 a year—$20,000!—that seemed like a fortune. I also loved the job, which was at a private university. Vince and I lived in a safe and clean—if vanilla—subsidized housing project. I had pulled myself up by the bootstraps, and the future looked like it would only get better.

Here is where I "mom up" to the next episode that blew us off course and (I think) screwed Vince up.

As I type the words, "And then I met a man…" I feel my palms start sweating and my stomach tighten.

***

Let's just call the man Kermit, because he was about as short, slippery, and spineless as a frog.

Kermit was originally from California and was finishing his neurosurgery residency in Minnesota. He adored Vince, the poor fatherless boy with the big brown eyes and quick wit, and Vince adored him. Kermit adored me, too, the spunky single mother with blonde hair and glasses who read novels by the pile. He only read medical journals.

Looking back, I guess I fell in love with him because I felt sorry for him. He had been abused by his mother. He told me about it in great detail. I tried to empathize by telling him about my abusive, alcoholic father who had died of an overdose. He said that wasn't the same thing at all—since my dad had died so long ago I shouldn't blame my problems on him. Besides, Kermit would say as he slugged down his fifth rum and coke, you can't hold an alcoholic accountable for what they do when they're drunk; they can't help it. Now, *his* mother was *really* abusive, and she didn't even drink! The Witch was still alive. Becoming a brain surgeon had been his plan to escape from her and never have to ask her or his dad, who was a saint, for anything ever again.

There were a few episodes of foreshadowing, like when he got jealous and hurled a can of Coke against my kitchen wall, and left me to wipe up the mess. Or when a cop pulled him over for erratic driving, and he flashed his hospital ID and told the cop, "You wouldn't want to throw me in jail, would you officer? I might be the one you need to operate on you if you get shot." He laughed about it when he told me later.

But then he moved back to California to join a practice there, and begged me to marry him and join him. I said yes.

He was living in a penthouse apartment overlooking the Pacific, and he hired a realtor who started sending me full-color glossy profiles of million-dollar houses. "Just get rid of all your furniture and move out there asap!" he'd say. "You can go shopping wherever you want and buy all new furniture!" He had bought a red Maserati, but he would buy me an SUV—a Mercedes, of course—not a Ford! Vince would go to a private boarding school, and wait—what? When I expressed hesitation, Kermit accused me of not wanting the best for my child.

Alarm bells were going off in my head but I ignored them. My friends and family were beside themselves that I had not only met a man, but a rich one—a doctor! And so I quit my new job, gave notice on the subsidized townhouse, and gave away most of my belongings. We were moving to California! What could possibly go wrong?

California Dreaming

-Anne-

And then Kermit changed his mind. He just wasn't ready to get married. It was too late for me to keep my job or housing. He mailed me a check to carry me over for a month.

***

So Vince and I never moved to California. Instead, we moved into a friend's unheated attic that winter until we could get a foothold and start over. Then we moved again, and that didn't work out, so we moved again. I started working as a freelance writer so I could say I was self employed instead of unemployed. Also because I was too depressed to get out of bed, so woodenly depressed that I wasn't thinking about Vince. Facing the impact of my behavior on him would have produced such massive guilt that it would have pushed me over the edge.

***

But wait, there's more!

I went back to Kermit, after months of him apologizing, begging, wooing, and having massive bouquets of flowers delivered to my door.

And so Kermit and Vince and I flew back and forth, and the hurled Coke can turned into me being hurled—hurled, punched, kicked, and strangled. Once, in the course of strangling me, Kermit broke his own thumb. I can still see him standing over me, as I choked and

200

gasped my way back to consciousness. "You bitch! Look what you did—you broke my thumb!"

***

A few years ago I had an x-ray for some reason, and the doctor asked me about my old neck injury. "Looks like you had a pretty significant injury," he said. I had no idea what it could be, until a few days later it dawned on me that this was probably from the time Kermit had tried to strangle me.

***

The only ones who knew what was really going on were the St. Paul Police, St. Paul Fire Department, and Vince. Actually, Vince tells me now that he didn't have a clue what was going on, but I find that hard to believe.

Kermit and I went camping in the Grand Canyon, where he beat me black and blue in our tent (but only where clothing would cover the bruises; he never hit me in the face). I escaped to the car, locked myself in, and shivered through the night. Back in St. Paul, I went to the police, who photographed my bruises. They couldn't do anything because Kermit was in another state, but I thought telling others would keep me from going back to him.

When I tried to cut it off, Kermit would call 911, say he was my doctor, and tell them he feared I was having seizures. Would they go to my house right away and check on me, breaking down the door if necessary? I would hear banging on the door at 3am and find firefighters with axes poised to smash down the door.

I kept flying out to see him, spending money I didn't have. That's right, Kermit never paid. One of his recurring accusations was that I was a gold digger, so although he made at least 10 times what I did, he never paid for my tickets. He did fly Vince out for the World Series, and they drove up to Oakland in a limo. He bought Vince an A's hat and jacket and full collection of baseball cards. Vince was in thrall to him.

Kermit and I took a road trip to Napa and visited vineyards. He bought expensive bottles of wine for his "collection," which never made it back because he drained them all. He told me he had access to drugs he could use to kill me if I tried to leave him, and no one would ever be able to figure it out because, after all, he was a genius.

I can't bring myself to write about how it ended, but it finally did, with an interstate restraining order against him.

Vince knew I had done the right thing but he was crushed to lose his idol. Was it this episode that set Vince on the road to prison—on top of not having a dad, growing up in poverty, having a depressed mom, and being genetically loaded for addiction, compounded by all his bad choices?

Appeal Denied

-Anne-

I got a postcard from Vince. Don't ask me why he addressed me as "Ms. M." and not mom.

Ms. M:

Well, I made it to Boot Camp. Everything is a bit stressful and overwhelming at first, but it's all designed with our success in mind. I'm picking up bits and pieces here and there but basically I have no clue what I'm doing yet. But it will come. I won't be to be able to talk to you for two months but I will be able to write more than I thought.

I'm more excited than nervous or scared. This is going to be really good for me, and everybody that knows me!

I'll write more soon,

Love,
Vince

***

My appeal of the visiting ban was denied. The warden wrote that she found "no compelling reason" to reverse it. I assumed it would be denied but it still made me furious when I opened the letter. And for some reason, the fact that the warden is a woman made me feel even more disgusted.

Vince cannot call me for two months now; that's a boot camp policy that has nothing to do with me. I can't call him, as ever. By the time I am allowed to visit him, it will be seven months since we've seen each other. He thought he wouldn't have time to write but now says he will. That's good. I can still email him. I am so grateful for that DOC email system.

***

Yesterday my sister had the left lobe of her liver removed. She had endured two months of chemo to shrink the tumors in it, and her doctor recommended they remove the affected part of the liver just to be on the safe side. Once she's recovered from surgery she'll have to go back on chemo.

In the movies, people get cancer and the next thing you know they're on their death-bed having a tear-jerking good-bye talk with their loved ones before they peacefully slip away. I did not realize that cancer can go on and on and on and on and on, with years of chemo, surgery, radiation, side effects, financial problems, and emotional highs and lows. I'm so grateful my sister has made it through so far, and I really hope this is it—that the cancer is gone for good.

What doesn't kill you makes you stronger? Bullshit. It makes you miserable. Well, check back with me in a year. My sister is a lot more of a naturally-positive thinker than I am. Maybe she'll bounce back to her rose-colored glasses, in-the-moment state of being if she can catch a break from cancer misery.

203

***

A friend emailed to find out how I was. "How's all that drama with your son and your sister?" he asked.

Drama? Drama is turmoil you create on purpose to draw attention to yourself, or to deflect attention away from yourself, like when you want to cover up something crappy you've done.

My sister's cancer is not drama. Vince being in prison is not drama. Their situations may be a bit dramatic, but that's different.

Drama is just what it sounds like: entertainment on the stage of life that distracts us or others from boredom, loneliness, inadequacy, or guilt.

Cancer and prison are horrible realities for real people I love.

***

Woah, what a downer of a post! You might think, from reading them, that I am a morose, miserable person but in fact I am quite content. My life is stable, my work is interesting, I am never bored, and I even have fun from time to time. Thing is, it's my dramatic experiences, probably, that have made it possible for me to appreciate what is good, but writing about how la-la-happy I am wouldn't make for very compelling blog reading, would it?

Buckling Down

-Vince-

Intense. The only word that comes to mind to describe Day One.

I've been here only 8 hours but my feet are already killing me. My socks are black from wearing my boots for 15 hours a day. For up to an hour at a time, we have to stand at attention, feet together at the heels, toes out at a 45 degree angle, thumbs pointed down and touching the outside seams of our khakis. Head forward, eyes up, staring at whatever point in the wall we choose. No eye contact, no movement.

The next few days we will practice marching, military bearing, and double timing (running) everywhere we go when we're outside.

There's a lot to learn in a short amount of time. But I already get the feeling that the COs here actually want us to be successful, even though they yell at us a lot.

***

First chance to write in two days. The stress is really mounting. It's my fifth day and I still can't figure out how to properly make my bed. My hands are blistered and sore from scrubbing my belt buckle with a 2×3" green scouring pad. I've worn through five pads so far. Scrubbed them down to raisins.

Yesterday we did two hours of drill and ceremony, during which we must have done 200 pushups, some of which we did on the CO's count. We go down on the count of one and have to stay there until he says two. Down doesn't mean we can touch the ground. We have to stay an inch off the ground. Very painful. I was trembling at the end. Today I am very sore, but it's our down day so I'll recover.

All that aside, I'm feeling good about myself. I know I'll succeed. All for now. Gotta scrub my belt buckle.

The KCQ

-Vince-

Learning how to iron. Learning to polish boots. Still scrubbing my belt buckle. Marching in formation is really difficult with 17 guys that have never done it before. People going in so many different

205

directions. It's absolute chaos, but we get to work on it every day. I'm exhausted, but dealing with it, as if my life depends on it, which it does.

We haven't started chemical dependency (CD) treatment yet, that's next week. But the general consensus from the people that have been in it is that it's different and it is working for them.

AA in my opinion has turned into too much of a faith-based 12 step program. I have no interest in religion and am generally turned off whenever the subject comes up in public (yes, AA isn't exactly public but I think I got my point across).

Anyhow, I'm excited to try out a different approach. Maybe this will be the one.

I can say this: they really come after us from all angles here. Mental, physical, emotional, and whatever other angles exist that I don't know about yet.

This is not just the beginning of the rest of my life. This is the opportunity to enjoy the rest of my life, be a good, honest person, and break free from the evil spell of my addictions.

Failure is simply the opportunity to begin again. This time more intelligently.

***

-Anne-

I got into trouble again, unintentionally, this time with Vince. For six months, I've sent him every blog post, no matter what the content. His, mine…this has been part of the deal, so he can see I'm not editing him, or he can change or clarify something if he wants. But then I got his first letter from boot camp:

"I maybe didn't clarify enough how important it is to never send me any posts, especially of the nature that you sent most recently. That subject is absolutely taboo. I thought you knew that. Send me the comments from everybody, and your posts. Sending me posts like the Kermit one could easily get me kicked out. No joke. So please think before you send."

He had not told me not to send any such posts. Given all the conflicting, capricious rules and difficulty of us communicating, he could be forgiven for thinking he had. God, I could have gotten him kicked out of boot camp in his first week!

So there I went again, middle-aged mom wading into the Kafkaesque correctional quagmire (the KCQ—good acronym!).

"Kafkaesque: having a nightmarishly complex, bizarre, or illogical quality, as in "Kafkaesque bureaucratic delays.""

The KFQ

-Vince-

It's really stressful here. People are constantly screaming at us. Today I was given contradictory orders by two different guards and I got in big trouble. I really felt like yelling back but I didn't. Then ten of us had to use spades to till up four garden plots roughly 50×100'. It took us two hours, non-stop, but we did it. I felt pretty good afterwards.

All right, I'm exhausted. Yes, we get up at 5:20am, Monday through Sunday, 182 days straight. Sundays are down days, but we're still active.

***

Today was a busy day. It's amazing how fast the days go when we keep busy for 16 straight hours.

We started out by taking about a three mile walk, at 5:45am. When we get back to our barracks, 58 men cram into the bathroom, undress, then rotate our way through the eight showers. Then we hurry to get dressed, all of us still in the small bathroom area.

It takes a lot to change because we have to

I don't even know where that last sentence was going. Those last two paragraphs were all I had time to write yesterday.

***

-Anne-

Vince wrote: If the plan is for me to live with you, then your landlord has to be made aware of the situation ASAP, and you need to have a landline installed by the time I get there, and you cannot have any alcoholic beverages on the premises. Start talking with your landlord now just in case there is a problem.

Aaargh. I don't want or need a landline. I really enjoy my beer or wine after work. And I surely do not want to have that discussion with my landlord, who I've never met but have only spoken to to complain about things that don't work.

"Hello, I'm calling to let you know that my son will be moving in with me; he's just getting out of prison for a drug sentence…is that a problem?" Right. That's gonna go down well. Would I be asking permission, or just informing them? Will they have the right to say No? Maybe I will have to move. Maybe if I just don't tell them, and don't tell Vince that I didn't tell them ….

I love my son and I want to support his recovery, but I really don't want to be inconvenienced by it. Does that sound terrible? Or am I already putting more into supporting him than most people would find acceptable? This is where the Kafkaesque Family Quagmire of family boundaries comes into play.

The Drill

-Vince-

I'm starting to settle in. But we are warned not to get comfortable. Our punishments for minor infractions like falling out of formation, forgetting to remove or put on our hat when going outside or coming in, are pushups. Those are meant to refocus our attention on paying attention. And there are no shortcuts allowed here.

Somebody was using a pencil to wedge his green scrubby pad into his belt buckle to get some hard to reach copper. A CO must have seen him cheating on the camera and they called him out, took his buckle, smashed it with a hammer, and gave him a new one. That was after five days of scrubbing. To put that into perspective, I have been working on mine for nine days and I'm still not done. Of course, I haven't been cheating.

My boots are not done. I've been polishing the leather tips of them with spit and ghost-coats of wax after applying a thicker first layer a week ago. I have spent roughly 10 total hours just making circles with a thin blue rag. I'm also getting really close to done on my buckle. When we're done, that frees up a lot of time for treatment and work crew.

The work crew consists of anybody that isn't in school or doing something else. Today they went into the woods and raked. They actually raked the woods. I can't really describe to you how pointless that seems, but that's just one of many way they keep us busy.

***

Day 10. Getting into it. What used to feel like chaos is what actually makes our days go so quickly. We're never in one spot for over two hours.

Schedule:
5:20 a.m. Wake up, Head-Count

209

5:25 a.m. Make our beds (with 45 degree angles everywhere), shave, brush teeth, get dressed, put laundry in bins

5:45 a.m. On alternating days, run or do aerobics for one hour. Stretch for 10 minutes before and after

6:55 a.m. Get back to barracks. 57 men shower, pee, poop, get dressed in our khakis, everything looking sharp, belt buckle lined up with our fly and shirt (gig line), boots laced tight and laces tucked into the boot at the top, lockers organized, clothes properly folded, etc.

7:20 a.m. Count. We stand perfectly still at Military POA (Point of Attention) for up to 30 minutes, usually less

8:00 a.m. Chow time. We file in, stand at Parade Rest (feet shoulder-width apart, feet at 45 degree angles, hands locked behind our backs, eyes and head forward, no movement), then slowly move through the chow line. We eat quietly then file out. There are many details I'm skipping, maybe I'll have time to write about them later.

8:40 a.m. Barracks cleaning

9:00 a.m. Some people go to school, others to morning treatment, some go to work. Work is either KP (Kitchen Preparation) or laundry (me), community work, all sorts of stuff really. I go to treatment at 1:00 p.m. until 4:30.

After evening meal, we do a lot of different stuff including more aerobics or running or going to the library or study hall.

Today we started treatment. Already I'm remembering a lot from my time in Hazelden 14 years ago. One similarity is that I still have to deal with a good number of people who don't want to be here or don't think they have problems. They weren't aware that this was going to be such a big part of boot camp. We shall see how long that lasts.

Thinking vs. Thinking

-Vince-

I just can't find the time to accurately describe our schedule. It does change daily.

Today I worked for seven hours doing laundry for all three barracks (182 men). Then, before I even had a chance to sit, we went out for drill and ceremony, where we marched for two hours.

Now I have to do my treatment homework, so that's it until later.

Later. I forgot to mention that the CD treatment here is called Positive Changes. It was developed for the Minnesota Department of Corrections by Hazelden. Hazelden Center for Youth and Family worked pretty well for me back in '01, so I'm hoping this cognitive thinking approach works for me because I just don't think the 12 step program is for me anymore. Not to say I won't go to meetings, when I get out, I just can't get past the God thing, and I don't like the idea of pawning my problems off on something that isn't real.

Way off track there. It's almost lights out time. Tomorrow is my down day. Good night.

***

-Anne-

I am a big fan of cognitive therapy, and it's not the same thing as positive thinking, so I wonder about this treatment program called Positive Changes.

Don't get me wrong, positive thinking feels a lot better than negative. If you are able to easily choose positive over negative thinking, why wouldn't you?

But in my 55 years of living I've only met two types of people who espouse positive thinking: 1) people who have never faced any serious life challenges, who tell the rest of us, "Just think positive!" and 2) people who are living in a fantasy world, whose lives would be considered by most people to be a mess but who exclaim, "Isn't everything great!" Actually, the name for this second one is denial—

it's a defense mechanism that protects us from harsh reality until we're strong enough to deal with it.

I went to Alanon meetings and worked that program for years. I got a lot out of it. I wish Vince could switch the word "god" to "the group" or some other support outside himself that is a support to his sobriety.

Back to the question of thinking, positive or otherwise. In Alanon there are a lot of slogans like One Day at a Time and Live and Let Live. There was one that was simply the word Think. For years I had no idea what that one meant. Think!? That's all I did! I worried, obsessed, and mentally gnawed on all my family's problems.

Then one day, maybe soon after I lost my belief in God, I realized it just meant what it said—Think, you idiot! Use the mind that God—or evolution—gave you. Thinking is different from obsessing or worrying. I found it helpful to reason things out with another person who was outside of the situation. It may sound simple, but in alcoholic families we are dealing with people who are not rational but manipulative, indirect, and sneaky. Alcoholics are often brilliant and charismatic, but they're also liars. People affected by them tend to be martyrs.

Alcoholic, Not Anonymous

-Vince-

Today is India squad's (my squad) down day. Already, we've been busy. Doing homework takes a lot of time. So does ironing. We need to have seven creases on our khaki shirts and four on our trousers. Oh, also making our beds takes a while. That is what I struggle the most with.

I am a perfectionist. I didn't really know that until I got here. Thing is, I can't do anything here perfectly, so I become frustrated and angry with myself. That can put me in a bad mood, which I communicate with my body language. Like brightly colored smoke. Stay away from me!

I tell myself I don't want to work on fixing my bunk because I know I can't do it correctly. And I don't want to ask for help because I should know how to do it by now and I don't want to look like an idiot. Do I make any sense here?

I'll be fine in a few more days. 171 days left. I will take advantage of every one of them.

***

I received the glasses my mom bought me a couple days ago. I've been told a couple times that Buddy Holly called and wants his glasses back, but they look much better than the ones I had.

Okay, this will be it from me for a while. It's time to focus on Me and my treatment plan. I hope you've all enjoyed my writing. There will be more, and when I get out in September I will have plenty of time to write about more of my life experiences and my time here and in prison. I have a lot to write about. I'm not exactly proud of where I've been and things I've done, but it helps me a lot to think and write about it all. Some of it is certainly entertaining.

Last thing. I know many of you have made comments on the blog. Thank you. Feedback, whether positive or negative, helps me. And if you really want to make my day, you can write to me directly at the address below:

Vincent Maertz 244296
MCF-WR/CIP
86032 County Highway 61
Willow River, Minnesota 55795
USA

"Don't take life too seriously. You'll never get out alive."
– Van Wilder

A Roof of One's Own

-Vince-

Ms. Maertz:

Over two weeks in! Things are getting better. Actually a lot better.

Now, to answer your questions.

It's true that I have to live in a half-way-house in Rochester, or with an approved relative in another city, yes.

The reason that we can't live with another person right away is that we don't yet have the resources to do so, and while we're here we don't have the ability to locate a place to go. Not to mention when we leave, we have nothing. About $400-500, a pair of jeans, and a white t-shirt. (no bed, no lamps, no furniture, etc.)

The no-booze rule is an intensive supervised release (ISR) rule. Ultimately, of course, it's up to us to maintain sobriety, but there can be no alcohol, drugs, firearms, bombs, etc. in your house while I'm living with you.

There are a couple guys in boot camp that will be in your area when I'm out. Eventually I will be working and will be allowed to move, I believe in as little as 30 days.

Your landlord has to know, by law, that I'm a felon, and my ISR agent will contact them before I'm approved to live at an address. If you own your own place by then it won't be an issue.

I can start looking for a job on day one. I can start work any time.

The money I get upon my release can pay for a landline. In a lot of cases, agents actually prefer us to have a cell phone because of the tracking ability. I plan on getting a phone right away anyhow for sober networking and job hunting.

Thanks for mailing me the blog comments keep 'em coming. Let's get our story out there, it's a good one.

Everything here is designed to transform every aspect of our lives. Starting with our thinking. I can't even explain it. It's better than Florida. How about that?

Love you, mom. Thanks for doing all the typing. I do see a lot of typos. Are they spell checked before they get posted? Also, we do NOT get body cavity searches here, FYI. I'm doing well. I like it here. This is going to change my life.

***

-Anne-

Typos? The nerve! I pride myself on my accuracy. But then, I have been under a bit of stress lately, which affects my concentration.

About 10 days after I moved to the new apartment, I found a condo I really like. Keep renting, or buy? That is the question. If I ever want to have a decent life in retirement, it'd be good to buy something very modest and try to pay it off. That seems very sensible. However I have to ask myself, "Am I making a $100,000+ purchase just to avoid talking to my landlord about my ex-con son moving in with me?

A Soul Restored

-Vince-

Ms. Maertz:
You should check out a guy named Mark A. Fagerwick. He has gone through boot camp and he writes (or maybe wrote) for the Pioneer Press. Just a thought.

***

-Anne-

Yes, Mark Fagerwick does write for the Pioneer Press, the St. Paul newspaper. I'm sharing his article here because it sums up boot camp well:

'Boot camp' prison alternative—for me, a life-changing program
As a recent graduate (survivor) of the Challenge Incarceration Program, I can tell you that this program was and is the single most physically, mentally and emotionally demanding, challenging and ultimately positive experience of my 55 years.

In 2010, I was convicted and sentenced to 48 months in prison on a DUI charge. I entered St. Cloud State Prison with an attitude of deep resentment toward a system I felt had failed me by unfairly, over-zealously, over-aggressively and harshly judging me. I also harbored and presented a stance of arrogant superiority over my fellow inmates — after all, I was a successful, college-educated marketing communications professional and a deeply spiritual family man. I had achieved amazing accomplishments and attained an outward appearance of success normally associated with right living. I was not a "criminal" deserving four years in a state penitentiary (or so I thought).

The first 24 hours of C.I.P. changed all that.

I was immediately struck with the reality that all of our creator's children make mistakes, poor choices and self-centered decisions that adversely affect families, loved ones and civilized society as a whole. And, that there are consequences for that kind of distorted thinking and the resulting arrogant, errant choices and behaviors. I am blessed to have been afforded the opportunity to participate in and benefit from this incredible, life-changing, life-giving program.

I owe a great debt of gratitude to the staff and supporters of C.I.P. for helping to realign my priorities, restore my relationships and reintegrate me back into a civilized society where I can affect a

216

positive change in myself and those around me through my experience and by example.

While it is an unfortunate reality that many of my peers in the program will likely reoffend and return to incarceration, the successes far outweigh the failures. And, in my opinion, one successfully saved life and reunited family is well worth the effort. We all deserve a second chance.

C.I.P. is an incredibly powerful and effective program in the much-needed reform of our criminal justice and "corrections" system. While the traditional system of incarceration and the isolation and segregation of certain criminal elements from society is necessary and has its place for many, there are also many otherwise responsible, respectful, repentant individuals who simply lost their way, made horribly poor choices and who sincerely desire another chance to prove themselves and make amends for the wrongs they have done. These individuals are irreparably damaged by extreme and unrelenting exposure to and influence of the traditional prison environment and the unremorseful, habitual and often-violent offenders confined there.

C.I.P. promotes and facilitates an effective combination of intensely regimented discipline, essential cognitive behavioral insight, intensive chemical-dependency programming, rigorous physical training and strictly controlled physical labor, all underscored by positive exposure to an uncompromising but sincerely dedicated staff and a group of program participants who are truly seeking positive change and a better way of life. Surely there are detractors who feel that C.I.P. simply represents a time cut for criminals who "deserve" to serve penance for their crimes — and to a degree that could very well be the case for some. However, for those who take the program to heart, who utilize the tools and skills provided, and learn from their past, society will realize a true and valuable asset — a soul restored, a family reunited, a man completed.

No Bars

-Vince-

Ms. Maertz:

There really aren't any rules and regs as far as when I get out. I'll be on an intense form of probation / parole for the first six months. As long as I'm doing well (passing my UAs, going to meetings, looking for work/working/going to school, they won't pay much attention to me. And those are all of the things I plan on doing.

The first day or two they usually let us go shopping and see family, that sort of thing. But we are expected to get looking for work right after that.

In five weeks, I'll be able to call you. I really don't know too much more than that, but I can't wait to talk to you.

Things are going well for me here. It's all manufactured stress. They like to see how we react to things. I usually do well.

***

It's been a crazy few days. Three days ago we got our red tags removed. Red tags go on our IDs and sort of make us stand out as new guys. It's the first real hurdle. We felt pretty good about it.

Well. Last night they made us put them back on. Our squad, as a whole, is a mess. Even for new guys. Some of us (thankfully, not me) still can't figure out left and right. Some of us (me) still can't make our beds with 45 degree angles and no wrinkles. And some of us (I won't profile) think it's okay to rap and use the N word and profanity.

It is now back to being incredibly stressful, but I think we're still on some sort of "right path."

Two days ago while on a work crew we went way out into the woods and raked up pine needles into piles for about an hour. Even though we were working, I felt completely at peace. The sun was hitting my face, a cool breeze making the dry leaves scratch each other in a game of leap-frog. The birds happily singing to us. And no fences in sight. No fences, no barbed wire, no bars anywhere here. I think of that moment when I get frustrated. I know that soon I will be able to find peace in everything I do.

And just writing all of that settled me down from today's frustrations. I'm grateful that people actually want to read this. Thank you. And stay tuned.

Easter Bunny, Denied

-Vince-

We were supposed to start running on Wednesday but the weather hasn't allowed it. We do the step tape for an hour every other day, and we have been speed walking on the alternate days to get prepared for running. As much as I fear running, I have been excited to see how far I can go, but now we have to wait until Monday for our next chance.

Getting in shape has been tough. When I got to St. Cloud, the first time I did anything for exercise was 35 minutes of softball (only five minutes of actually doing anything) and I could hardly walk for three days. Now I can do the step twice, about 55 minutes of constant motion. It's a great workout. I started using 1 pound weights and I couldn't believe how heavy they felt afterwards.

***

I'm sitting in a chair next to my bunk feeling drained. I couldn't estimate how many miles we've logged marching and walking to various places to clear brush.

219

At one point we had to run a half mile wearing our full-length khaki uniform, boots, coveralls, gloves, wool cap, and hard hat. The whole time all I could think about was that I had to take a %$*#)@. Thankfully I made it back in time.

After our weekly haircut we ate lunch, then went out for drill and ceremony for two hours. Marching, counter column march, rear march, left oblique, right oblique. It's really hard. I'm pretty good at it now, some people in our 16-man squad just don't seem to care. So we argue, bicker, yell. And in the end we've somehow grown closer.

Some of them won't make it. Some of them will never care about anything in life. So I have to focus on me.

So here I am in my chair. Exhausted, quiet, challenged, and hopeful. Time for dinner.

***

-Anne-

My 80-year-old mother wanted to send Vince some money at Easter. She sends each grandchild a card for their birthdays and other holidays with $10. I read off the two addresses, twice. One for sending Vince the card, another for sending him the money order, which would cost a couple bucks.

She called me later and asked me to re-read all the information because she couldn't keep it straight. I typed it and emailed it to her, thinking that would be clearer.

But she sent the money order in the card, so it all came back. So I explained, again, how she couldn't send ANYthing with the money order. She had to mail the card to a different address. Why? I don't know, mom. I don't know. You just have to do it that way.

Vince's grandma with her youngest grandson

Down Day

-Vince-
Sunday, 6:01 am. This is the hardest day of the week for me because it's our down day. We don't do any morning exercises, and there's no mandatory physical training, no school, treatment, or work crew. So we just sit next to our bunks from 5:20 am until 7:20 am. No breakfast, no coffee. I'm writing to combat my fatigue.

I've been working on some mini-meditations we learned in our Thinking for a Change class in which I channel positive thoughts into my subconscious mind. I tell it I have energy, I'm wide awake, and so on. It seems to work. But it doesn't last long.

***

One of the problems that has carried over to each facility I've been in is the unreliability of our canteen orders.

221

Last week I ordered five postcards and five envelopes. I got two of each. I was charged for all of them, and also for two pair of socks, which I didn't order or receive. I will get credit but not in time to order this week. So I'm stuck with what I have for two weeks.

I spent a couple hours playing cards and walking the track with one of my friends that I met in Moose Lake. He is going to St. Paul when he gets out, two months before me. Anyhow, I'm already starting to build my network in here for out there.

***

I remember the first time I went to treatment for the right reasons, and stayed sober nearly five years, I didn't know what to do when the using thoughts started drifting through my head.

Relapse starts well before the actual using. Here, I can look back on all of my actions and feelings and put that together with the tools I'm getting here to not just be sober for a while, but live sober forever.

I've collected enough evidence on the outside to make me sure that I'm not the guy that can just have "a couple of beers" or just a couple lines. I use until I physically can't anymore. I do not stop.

Arbeit Macht Frei

-Vince-

11 am: So far today we've run … eaten breakfast, raked up pine needles in the woods, wheel-barrowed pine needles to the gigantic compost piles, back and forth. Back and forth. Folded the first 2/3 of our laundry, went to lunch, marched back and forth from the chow hall to the barracks in the rain, and then I sat down to write this. Well, right after standing at POA for 20 minutes for head count. In 35 minutes, we go to CD treatment until 4:30. Then dinner, then Thinking for a Change (henceforth TFAC) from 6:30-8:00. And then

we spend the rest of our night polishing our belt buckles and boots. Oh, I have to find time to iron my clothes, which I will do now ….

5:20 pm: I still haven't had a chance to iron.

***

I never ironed yesterday.

Today I spent my first eight hours doing the laundry for all 180 offenders. Standing on my feet all day is harder than most of the other work they have us do.

Well, except for today. We had to move compost from one spot to another. Two and a half hours going back and forth with wheel barrows full of what smelled like feces.

After that, six of us went to the administration building to clean for another hour. Then we ate.

When we came back from chow, our bunk areas had been torn apart. If they find anything wrong they tear it all apart. I had to remake my bed, fold all of my clothing, re-organize. If it sounds like I'm frustrated today, I am. Breathe.

***

It's our 25th day. Sunday my off day. We still get up at 5:20 am we still have to get dressed and ready. Ready to sit in our chairs for two long hours. It's the most boring day of the week.

By comparison, yesterday was one of our two work crew days. I personally kept moving pretty much all day. Part of boot camp is on Department of Natural Resources land. In trade, I'm sure for payment of rent, we clear the land of brush, sticks, logs, and garbage. Yesterday was a wood hauling day.

I wheel-barrowed roughly 75 pounds of tools 3/4 miles to the site where we then gathered dead trees from the woods and cut them down to 16 inch logs. We loaded up all of the 50 wheel barrows, and began the trip back. The last 300 yards was all sand. It's one of the hardest things I've ever done. We were all exhausted. But there was more work to be done.

We took a break to eat lunch and get our hair cut. Then suited back up to go chop all the wood we brought back. Funny thing, the splitting mauls are all dull by design. Rather than a sharp edge, they are filed down at the very tip so we swing, I'd guess, three times more than should be necessary. Ugh.

I'll say this, I'm already in the best shape of my life. And it goes up from here. I'm tired, sore, humbled. And I feel great.

Stylin'

-Vince-

Two weeks short of 14 years since I entered Hazelden Center for Youth and Family. I have a lot of fond memories of that place, partially because I actually have clear memories of it. There are many similarities between then and now, and here and there, and a few substantial differences.

The toughest part here at boot camp has been being surrounded by people at all times. At no point in the day do we have any privacy. If I take a shit, there are people in front of me, brushing their teeth, sometimes staring back through the mirror, sometimes trying to engage in conversation.

We have two-minute showers in the morning after PT. Sixty guys, all naked, clothing everywhere, people arguing, some using the toilets with people changing a foot away. Sinks all at once being used for teeth (inside and outside of the mouth), shaving, hand washing. On occasion timing is off and somebody will spit out blood and toothpaste onto a razor. It's chaos.

224

I have been here only three weeks, and time is flying by, and I'm getting a lot out of it, but I can't wait to take a real shower. Use real hygiene products. Poop behind a door.

Imagine being wherever you work. Now, imagine every other co-worker on a toilet, or naked and trying to talk to you. It's really something else. Way more eye contact than necessary.

Today is group (our squad consists of 16 guys. We're in everything together, including CD treatment). I shared my first written assignment. We were asked to write a 1-2 page paper on our worst 24 hours. I put it all out in a 4-page story of my arson conviction back in (I think) 2000. I may or may not share that story some day.

A side note: The last song I heard before I came here from Moose Lake was "Style", by *Taylor Swift*. The bass line and chilling, beautiful voice have been in my head ever since. I do not actually know the words though, so my mind just replicates the tone of her voice in its own cadence. That's all I can really say about that situation.

Still Prison

-Vince-

10:45 pm
Another day done. Tomorrow morning we run. I still haven't been able to go more than two laps, but that's two more than I could have done 9 months ago. I will give it my best shot tomorrow to go three laps, which is two miles.

The "A" run is a distant goal. They run 7 laps, just under five miles, and they go fast. Under eight minutes per mile. I think I'll be able to join them in two months. We shall see.

5:53 am

Due to either weather or lack of staff there will be no running this morning. This happens roughly half of our running days. So we only get to do half of our aerobic workout which is why I'm writing now, sitting doing nothing.

***

On Friday we were allowed to go to the library for the first time since our arrival. Only for ten minutes, we all (16 guys) scanned through maybe 500 titles, mostly religious. I found two works of fiction to my liking: one I've read already during my incarceration. "Prey" by Michael Crichton, and "Lord of the Flies" by William Golding, something I've read but don't remember where or when. I think maybe grade school.

So today (Sunday) during my down day, I spent a few relaxing hours in the barracks with my ear plugs in reading. It was quite nice. I needed it.

I also played a few games of cribbage, all of which I lost, with one of my friends that will be in St. Paul when I get out. Then I caught up on ironing, polishing my boots and buckle, treatment work, and writing.

***

Today was rough. Tomorrow will be rougher.

I finally broke my personal record for running. I'm still struggling with it, but today I ran 2.1 miles. That's half of what is expected, but more than some people can do.

Also today we used the same little green scrubber pads we use for our belt buckles to scrub the baseboards in the gym. Back breaking labor, I think it could be referred to as. It wasn't really that bad.

I've been here over a month now. Man has it flown by. Tomorrow is our first review. We're going to be yelled at, we're going to be scolded. And they won't really say nice things. But, hey, this is still prison. And I still have a lot to work on. 153 days until the real test.

I really miss talking to my mother. I think we were getting closer than we ever have been, quite frankly I think as a result of the blog. I've wasted so many years away from my family. I hope I can become as close to them as I should already have been.

Whole Lotta @#%$

-Vince-

About twenty minutes ago we had our first monthly review. I had high hopes that the worst of our group would be called out. They were not.

I was pretty much passed by. Mostly because I don't get into too much trouble. They did say that I need to challenge myself and run more. To do that, I'm going to run on my off day, to see if I can build my stamina. I've made a lot of progress since I was locked up nine months ago, but not enough.

I lost about two pounds and lost 1% body fat since I arrived here at boot camp. It's a start. I can see in the mirror that I'm becoming muscular, toned. I must work harder. I will work harder.

***

30 days in boot camp and I can make my bed, iron nice creases into my khakis, and run farther than I ever thought I would. If you would have asked me two years ago if I would ever run two miles total in my lifetime, I would have said, "Hahahahahahahahaha." You get the picture.

The point is, that I—we—are conquering the obstacles that seemed so daunting just a month ago. We're even starting to get along. We still bicker, but what else could be expected, we live in the same room, shower, @&%$, and shave together.

***

My mother brought up a man named Kermit. She didn't include his last name or real first name but when I said them in my head, I became angry, which rarely happens.

Yes, I got to see the Reds [baseball team] win the 1990 World Series right in front of my eyes. It was cool as hell. But that was probably the only highlight of that period of my life.

I remember where I was standing, on the back porch of our green apartment building on Dayton Avenue when she told me I had a brother.

The third of four places we moved to in one year after the Kermit debacle

***

In that same apartment, I remember getting a dog. He was a sheltie, and I named him Flash. He was ... special. Maybe flat out retarded. And one time-oh god it hurts me still to think about it-he ate an

228

entire box of giant chocolate bars I had to sell for a school fundraiser, foil wrappers and all.

I know I don't remember the correct sequence of events, but I know this: he @&%$ everywhere. He @&%$ outside, he @&%$ on himself. He @&%$ on the piles of @&%$ that he had @&%$ on himself. That was just outside.

Hoping he was done, we brought him inside so he wouldn't freeze to death. We shut him in the bathroom for the night, and when we opened the door in the morning, I will let my dear Mother take over from here because I am not allowed to use profanity in my writing. Holy flippin crap. Nobody will ever see what we saw that morning.

***

-Anne-

I don't care to elaborate on Vince's dog story. I am not a dog person, but I thought every boy ought to have one, right? Especially after what I had put Vince through with Kermit. I was wrong.

Vince says he rarely gets angry. Elsewhere in this blog, he writes about "anger coming off me like steam." I wonder if he's dulled his anger for years with chemicals, is just now experiencing it unfiltered, and doesn't even recognize that?

Cripple Girl

-Anne-

Mother's Day has come and gone. Vince had told me he wouldn't be able to make any phone calls from boot camp for two months. That's standard procedure. Why? Who knows. Maybe they want them focused on the program and not distracted by family and friends who could be unhealthy influences?

Vince sent me a postcard telling me he'd be able to call me on May 10, and to have my phone switched on and close by because he would call as early as possible and he was really looking forward to talking to me. May 10 happened to be Mother's Day. It was clear he had no idea it was Mother's Day. After all, they have no television, no radio, no internet, no newspapers. One of his big requests recently was for me to send him the weather forecast for the week so he could sort of know if he'd be running outside or not.

I thought it was a nice coincidence that the first day he could call me would also happen to be on Mothers' Day.

Mothers' Day came and went and he didn't call. May 12 would be exactly two months since he entered boot camp, so maybe he would call me that day? But no. Then I got a postcard from him saying his first phone call "should be" May 17. I guess it's SNAFU at the DOC. At least I am not going straight to the worst-case-scenario assumption, like I did for years: He's dead! They beat him to death and are covering it up! They're probably burying his body in the woods right now!" And so on.

***

His postcard went on to say, "I can't believe how much progress I have made. I've lost 25 pounds and I'm now at 11.2% body fat. Physical training, as it turns out, is beneficial in so many ways. It's the first thing we do every morning and it really sets the tone for the day."

Well duh. I've been an exerciser most of my life, and I can't imagine life without it. This is, I think, thanks to being diagnosed with scoliosis and having to wear a full body brace, 23 hours a day, for several years starting at age 12 or 13.

During the 24th hour, I could take a bath (not a shower) and do my physical therapy. The doctors and my mother warn me that if I didn't do my PT I might have to have surgery to implant a metal rod alongside my spine. In retrospect I think surgery would have been easier, socially, than wearing a brace. It's no fun being called "cripple girl."

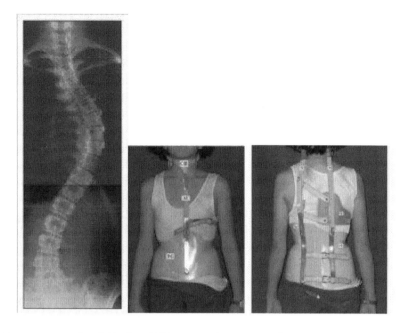

But guess what? Doing PT every day year after year created the habit of exercise. So that brace was good for something, because now the medical profession knows that bracing doesn't have any lasting straightening effect on scoliosis.

When I turned 16 I told the doctors at Shriners Hospital for Crippled Children to go fuck themselves. I wanted a boyfriend. I found one. I became a mother.

Vince moans and groans about the enforced exercise, but maybe the theory is that it'll become a habit. A good one, for once.

Rainbows and Unicorns

-Vince-

1800 hours. I'm sitting next to my bunk, facing a window that is letting in the most beautiful feeling I've had in awhile: Sunlight.

Spring has sprung. Soon we will be spending a large portion of our days outside. The work they have us doing can be tough, but everything seems a little better when I'm outside. I'm ready to

Not sure why I didn't finish my thought there. Sometimes we just have to drop what we're doing and go.

Today we moved the wood pile we created last week to a different spot for no other reason other than work as punishment. Two hours I went back and forth with loads of wood. I'm going to be a beast when I get out of here.

***

Ms. Maertz:

Every letter or card we send out has to be started with Mr, Mrs, Ms, etc. Just policy.

Today I ran 3.3 miles. I couldn't believe it. I'm pretty much the worst in my squad at running, but they were all cheering me on. I am really good at marching. You will get to see that at my graduation…assuming all goes well. September 9th.

Today two new squads came from Moose Lake, so we're not rookies anymore!

If you do know exactly or approximately the end date of your 6 month ban, be ready to send in another visitor form so you are approved to come to my graduation ceremony. I keep hearing people talk about staff at Moose Lake banning people for minor issues. I don't get it, but I'm not there anymore.

I hope my writing is still entertaining enough for people to want to read.

Love,
Vince

***

-Anne-

I worry that, now Vince is doing well and appears to be on the road to a shiny happy life, people will get bored with the blog. Aren't horror stories more entertaining? Then I remind myself that Vince is a real person, not a character in a fictional narrative. I wish he would write more about his inner processes, or philosophize like I do, but he is not me.

It also doesn't take me long to recall that the real test starts once Vince is released. Right now, his food, shelter, and clothing are provided. No bills. No liquor stores or bars. No music with drug references. No women, and all the potential relationship difficulties that could go with them. When he's released, it will be with the clothes on his back and about $400, and every landlord and potential employer asking, "Have you ever been convicted of a felony?" So on second thought, I'll try to appreciate the present, positive moments.

That Confounded Bridge

-Anne-

My Palestinian colleague is going back to Jerusalem this weekend. When I was there with him a few months ago, I wrote about what that involves, but I didn't mention that he was strip searched three times while I waited for him on the other side of the bridge crossing. At the end of an email exchange in which I expressed my concern about him crossing the border again, he wrote:

"Steadfastness 'Somod' as we say is a good peaceful weapon. When I feel disempowered, I think of others who experienced harder situations and kept strong along with my believes in justice, freedom, dignity, and integrity. I will need to find ways to express my rage, although I always believed in constructive actions that can bring change. In solidarity!"

There are parallels between his and Vince's situations, not least of which, they're about the same age.

I went through a long process of change when I was sent to the Palestinian Territories for work. My first reaction was, "Are you F—ing kidding? I'm Jewish!" Since Vince is no longer at Moose Lake, surrounded by skinheads and brothers of the Nation of Islam, I can say that.

Over a period of six months, "my thinking evolved," as Barack Obama said about his position on gay marriage. I found some like-minded Jewish American activists who saw no problem with holding Israel to high standards. My rabbi said, "Maybe God thinks you're the one to do this." I don't know about that. But he didn't think I was a traitor to my people, that was a huge relief to me.

I could write volumes about this, but for this blog I'll just say that I credit all my work in Alanon for helping me develop an open mind, a radar that tells me I'm in denial, and a willingness to try anything to feel better and get clarity. I am so glad I went on the trip. I could have refused to go, and missed a life-changing opportunity.

***

I moved less than a week after returning from that trip. That was two months ago, and now I will move again in three weeks. Yes, I found a condo to buy just a few weeks after I moved into my new apartment. Sometimes timing just isn't great. But an unexpected benefit is that I won't have to have the conversation with my landlord about Vince moving in.

In fact, when I called my landlord to find out about getting a subletter to finish out my lease, she told me the person would have to have 2.5 times income to rent, "and of course we don't want any felons!" she laughed. She said it so lightly. She obviously isn't related to any of the 47,000 ex offenders in Minnesota.

***

-Vince-

> *Ms. Maertz: Good news about getting the condo. I know it's nice to have a glass of wine or a beer in your own home. But if you do while I'm there, I will get sent back to Moose Lake for 18 months. So decide now if you think I should look for another residence. Love, Vince*

Vince's Big BM

-Vince-

The stress is getting to me finally. They really pile the work up on us.

I'm having troubles in more areas that I thought and it was brought to my attention over the past couple of days.

Thankfully, it happened on the side by a CO. He didn't point anything out but he talked to me and when I answered his questions I realized then that I'm not perfect, I have residual anti-authority issues from being a criminal for a good portion of my life, and that I still negative-talk myself a lot. I kind of still hate myself for wasting my life away using and dealing drugs. Sometimes I want to give up. I want to leave this place because it would be easier than staying.

The CO and I talked for a good half hour. He wouldn't let me walk away. He wouldn't allow me to use the self-pity stance. And he almost got me to cry.

He took me aside to talk because he knows I do try. That I'm not a trouble maker. And mostly because I really needed to be heard. I was able to open up and really dig.

And we found some problems I've been having here, that I couldn't see.

I'm controlling, manipulative, and a perfectionist, which is why I hurt so much inside. I'm full of shit. And I don't want anybody to know. I use deceit to control. I will lie, cheat, steal, tell half truths, and beg to obtain and continue using drugs on the outside. And in here I'm defensive, I'm always right, to keep others off balance. Then I point out their faults. I need to quit all that now.

I hope some of that made sense. Sometimes I just write to vent. I feel better getting that out.

***

Today is the first day of our 6th week. We are no longer lowest in seniority; we got new guys today.

Today's date seems to have some significance in my life. Nine years ago, it was still my sobriety date. Before that, I don't remember how long ago, I had the chicken pox, and another time I was an usher in my aunt's wedding. Today, I ran over three miles and didn't die.

I ran three straight laps around the big track (two miles). Then I had to walk twice around the small track, but then I fell back into the run, and completed two more laps (one and a third miles). I am so sore. But I feel great.

This last Friday I only made one lap running and then walked for the rest of our PT time. I felt like a failure. I thought about it over the weekend and decided I need to push myself harder. So I did.

Tomorrow we do 40 minutes of aerobics, then we run again. Completing the run consists of six full laps. That's 4.1 miles. That's the "B" run. Then there's the "A" run. A faster pace, and I think 8 laps. I don't know the math on that one.

***

Vince has the wrong date, but yes there is a date on or around on
which all of these things happened, not to mention his bar mitzvah.
That was a lot of fun. There were a lot of jokes about "your big BM"
and afterwards there was karaoke and he and his friend David
inhaled all the helium from the balloons—lord, did that contribute to
his future waywardness?

Breakthrough

-Vince-

It's been a crazy two days. The new guys have been getting yelled at constantly, which does take some pressure off us, but we are also feeling the pressure of trying to set an example for them.

Most amusing to me is seeing what we looked like a month ago. Completely disoriented, disorganized, and disheveled. We have made enormous progress in just over five weeks. We also have a long way to go.

Today, I really blew it. I talked myself down and out of the running group. I used every excuse I could think of to make myself okay with doing only two laps (1.5 miles). Now, of course, I feel stupid. I have a lot of trouble still with motivating myself to run. I don't like any part of it except for how I feel when I'm done. That's the only way I can explain it.

***

I received a postcard from my Mother today from Petra, Jordan, postmarked two months ago. So that took a little while. Well, it's been a long day. Time for dinner soon. Tuna casserole.

I'm going to apply for a lead cook job here. It doesn't pay, but it would be great experience.

The tuna casserole was actually quite delicious.

It's Friday night. We don't really do too much. Study hall for 1.5 hours at some point I think.

Then comes Saturday. My least favorite day. It's the day we're all on call for any dirty job they come up with. Trending this week is the gigantic compost piles. Tons and tons of decomposing organic matter we get to move around over and over, and over. If you don't know what compost smells like, think of the smell of feces, and then don't change anything. That by itself isn't so bad.

When we're working we are dressed in our full khaki uniform, long-sleeves and legs, and coveralls, gloves, and a hat. It's not even hot out yet and we're sweating like crazy. I'm not complaining; I signed up for this. Ugh.

***

-Anne-

Vince called me today, the first time in over 2 months. He is allowed one phone call every other Sunday from here on out. Except, he explained, that this month has five Sundays so it'll be three weeks until he can call again. I've been trained by the DOC now, not to ask "But why?"

Vince is allowed one 13-minute phone call, and he called me. That tells me I must have done something right—right?

To me at least, once we got talking it felt so natural, like we had just talked yesterday. I think that's a sign of a close relationship, when you don't need to be in constant contact to feel comfortable talking to the person on the other end of the line. It wasn't always that way. For years our conversations via text and in person (Vince didn't have voice service on his phone) were stilted and extremely uncomfortable. I was always hinting and probing and hoping for some sign that he wanted to change, and that was the last thing he wanted to do. This is huge, I realize as I write this. Happy Day! And maybe this means that someday he can have a healthy romantic relationship too.

Fact-Resistant Humans

-Vince-

It is such a beautiful day. Fortunately we spent a lot of it outside. For an hour we marched. We're getting pretty good. We can do counter columns, rear march, left and right flanks and obliques. In 4 and 2/3 months we will get to show our moves at our graduation. Time moves so quickly.

After marching we spend about 3 hours sweeping the running rack and transporting leaves and pine needles from the woods to the compost piles. I didn't even feel like I was working, it was so nice out. But as I write this I'm quite sore, and I have a huge blister on the palm of my hand.

***

I've been lazy all day and I loved it. I won five games of cribbage. I've done a little bit of treatment work. I'm hoping that not doing anything physical today will help me in my running tomorrow morning. I'll let you know in the next sentence.

***

Nope. I only ran two miles. Still an improvement from ten months ago, but not where I want to be. I need to try harder, but it's hard to try harder. And my legs hurt.

I got my Initial Treatment Plan (ITP) last Friday. I hate it because it's spot on. As it turns out, I'm controlling, I just didn't know how bad I was.

I use my body language and anger/sarcasm to control the people around me. For example, if somebody close by is doing something wrong, I try to look like I'm upset and I might even point them out to somebody else instead of talking to them about it.

Another example: If I'm having trouble with making my bed, I will exaggerate my frustrations to make it look like I'm having trouble so people will try to help, instead of me just asking for help. And sometimes when they offer assistance, I get annoyed and tell them

240

off, which makes me look like an asshole. Ugh. Treatment is hard. I like it.

***

Today I noticed that I quit biting my nails a week ago. I didn't even do it on purpose, it just happened. I wish I hadn't noticed it, I can't stop looking at them now…I must change my focus.

Here's a good one. The other day in our cognitive thinking class, where we are invited to ask questions about anything, someone asked why the asteroid that killed off the dinosaurs didn't kill all the people too. Then: dead silence. I was the first to laugh. He's not a smart man, and every week he has mentioned that he "doesn't believe in dinosaurs," as if they were mythical creatures.

Maybe not such a crazy thought considering our teacher says we're all descendants of aliens—35-40-foot-tall aliens.

***

-Anne-

When I spoke with Vince on Sunday, he told me about this instructor, Tim Peebles. Vince is enthusiastic about the Thinking for Change class Peebles teaches. He said it's all been developed by Hazelden Betty Ford, which is a well-respected chemical dependency treatment, publishing, and research center. But aliens? How can you lecture people about thinking rationally, then (as Vince described) spend the remainder of the class telling stories about the aliens you saw at Roswell? I believe there is life elsewhere in the universe, but until there are facts in front of me, I don't claim to know what form they take.

***

It's Memorial Day, so here's a post about death.

Am I the only one who thinks about death all the time? Bear with me. Honestly, I'm not depressed and I don't find it depressing to think about death. If you do, maybe you should skip this post.

Death has been a preoccupation of mine since my dad died, when I was eight. When Vince was missing for that first worst year, all I could think of was him lying face up behind a garbage dumpster, eyes staring, with a bullet hole in his forehead. Ok, I also imagined him dead in a gulley, in a corn field, in the river, and any number of other cold, isolated, lonely places. But that's not the kind of dwelling on death I'm talking about here.

My mother is continually clearing out her house, shifting mementos onto me and my siblings. She had a shoebox of loose family photos that we looked through together. Birthday parties, picnics, and school plays from the 1930s, 40s, and 50s. "This is my cousin's fifth birthday party," she explained, showing me a black and white photo of small children assembled around a cake on a picnic table in someone's back yard, wearing birthday hats. Little girls with Shirley Temple curls and elaborate home-sewn flouncy dresses. Boys with bow ties and their hair slicked down like Alfalfa from The Little Rascals. The cars parked in the background had gorgeous fins.

"My cousin and another child got sick after the party and they both died the next day—it was meningitis." Her finger traced the circle of five-year olds. "I don't remember who the other child was. We had to be quarantined, so they ran a yellow QUARANTINE tape around our yard. We couldn't leave or have visitors for a week. Mr. Goldenberg, who owned the five-and-dime at the end of the block, would bring a box of food, set it near the back gate, and run back down the alley."

Let's face it, all these photos will be pitched into a dumpster when she dies. I won't remember who any of the children are.

And so it goes. We are born and, if we're lucky, someone loves us and takes care of us. Lots of photos are taken to celebrate our milestones. When we enter adulthood we are so focused on achieving goals that we don't realize we will never be this healthy, energetic, or attractive again.

Now at 55 I have dozens of photo albums that will go into a dumpster when I die. I have thousands of photos on Facebook that will likely sit in cyberspace as long as servers exist, of interest to no one except maybe some future social anthropologist.

And so I—my whole life—my loves and dramas and losses, my story, all my brilliant ideas and daydreams and real dreams, my travels, my elaborately decorated dining rooms for dinner parties and painstakingly tended gardens, the thousands of miles I have walked and millions of reps I have done at the gym, my friends far and near, the millions of dollars I've raised for good causes, maybe even those good causes and their organizations themselves—will disappear.

We're all on a conveyor belt. We move along it, conscious of it or not. We can't get off, we can't go back, and we don't know when we'll reach the end of the belt and fall off into … ??

A lot of people are sure they know the answer to that but I'm not one of them.

Again, I don't find any of this depressing, or feel sorry for myself—I just find it intriguing. So what should we do while we're here? The only conclusions I've reached for myself are: 1) it feels better to do good things than bad ones; 2) it's important to have fun while you have the chance; and 3) if I ever stop seeking the answers to life's imponderable questions, I'm as good as dead.

Cleaning Up His Act

-Vince-

I got to leave the grounds for the first time today. Myself and five other volunteers took a short van ride to a YMCA camp type of area thing place. We cleaned up after some sort of event, folding tables,

243

stacking chairs, sweeping, mopping, etc. Nothing too exciting but just for half an hour I felt like I wasn't in custody. It was nice.

We've been here a while now and more of these opportunities will come. Count me in.

It's been snowing all day. It all has melted on contact with the ground, but we still haven't been able to get outside much. That's why I'm able to write so much sometimes.

***

Twice now I've made it four laps around the big track. Three miles each day is definitely an improvement over, well, anything I've ever done. My lungs are sore. My ribs hurt. My calves are tight. I have an abundance of energy, but am too sore to do anything with it. And I'm starving! Soon we will eat.

It's my down day. It's been quite frustrating so far.

It started at 0800. In line waiting for breakfast, the notorious Officer Weston was looking at everybody's boots. Mine, along with several others, were not up to par. They should be inspection-ready at all times, so I can't blame it on anything other than me being lazy. He made me go back to the barracks and get a shine on them before I could eat.

After breakfast, he lined us up in the main hallway and took us one by one into our respective barracks to our bunks to inspect our personal areas. Mine was not looking too good.

It's hard—nearly impossible—to have every area perfect. 2 bins; clothing in one, books, folders, mail, medications in the other. He unfolded all the clothes and tipped the other bin upside down on my bed. Then he took all of the clothes off my hangers and shoved them into the top part of my locker (our display area for hygiene stuff) so I had to start everything from scratch.

It took me two hours to fix it all. I finally got to go play some cribbage outside with a friend. When I came back in, a different Officer had un-made my bed for me. I don't know why. Ugh. I need to focus more I think. Just when I thought I was doing well ….

***

-Anne-

I am a neatnik, although I've learned to ease off. I used to be such a clean freak that I think people were uncomfortable in my house. And Vince was the opposite, maybe in unconscious rebellion? His slovenliness was one of the things that bothered me when I would visit him in Lanesboro. His apartment was strewn with dirty clothes, empty beer cans, and trash. The carpet was stained, the blinds were crookedly half-raised so it was always dark, the bathroom was, well, let's just say I preferred using the porta-potty at the nearby campground. So now he's learning to take care of his things, to make his bed, to keep things tidy. It'll be interesting to see if he continues that once he's released.

Nodrinkalotine

-Anne-

There seems to be all sorts of momentum to reform drug sentencing, to reduce mass incarceration, and to make it easier for ex-offenders to make it on the outside.

There was a full-page article in my favorite magazine, The Week, entitled "Opening the prison door: A new, bi-partisan movement is challenging the notion that jailing millions of Americans makes the U.S. safer." It cites the stats: taxpayers spend $80 billion a year to keep 2.4 million prisoners locked up. It examines what's going on in various states, including the reddest of red states, Texas. I never thought I would admiringly quote Texas Governor Rick Perry, but he said, "The idea that we lock people up, throw them away forever, never give them a second chance at redemption, isn't what America is about."

Current affairs geek that I am, I enjoy watching 60 Minutes on Sunday evenings. I hate it when it is delayed for some stupid sporting event, like football. ANYway, a few weeks ago they did a story on TED Talks, and one of the TED talkers they featured was Bryan Stevenson, a public-interest lawyer and the founder and executive director of the Equal Justice Initiative, which is challenging racial discrimination in the criminal justice system.

The Minneapolis Star Tribune is full of related articles. One is about a couple of drug reform bills that failed to pass. Hennepin County Attorney Mike Freeman is quoted: "Those people who possess large amounts [of drugs] for sale suffer from the disease of greed, and the answer to their problems isn't treatment, but the big house." The big house? Is he living in a Jimmy Cagney movie or what? Regardless, most people in prison on drug charges, including Vince, were busted with small amounts of drugs.

There was an article about how the DOC has succeeded in banning journalists from taking photos or video inside prisons. To me, this sounds very much like the DOC has something to hide, and also like a slippery slope toward becoming more like North Korea or Iran. I mean, freedom of the press is a pretty fundamental part of democracy, and nowadays visuals are so much more vital to reporting than ever.

There's an editorial, "Restore voting rights to former felons." This is a hot button issue for me. Because Vince was convicted of his first felony shortly after he turned 18, he wasn't allowed to vote until he'd cleared his record–when he was 30. It so happened that this was the year Barak Obama was elected, and Vince was jubilant. "My team won!" he exclaimed. I was so happy for him. Now he'll start from square one.

At work, I see all sorts of funding opportunities for studies of addiction. These are just two that I saw in the same day: "Second Chance Act Strengthening Families and Children of Incarcerated

Parents" from the Department of Justice, and "Human Studies to Evaluate Promising Medications to Treat Alcohol Use Disorder" from the National Institutes of Health.

So there really does seem to be a movement to end mass incarceration, and there is promising research being conducted to get at the root causes of addiction. Someday maybe, when you take your 10-year-old kid in for his annual exam, the doctor will run some routine genetic tests. "Mr. and Ms. Jones, I'm afraid your son has inherited your family's gene for addiction. The good news is, we can tweak his DNA, or put him on a course of Nodrinkalotine. Let's discuss the pros and cons of each."

Fit, Fat, Ffffttt

-Vince-

This morning at 0645 hours I finally achieved my goal of completing a run. I ran 4½ miles without stopping. It hurt a lot, especially with some cramping near the bottom of my ribcage, and general soreness in my knees and thighs, but I was too happy to care. I did it.

I don't know if I'll be able to do it every time, but I do know now that it's possible. On a side note, I started taking a probiotic supplement today. I think it's supposed to help me with my poops. But for now it just makes me fart a lot. More on that later.

***

Two days later, 0633 hours. My down day, my second least favorite day. Yesterday was tough. For the first time since my arrival we did not go out on work crew assignments. We did, however, practice marching. The worst was from 1415 to 1610 [2:15-4:10pm] when we did half step march (120 steps per minute) up and down the side of the track. Half step is difficult because it's faster and we have to pick our boots up about 6 inches from the ground every time to keep us all in line. It looks nice, but doing it for two hours hurt.

That wasn't the worst of it. We had to wear our full khaki uniform and work gloves and a hat. Ugh. So hot. My gloves were soaked by the end. We did a total of five hours of marching yesterday. I'm still alive.

***

I completed the run again. 4½ miles. I even felt great afterwards. This is especially good because our brown hat review is in a few days. It's the second of four big reviews. We will have a meeting with our case manager, counselor, squad officer, and physical trainer. We will go over everything positive and negative from the past month. If all goes well, we get upgraded from red hats to brown hats. That means our seniority goes up, and we have more responsibility. More on that later.

We had our monthly weigh-in this morning. I went from 194 pounds and 13.4% body fat to 189 pounds and 11.2% body fat. That's pretty good for a month. It means I'm turning fat into muscle, I think.

***

-Anne-

Eleven percent body fat!? That's so unfair! I signed on with a personal trainer for the first time in my life about a month ago, and she measured me at 34% body fat. Ugh. I've always loved weight training, and she has added all sorts of cardio, which I hate because I hate sweating. But I am doing it. And after three weeks Ta Da! Still 34% body fat, no weight loss, not an inch lost. Again, ugh. She told me not to be discouraged, to keep it up. I mentioned that Vince is at 11% and her jaw dropped: "That's really, really good for a 36-year-old man," she said. Skeptical analyzer that I am, I wonder if the devices at the Y and in prison are different? Maybe I could find some way to have them test my body fat when I finally get to visit Vince? No, that's crazy thinking. Now I understand why there's such an obsession with naming things "boot camp," if it gets those kinds of results.

248

Red Hat Days

-Vince-

We still haven't had our red hat reviews yet. This is very disappointing because two squads left today, and we would have been given our brown hats today. Hat color means a lot around here. Without brown hats, we get no weight room, no visits, no phone calls. There's still time, but it's kind of annoying. If we were late for anything, they would treat us as if we were idiots. Oh well. Only four months to go.

***

Our red hat review was postponed until Monday. We've been nervous about it all week, now we have to make it through the weekend. I'm not actually worried about anything, but a few of my squad mates are. Because, of course, they aren't doing very well in one or all aspects.

I finished my fourth run today. I'm still amazed at the end. I've come so far.

***

Here are a couple things that are difficult, even after two months. The first one is a position we hold briefly before we march that gives us our proper alignment. It's called "dress right, dress." Upon the execution command of the second "dress," we snap our left arm out straight left, and look directly right. Then we all move to touch the fingertips of the guy on the right. If we don't do this correctly, and somebody wants to be mean, they will make us stand in that position for five minutes, without touching anybody else. You should try it at home. Just put your arm shoulder height, straight left, and see how long you can hold it.

***

Day 60. 1/3 of the way. 120 days to go. 360 meals, 52 runs. However I want to put it, I'm getting there.

Yesterday, 18 of us went out on a mission to plant trees on a Department of Natural Resources tree farm. We walked two miles on dirt and sand in our full khaki uniforms, coveralls, hat and gloves while carrying shovels. It's a lot of work just to get to a job site.

Along the way, a few of us found a pretty good number of agates, which we tossed back to Mother Nature, as we are not allowed to have any contraband.

The planting trees part was actually quite peaceful. Quiet is what I enjoy most in any prison/jail setting, probably because it is so rare.

So the 18 of us planted 250 1-foot tall pine trees in an area similar in shape to, but twice as large as, a football field. It was warm out, but I hardly noticed anything but nature. It was a good day.

Dying for a Smoke

-Anne-

I've written about how I'm so lucky / grateful to not be an addict. However, quitting smoking was the hardest thing I've ever done in my life, so I guess that makes me … a recovering addict. Is having a Swisher Sweet cigar once a month a slippery slope? This is something I started in the last year or so. I don't inhale. But I must get enough nicotine to give me that instant stress reduction effect. I go down to the river with a beer or a flask of tea and smoke one little cigar and watch the water go by. Is that really so bad? Can't I just enjoy one vice, once in a while?

***

I tried everything to quit. Setting a quit date. Cutting down. Smoking myself sick so I'd never want one again–until the next day. The patch, the pills (which caused frightening hallucinations), chewing on cinnamon sticks. Willpower. Phone counseling through my insurance plan. Not smoking til after I'd worked out for two hours. Never smoking in public. Never smoking until after work. Meditation.

I quit over and over. I'd quite for six months then cave in. Once I quit for FOUR YEARS! And then I started again after Dr. Wonderful broke our engagement. I was so sick the next day, after smoking one cigarette. But I started and kept on smoking for another 10 years.

In the end it was a silly thing that got me to quit. I read somewhere that the average age of women who get lung cancer is 42. So I'd had that in my mind for years—that I had to quit by the time I was 42. And I did. But as with the depression that I battled for decades, I think it was all the things combined, plus this final silly thought, that made it stick. That was 14 years ago.

Meditation helped, too. After all, it involves inhaling and exhaling, just like smoking. I still found myself tearing off the nicotine patch so I could have "just one" cigarette, then slapping the patch back on and yelling to myself out loud, "No—NO!!"

I know I can never pick up a cigarette again, not even to have one drag. I went to Jamaica with a friend 15 years ago. She had quit smoking years earlier. But I was smoking, and she picked up one of mine, just to have a few drags—we were on vacation, after all. She smoked all week and has been smoking ever since. My sister smokes. Yes, the one with cancer. Yes, she knows that smoking can be a contributing factor to colon cancer. She tries and tries to quit. Now there are e-cigs, and she says they're ok up to a point and then she Just Has to Have a Real Cigarette. I don't blame her. Like I wrote above, they're an instant stress reliever. Until you think about lung cancer and heart attacks; that'll raise your stress level.

There has been no smoking allowed in Minnesota prisons for over 20 years. This is good; Vince's lungs will get a chance to regenerate. But will he light up again the minute he's out? He didn't fight to quit, like I did; he was forced. And he wonders why he was so moody the first few weeks he was inside.

Brown Hat, Hurrah!

-Vince-

We finally had our red-hat reviews. A week late—better late than never.

I did about as well as I thought I would. No formal discipline. No major issues in Physical Training, Chemical Dependency, or Military Bearing. I will get my brown hat tonight.

What does that mean? Well, all of us that passed (14 out of 17) will have a higher level of responsibility.

We will be lifting weights now twice a week. And we have to do 30 pushups when we are informally disciplined. It's time to really step it up. I will.

The three members of our squad that didn't make it will have a chance in a week to get their brown hats. They accumulated too much discipline over a short amount of time. My prediction: one of them will be held back a month. He hasn't lost his attitude. But it's not my job to worry about him. I can only control myself.

***

We got a new squad in our barracks. There are 12 squads, four in each of the three barracks. Two squads leave and arrive each month. Anyhow, it's amazing to see the new guys and see how far we've come in 2½ months. They are a mess. They have a constant look of fear about them and are totally disorganized. I can't believe we were like that, but all new squads are.

***

Yesterday I worked KP for the first time. It was nice to be back in a kitchen setting, however I was quite disappointed with the overall operation.

First, for what their labor cost is, it should have been the cleanest place in the world. But I saw obvious signs of neglect. After breakfast, lunch, and dinner service, I spent my time cleaning nooks and crannies using only a large towel. There are no useful cleaning tools (like steel wool or green scrubbers). And we aren't allowed to spray cleaning chemicals, only pour them on towels.

The worst parts were two equally horrible things:

1. I have never seen so much useful food thrown away in my life. Hundreds of pounds of cooked, edible food, tossed in a garbage can. They only let the offenders eat a certain amount of food. It's plenty, but I don't see a reason to not let us get seconds on things like broccoli, bread, or salad. Or how about doing something cliché like somehow getting the extras to homeless shelters? I dunno. Things like that get to me. What a waste.
2. The kitchen staff (not state employees) use the power they have to degrade and belittle the offenders. Unfortunately I can't write more on that, but I will when I am a free man.

***

-Anne-

I kind of feel like one of the old geezers on Sesame Street, commenting from the peanut gallery on Vince's posts. But since we only get 13 minutes to talk on the phone every two weeks, we don't waste time clarifying the finer points of the blog. So. I don't get why he was so looking forward to getting his brown hat. It sounds like it just makes life more demanding—I mean, 30 pushups? I can barely do three.

I think this goes to show that many of us thrive when more is asked of us. I see this at work with volunteers. The ones whose supervisors "don't want to overwhelm them" by giving them too much work usually don't stick around. The ones who we pile work on, rise to it and usually do even more than we asked of them.

I always thought Vince's problem was that he couldn't handle stress; that was why he lived in the boon docks, didn't own a car, never aspired to become a chef rather than a cook. But maybe I had it wrong. He seems to be thriving under high expectations. It'll be interesting to see how he manages when he's outside, with just the minimal expectations that he not use chemicals and not break the law.

A Room with View

-Vince-

Today we watched a movie in treatment called 7 pounds. (The number is shown in that form in the title so I can't be faulted for not spelling it out.). It stars Will Smith. And it's one of the better movies I've seen in a long time. It's really sad. Funny in the right spots. And at one point in the beginning he says to a man when asked why he was deserving of his help, "Because you're a good person, even when you think nobody is looking."

I liked that. I want to be like that.

Throughout my life, I have always thought of myself as a good person. Unfortunately, I haven't actually acted like one very often.

From dealing drugs to stealing anything that wasn't nailed down, to abandoning friends and family alike, I've done nearly everything possible to be a bad person.

I've looked into that a lot over the last two months, done a lot of soul searching, taken my moral inventory. I can see the harm now in the things I've done. Now I'm starting to build myself back up. To gain the confidence I never had. I can be that good person I've claimed to be. I am going to be a good man.

***

Last night at 2100, like every other night, we stood at the POA at our bunks, waiting to be counted. This time I noticed that it was still light out. It reminded me of my childhood in Aspen Glen, the suburban subsidized housing complex we lived in until my mom met Kermit. I remember staring out the window at the other kids still playing outside. I don't remember how old I was, or what time I had to go to sleep, but I do remember hours of boredom.

No boredom here. Today we were allowed to raise our Reebok Step up to ten inches. Ugh. What a difference. For 40 minutes, the extra two inches made me sweat like a hog. (That's what she said?) It was a good workout.

***

-Anne-

I feel myself getting defensive as I read Vince's memory of Aspen Glen. There must have been hundreds of kids who lived there. We moved in when Vince was four. Maybe he was staring out the window at the other kids because he was four and I actually enforced a bedtime, unlike a lot of the other parents. There were good parents there, but there were terrible ones too. And a lot of them, like me, were completely overwhelmed and exhausted with work, school, household chores, and parenting. Sometimes I couldn't stay awake past 9:00. Unlike me, Vince is a night person, so I can imagine he was bored because he couldn't go out and play and he couldn't go to sleep. But it's not like I kept him locked in his room and slid trays of food under his door—just to be clear.

All Those Pizzas

-Anne-

The last post, in which Vince and I recalled Aspen Glen, reminded me of a vivid memory from that time.

Vince came rushing in the door from school; I think he was in first grade so he would have been six or seven. Before I could turn around from whatever I was doing in the kitchen to say hi, he was out the door again.

About an hour later, he came flying back in and flung himself to the floor, crying pitifully. "What on earth is the matter!?" I asked in alarm. Still prostrated on the floor, he sobbed, "We have to sell pizzas for a school fundraiser, and I went to every house in Aspen Glen and didn't even sell one! How am I ever going to sell all these pizzas!?"

I hid my laughter. Every unit in Aspen Glen had kids, and they all went to his school. Why would anyone buy a pizza from someone else's kid, especially since we were all on food stamps?

***

I think about this story when I'm feeling overwhelmed. I say in my head, "How am I ever going to sell all these pizzas!" and chuckle to myself. It reminds me that nothing is that important that I need to fling myself onto the floor and sob.

But I do wonder if this little episode is emblematic of Vince's personality traits that may have made drugs appealing. I know, this is called "taking someone's inventory." I am only supposed to take my own inventory. But still.

256

Another example: Vince bought a pair of roller blades with his bar mitzvah money. He laced them up, hobbled outside, and 10 minutes later crawled back into the house, ripped off the skates, and hurled them across the room, screaming, "I'll never learn how to rollerblade!" Of course he was a master of it within a week, skating backwards and doing pirouettes in the street, which made me shudder.

He often complained of being bored. Lots of kids say, "I'm bored!" but he was saying it up until he was arrested, at age 35.

Okay I'll just say it: I think Vince is impatient and impulsive. He needs stimulation and instant results or he complains of boredom or finds something to fire him up. Just a few years ago, he took a dare to eat a tablespoon of dry cinnamon. Dry cinnamon! Maybe a tablespoon doesn't sound like that much to you, but try it some time. No, don't. He was sick for days. Why would anyone do that, if they weren't looking for a little excitement and they didn't care if it was positive or negative?

I am never bored, so it's hard for me to understand. I am also a high energy person, up at the crack of dawn, on the move, tackling my to-do list—go, go, go. That has its own downsides. But that's why I've never even been tempted to try a drug that would pep me up, like cocaine. I don't need to be any more hyper.

If it's true that Vince's personality traits feature impatience, a need for constant stimulation, and impulsivity, how will he manage when he's out, when he has every opportunity to relieve his negative impulses?

Tweaking is the Best Way to Travel

-Vince-

2005 hours

I got a letter yesterday from an old using friend. I wrote him about four months ago telling him I had made the decision to be sober when I was released. He was happy for me, but sad to lose a friend.

The letter I got was very sad. The day before Easter, he fell asleep while driving (very common among meth users) and flipped his vehicle three times. He doesn't remember any of it. He also didn't remember being saved by the Jaws of Life, but that's how he got out.

He was air-lifted to the Mayo Clinic where he was in the Intensive Care Unit for 9 days.

His collarbone was spider-web fractured from far left to far right. Femur shattered at the hip socket. Three broken ribs, two punctured lungs. Staples and stitches to hold his fractured skull on.

He said the worst part was waking up several times upside down, still strapped in his seat, and passing out from the pain. Ugh.

On the plus side, he says, "I have decided that the Good Lord saved me for a reson (sic). I will go to my grave straight and sober." I hope he does. It's amazing what a meth addict can survive and keep using.

***

About 9 years ago, I had left Winona after selling some meth and was nearing the town of St. Charles. It was early on a Monday morning, during what could be considered rush hour, heading toward the direction of Rochester.

When I woke up, the speedometer said 68 but the road was green. It took a split second to realize I was in the ditch. There was no time to react to what was ahead of me.

Out of the culvert I came at a quick pace, but a gradual incline. I went airborne and cleared the first driveway by about ten feet. I landed perfectly straight in the next ditch, and up ahead I saw trouble. I was headed straight toward a 3 foot cement drain pipe.

Speed unknown, I smashed into it, destroyed it, and once again I became airborne, this time I landed on the driveway and stayed there.

During the impact, the airbag deployed which, in tandem with my seatbelt, surely saved me from death and/or serious injury. If you ever have the opportunity to see an airbag deploy in your face, pass that up. It's so quick and loud, it's like a glitch in an old black and white film. It wasn't there, then it was.

***

The aftermath.

I thought the car was filling up with smoke, but it was some kind of dust from the airbag. Either way I got out quickly. That was when I realized that I had my dog with me. Willie jumped out after me and ran across all four lanes of traffic and the median, somehow avoiding every car, truck, and semi on the road. He appeared to be uninjured as he disappeared across the road. More on that later.

A car pulled up behind me, the lady jumped out and said, "Oh my God, I can't believe you're alive!" It turns out she was a nurse at the Mayo Clinic. I asked her to call 911, she talked with them and said I appeared to be in shock, but otherwise okay.

Looking at the car I first noticed the front, driver side wheel gone, and the engine resting, smoking, on the ground. Everything "accordioned." And that was really all the damage to me and the car.

When the cop came, I sat in the front seat with him and answered some questions. I was very nervous because my pockets were full of felonies. But I'm a good liar and he didn't suspect a thing.

The car I was in had no insurance so I ended up losing my license for a couple years, but I got it back and still have it now. End of story.

That was the first of three similar accidents, two of which happened more recently, within the last three years. All related to dozing off while driving. I do consider myself lucky to have never hurt anybody.

A week after the accident, after calling around various animal shelters, a friend of mine located Willie at the St. Charles veterinary clinic. He was just fine, and now up to date on shots! He was so excited to see me I cried a little bit when I saw him. End of story, again.

Toadally at Peace

-Vince-

I lifted weights for the first time in years this morning. They're still heavy like I remembered. Free weights make a guy feel a bit awkward and off balance, but they really do a good job. My goal was to lift 10,000 pounds, but I lost track after my first set. I think I did a bit more though.

I saw myself in a full length mirror today. My body has transformed considerably for just 2 ½ months. I've lost most of my gut, and my chest sticks out by itself. Most guys in prison stick their chests out to appear more threatening, much like a dog bares it's teeth. Now I don't have to do that! Either way I pose no real threat.

Today I'm feeling good about myself.

***

Today I left the grounds on RJWC—Restorative Justice Work Crew. I spent six hours working very hard at a bible camp/retreat/campground sort of place. My favorite part was being completely unsupervised for about an hour while I groomed a trail in the woods around a pond.

It was quiet. I was surrounded by nature. I spoke briefly with a couple toads. They said nothing back, of course, as most toads and frogs speak little to no English.

The rest of the time I spent stacking wood, and raking up concrete and Styrofoam from an old shuffle board court. I was with seven others from the India squad and we all sort of moved around to different projects.

It was a very fulfilling and productive day. I will have the opportunity to be on RJWC every week or so for now, and it's usually something /somewhere different every time.

***

I miss my dog, Willie. I think about him a lot, and I wonder if he still thinks about me.

He was with me shortly before I was arrested, which is usually a sign that that person set you up to be busted, but I know he wouldn't do that to me. He's not even a person. He is, however, probably more loyal than most of the people I know in the meth world.

He is with my dear non-meth-using friends in Fountain, Minnesota. He's been living there without me for about a year and a half. I just got a few pictures of him and my friends and it took everything I have not to break down crying in the middle of the other 5 guys in my barracks.

There's so much of my life I wish I could do over.

Victory Lap

-Vince-

Sitting in my blue plastic chair, here's what I see. Three feet in front of me, my bunk mate is sitting in his blue plastic chair, facing me. He also has folders on his lap, which we call our "desks."

To my immediate right is our bunk. My bed is on the bottom, our combined four foot lockers under my bed (not four feet long, four of them). Blue blankets stretched flat with 45 degree angles on the foot end, our brown blankets stretched over our pillows with a 45 degree angle at the top.

To my left, three feet away, is the same thing. To my right, the same thing five more times. Like one of those infinity mirrors where the same scene seems to go on forever and ever.

Everybody is talking in different directions, some talking over others. It's louder than one might think. A Correctional Officer just walked by and dropped somebody down for working on personal letters. So that's all for now.

***

Every other morning, well, actually every Monday, Wednesday, and Friday, I tell myself over and over that I will finish the run. It's still kind of tough, but I've only dropped out once in this past month.

Today, I struggled. I really wanted to fall out after the first three laps. Lap four came and when we were almost to the point where we have to yell, asking for permission to fall out, there was a C.O. walking around the small track, right where I would fall out. I didn't want to have to answer a bunch of questions about my motivation so I continued on.

It was very humid out. I was drenched with sweat, and cramping up in my stomach. All sorts of reasons to quit. But I made it through lap six. Then, the physical trainer leading the run decided to bring us around one more time. It was the hardest lap of my life, but I did it. Five miles (4.9, but we call it five). I've felt great ever since.

So. That's what I did before 7:00 am. How about you?

Sticker Trippin'

-Anne-

I thought I would show you some of the envelopes that go back and forth between Vince and me. First, here is the standard return address on a letter from him. Just in case I've managed to keep his incarceration private from a few people, the DOC makes sure that the US Postal Service and my neighbors in my apartment building know he's in prison.

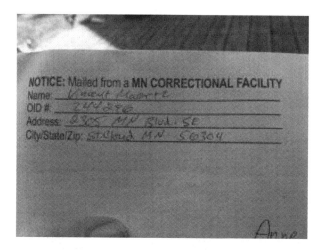

I know, I know. I could be a battered woman who wants nothing to do with her abuser, who is locked away in Moose Lake. It just seems like most people are suspicious enough that they would see a letter from someone they don't want to hear from, a mile off, without the use of MN CORRECTIONAL FACILITY. I mean really—all caps? Who uses those anymore unless they are angry?

On the positive side, here is the standard postcard they send. I like the tree, nice touch.

Here is a sample of a letter that was returned to me. Why? Because I used a return address sticker, apparently.

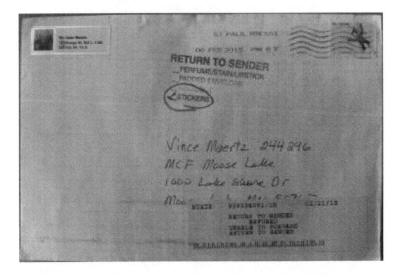

Again, I understand that every one of these "rules"—I use quotation marks because they are enforced inconsistently—probably originated from some incident. In this case, the myth is that someone tried to send the offender LSD using address stickers. Apparently you might try to send LSD in lipstick, perfume, bubble wrap, white out, or even create a fake stain. It's true that a lot of criminals are pretty imaginative.

Imaginative, but dumb. If you wanted to get high in prison, and I can understand why you would, would you really want to go on an acid trip? I've never dropped acid. If I were going to, I'd want to be in a

264

lovely cottage in the countryside somewhere, where I could safely ponder bunnies and fawns.

Tripping in a prison cell? That's one of the ways our clients where I work have been tortured. They're shackled to a bed, forced to ingest acid, then tormented in an endless variety of ways.

A Room with a View of a Brick Wall

-Anne-

I moved again. It was exhausting. I hired my nephew and niece to help me, thinking, "If I'm going to spend hundreds to move anyway, why not keep it in the family?" But here's a tip for free: rent a big truck, even if your nephew has a truck. All trucks look big to me. But even though I was only moving about two miles, it took 7 hours to move most of it because the bed of his truck wasn't all that big. I spent two more hours after they had to leave, schlepping the rest of the odds and ends in my Mini. Then there was the cleaning up at the old place. Fortunately I had learned an important lesson from the first move: don't buy cheap packing tape. So this time boxes didn't spring open and spill all over the truck.

The highlight of the move was when they couldn't get my dining-room table through the back door. They removed the center legs. They tried to remove all the legs, which didn't work. They tried opening it all the way (it's huge—it seats 12 people). This resulted in some fairly deep gouges in the top. They tried taking the door off the hinges but the screws were rusted in place. They finally loaded it back in the truck, drove around the block, and brought it in the front door, which required carrying it up about 5 flights of steps.

But I'm in. If I am really disciplined, I can pay it off and not have a mortgage or rent payment when I retire.

It's not just the moving that's such a pain. There's changing your address for everything—which I had done three months earlier.

Here's another tip: walk into a post office and do it. Don't do it online. I've tried it twice now and it doesn't work.

I took the opportunity of moving to liberate myself from KomKast. I now have an antenna and can get about 10 TV stations. I switched internet providers, to CenturyLink, and am so far pleased with them. I named my new wireless network "I'llNeverMoveAgain."

***

So now I live in a gorgeous old wreck of a place; below are some photos. Another niece, and my cousin and her girls, came over before the move to help me paint. Tip number 47: get the right height ladder. Trying to paint 10-foot ceilings when you are 5'3", using an extension pole while precariously balancing on a counter top on a wobbly footstool … well, I feel lucky I just had a sore neck and back for a couple days and didn't break either.

When I sold my last place six years ago, I swore I would never own again. I would never spend a sunny Saturday morning at a big box home improvement store. But the economics of renting vs. owning changed with the Great Recession. So here I go again, buying all the stuff like drills and putty and ladders that I got rid off back then.

Now I lie awake at night thinking of all the things I want to do. I want to re-do everything, basically, with no money and no time and no expert help. I just try to observe myself, have a little laugh at my own expense, try to be kind. Tell myself, "one thing at a time." My favorite feature of the place: a big south-facing window with beveled glass.

The dining room, with the troublesome table, which looks amusingly tiny now.

I think this layout, with a long hallway, is called a Pullman.

The kitchen is horrid. I have a grand vision for remodeling it but that will have to wait.

This will be Vince's room on September 9. It's a work in progress, like the rest of the place. I hope the view of the brick wall doesn't make him feel claustrophobic. At least he'll have his own room with a door he can close, and a bathroom he can use by himself, with a door he can close.

Life Imitating Work

-Anne-

Once or twice a year, my organization sends out a list of items that our clients need. I got the latest list the first week in June. It had the usual things on it, like Target gift cards, quarters (for laundromats), umbrellas (they travel on foot or via public transport and it's been a rainy spring), and shoes (in this case, men's size 8, "preferably tennis shoes").

Someone needed a suitcase. As an asylum seeker he is not allowed to work and he also is not eligible for any public benefits, like housing. So he is sleeping on someone's couch—probably a friend of a relative of a friend who is the same nationality as he is. The most common nationality we see right now is Ethiopians.

I had a giant suitcase that I was never going to use again so I arranged for him to have it. Win-win situation: I didn't have space for it; he needed it, good deed done. I am so glad I'm not a social worker; our clients' needs are endless and their stories are so sad.

A week later I got this letter from Vince:

Ms. Mom:

I've been doing a lot of thinking about my release. I've been here 100 days. 82 to go.

I've mentioned before that I won't have much when I get out. Nothing really. But there are some necessities and even some convenience items I will need your help with. You're the only one I feel comfortable asking, but you may know some others that are willing to help.

So here's my list of things. Some of them explain themselves. Some may not, so I will:
Bed and bedding related items
Clothing (from the ground up, figuratively and literally)
Eye exam and contact lenses
A vehicle and insurance. For this I may (will) need to take out a loan from a loving family member. With only four hours

of personal time per week, not to include AA meetings or physical activity, time management is going to be critical. For me, a vehicle is one of the more important needs. We'll talk.

Gym membership. We've talked. [I told him the YMCA has a sliding scale system.]

Cell phone, if my ISR agent allows one. I think I can pay for it.

Well, that's a good list so far.

This list wasn't entirely my idea. We are all encouraged to write to family asking for help when we get out. They know we leave with nothing, and it's good to prepare as soon as possible.

I have a new copy of my driver's license in my file here, and soon I will have a new Social Security card, so I will leave here with the requirements to obtain legal work anywhere. My chemical dependency counselor says it would be good for me to get work outside the foodservice industry, so keep your eyes peeled for factory work or anything really that you think I could do that would be felon friendly.

I'm not intentionally trying to add stress to your life so if I am, say so. They say the more we prepare, the better our chances. And our resources here are limited. I know I'm going to be a bit of a burden for a while. But I'm willing to pull my weight however possible.

I'm coming home with a positive attitude, a good work ethic, and a desire to be productive always.

I need to fill 90 hours of community service/volunteer work. You mentioned a good volunteer is hard to find. I volunteered in a nursing home the other day in Moose Lake. It was very rewarding.

I love you, Mom. Thank you, again, for all you continue to do.

Vince

Money for Nothing

-Anne-

Today, June 26, is United Nations Day in Support of Victims of Torture. Today also marks one year since Vince entered prison.

My organization will host a potluck supper at our clinic in St. Paul. We're supposed to call it a healing center, not a clinic. It's in an old renovated Victorian home. I think it's actually Edwardian, but in Minnesota, we call everything Victorian if it's more than 100 years old.

You would think I'd be used to dealing with the corrections system by now, but it still has the ability to throw me off guard. First, in keeping with my accidental theme of critiquing every word, why can't we call it the prison system? Just what are they "correcting"? I have an image of them straightening out Vince's limbs and brain with ratchets and wrenches.

On June 23 I got the following message from the corrections system email provider:

> *This email is to inform you that effective June 30, 2015 the Minnesota Department of Corrections will no longer utilize CorrLinks for inmate message transfers. The MNDOC agency option will no longer be available effective June 30th.*
>
> *If you would like to request a refund of your balance you may do so by removing all of your contacts and closing your account.*

Sincerely,
CorrLinks Support

I so wish I could be an emotional ninja all the time—ducking serenely to avoid upsetting news like this—but instead I flipped out.

UNBELIEVABLE! was my immediate reaction. CorrLinks is the one thing about the entire MNDOC that has actually worked. It's affordable, simple, and it's the one effing way I could reliably communicate with Vince.

I assumed they had found another vendor that would cost five times more and was owned by the warden's brother in law. Or were they just going to discontinue the email option completely? What a joke.

***

I checked the DOC website and it had no information about the change. So I called them. The person who answered knew nothing about it. She put me on hold and when she came back read me a memo she had managed to track down that said the same thing as the email. But it did go on to say there would be a new system called J Pay. (I wonder if J is for Jail?) It will cost 40 cents per message instead of 30. Okay, I guess I can afford that.

I currently have a $4 balance with Corrlinks. Am I going to bother requesting a refund? Hell no! I'll bombard Vince with emails—articles from the Atlantic are good for using up words.

But I bet there will be thousands of people who don't ask for refunds. Let's face it, one week's notice is not very much, especially for wives of prisoners who are working full time and have kids. So let's say there are even 1,000 people who leave $4 on the table. That's a cool $4,000 for Corrlinks, or for the DOC. In fact, I wonder if they switch systems every now and then just to get some quick cash.

I am so cynical! Probably the money will be donated to some prison-related charity, right?

The Restorative Powers of Kittens

-Anne-

When Vince and I started blogging, I didn't realize that a theme of redemption would emerge. Vince's transformation is probably obvious. Mine is subtler and has unfolded over many years.

I have been thinking about this lately because in the spring and summer I get dozens of emails a day from the Humane Society about stray kittens. What does this have to do with redemption?

I signed up to do foster care of kittens a couple years ago. These kittens are born in warehouses or barns or even under car hoods. The mothers, if they survive, are emaciated and barely old enough to conceive. So that's part of what makes fostering redemptive for me—giving care to vulnerable teen moms that I didn't receive myself.

I keep these kittens, with or without moms, until they are old enough to be spayed/neutered, then turn them back to the Humane Society. It's not all fun; I've had entire litters die because the mother was so dehydrated. Kittens have been smothered by their litter mates. One lost an eye to the claws of a litter mate. So it's kind of a nature-tooth-and-claw experience.

People wonder how I don't get so attached to them that I want to keep them. I think fostering is the ideal setup—I get the cuteness of kittens and the Humane Society pays all the vet bills and provides the supplies. I travel too much to have a permanent pet. When I turn them back in, I know they will be adopted immediately—there's a huge demand for kittens. And I'm not even that much of a pet person.

So why do I do it, and what does it have to do with redemption? I think it goes back to one of the few memories I have of my dad.

274

A few weeks before he left home forever, he had been gone for weeks and showed up with a black kitten. I must have been seven, and my three siblings, younger than me, were thrilled. I was too, but also leery because I knew my mother was not happy. I can see now that the kitten was my dad's wedge to get back in—if my mother had demanded he turn around and leave, "and take the darn kitten with you," she would have been the bad guy.

I remember dad telling us to hold her gently and not fight over her because she was a living creature with feelings. He said her name was Surprise! and told us to always say it that way, like there was an exclamation point.

So then dad was back home, and the next day he went out to buy some cat food and kitty litter. He was gone all afternoon and missed dinner. My mom tried to put us to bed early. We did what we usually did, laughed at her and ran in four different directions. But I also can still feel how anxious we all were.

Dad made his appearance just as the cat had crapped under someone's bed. My mom began to reproach him because he was drunk and hadn't brought home any pet supplies.

We kids were giggling until dad roared, "I'll get that goddamn cat!" He ripped the kitten out of my sister's hands, strode to the top of the stairs, and hurled her down the staircase like a fastball, screaming, "You goddamn piece of shit!" He raced down to the landing, grabbed Surprise! before she could get oriented, and sent her hurtling down the second set of stairs to the first floor.

We huddled at the top of the stairs. Someone was whimpering but I had learned to be silent, no matter how frightened I was.

That's when I had the thought that would teach me to never make wishes: "I wish he was dead." A few months later, he was.

Surprise! not only survived but had a litter of eight black kittens six months later.

Much later, there was a (nonviolent) incident involving cats and Vince but that's his story.

Who could not feel their soul restored by kittens?

Have a Nice Day

-Anne-

The drum beat of stories about prison continues.

Last week, every day on my drive in to work, I heard a different story about prison on National Public Radio's Marketplace Tech Report. At the end of each segment they said, "Go to our special website for this series to read more" but I can't find it. The series is called Jailbreak (clever, huh?).

In the process of trying to find the Jailbreak series I found a dozen great short podcasts on NPR. There's one called, "Connecting inmates with their children through books," another about for-profit prison companies adjusting to a new era. Apparently the prison population has decreased slightly, which is bad for their business model. What a shame!

There was a story about keeping mental health patients stable and out of jail. I don't expect you to listen to all these stories, but they are a good representation of the economic, health, and social issues that all intersect in prison.

There was one story I could barely stand to finish listening to. From Solitary to the Streets was much as the title implies: prisoners, kept in solitary confinement for years, then set free with no support or resources. It's an 11-minute podcast that will break your heart. This is the kind of story that gets me so mad and upset that I worry I might drive off the road. Vince was in solitary confinement for less than a week and I think he would say it was the worst part of his one-year in prison so far.

This same week, there was news that Ross Ulbricht, creator of the Silk Road black market website where people could buy drugs and fake IDs, launder money, and conduct all sorts of other nefarious activities, was sentenced to life in prison. Life in prison. He's 30 years old. Obviously the guy is a jerk with no moral compass. But life? I don't know enough about the story yet to be suspicious about the government's motives, but I'm sure that will come.

Back to the subject of jail breaks, the story that's been fascinating to me is the real New York prison break. I won't post a link because there are frequent developments. How did they get power tools? How did they communicate with each other and their presumed accomplices to create such a brazen and fine-tuned plan? How did they cut through the walls of their cells and the steam pipe without being heard? And the smiley face! Was that part of the plan that they snickered over for months, or was it spontaneous?

I have caught myself cheering them on, then remind myself that these guys are murderers. I have to check my allegiances; I firmly believe in the rule of law and the 10 Commandments. I'm pretty sure I wouldn't succumb to the sweet-talking B.S. of a lifer and smuggle in power tools to help him escape. But I can't wait for the book and the movie to come out.

Nap Denied

-Vince-

They tore up part of the running track last week and never put it back together so I haven't been able to run for a week. Some people are happy about it, I am not. But, there is nothing I can do about it. 78 days to go.

The list of "Things I will need" that I sent my mother a few days ago, well, some of them will be easy/cheap at the Salvation Army or Goodwill, I think. I have a lot of resources at my disposal, but I don't want to take advantage of the system unless I have to.

I will qualify for food stamps and maybe unemployment still, so those may help.

***

Restorative Justice Work Crew, basically community service. Earlier this week I got to leave the grounds for only the second time in three months to do some work in the community. Specifically, in the city of Barnum. Our job: clean out 10 school buses, only the insides, from front to back.

It was particularly hot out, 90F, and most of the buses had routes that utilized gravel roads for the past nine months, so we were quickly covered in dust.

Nine men, six hours, 10 clean buses. My job was to vacuum the area around and on the driver's seat and to clean the windows and mirrors. It was hard work, but it felt good to be doing something productive.

And of course it was nice to be out and about, almost like free men. As in St. Cloud, I only realized how long it had been since I last heard music when I heard a song. It was some crappy pop song, but it was beautiful. The radio was on for the ride there and the ride back, 25 minutes each way.

***

I'm exhausted. I haven't taken a nap for over 90 days. But it's less than 90 days until I can. Naps, and good food, are what we talk about on boring days. Today is boring. I want a nap but they're not allowed.

We got some new guys yesterday. This time they're in the bunks next to ours. They're loud, confused, and completely unorganized. Three months ago, we were them. I better go help them out.

No Good Deed Goes Unpunished

-Anne-

Today is Independence Day in America, or what we popularly call "the 4th of July." I thought I would write something profound about freedom and democracy and human rights and the intersections of race and class, but instead I am too busy to write much because I am fighting off a flea infestation in my new home.

The day after I wrote that maudlin post about kittens, the Humane Society was sending email after email about kittens that needed fostering, so I raised my hand to take a trio of month-old motherless kittens. Oh they were so cute, so cuddly, I held them in my lap for hours.

I spent the next few days and nights scratching myself and waking up at 3am exclaiming, "ouch!" I won't go into detail but let's just say that fleas like the warmest parts of the body.

I spent yesterday at a doc in a box, then went to a different pharmacy from my regular one to fill the prescription.

Then I returned the kittens to the Humane Society. They were very apologetic. This is the biggest year for kittens in anyone's memory, so they screwed up and sent a litter out without flea-bombing them, or whatever it's called.

"And if they ingested any fleas, then they have tapeworms, too," the vet tech said sadly. I can only imagine the look on my face, because she started repeating, "I'm so sorry!"

Fleas are a nuisance and make you feel like a hillbilly, but I draw the line at worms. I find worms of any kind horrifying. Guinea Worm, a disease found in Africa, would be my worst nightmare. I won't provide a link because I know images would pop up. Tapeworms would be a close runner up for horrifying conditions.

"Does that hold for humans, to?" I asked. "If I accidentally ingested a flea could I have tapeworms?"

"I don't know. Probably."

She didn't know. Probably.

On the bright side, it's not bed bugs, which was my first fear. Apparently they are almost impossible to get rid of.

You get rid of fleas by poisoning them, heating or freezing them to death, suffocating them, or vacuuming them up. So I have spent my 4th of July holiday washing every fabric item I own, vacuuming, stuffing things into airtight plastic bags, stuffing my freezer full of pillows. I am coated with Permethrin cream from head to toe.

Here's a photo of the little buggers when I dropped them off.

The One I Love

-Vince-

I passed a drug test and breathalyzer. I knew I would, but I did get a little nervous. Well, nothing to fret over now.

***

I remember a lot of good from Aspen Glen, our subsidized housing project. Twenty plus years later, I still think about my daycare family—Duane and Mary and their three kids James, Shawna, and Michael. I spent years with them after school and playing with the kids on weekends. Even after we moved I stayed in touch for years. I really do miss them. I wonder if they wonder about me.

I also remember fondly my years at Bel-Air School. Years later I drove by it, and was surprised at how small it was. Everything is big when you're a kid.

I remember when the suburb of New Brighton itself was small. Woods everywhere. Again, driving through years later, it looked commercialized. The town I grew up in, plastered with big city names. Big City businesses. I remember when the employees at the Red Owl grocery knew me. That was the first place I ever stole from. I got caught the first time. Oh, how things change.

***

I went out on another Restorative Justice Work crew. We spent five hours at a nursing home in Moose Lake. We cleaned all the exterior windows of the facility, then picked at the never-ending supply of weeds in the various gardens. I found quite a few agates in the landscaping. We're not allowed to keep them so we put them in a bird bath for all the residents to enjoy. They always look nice underwater.

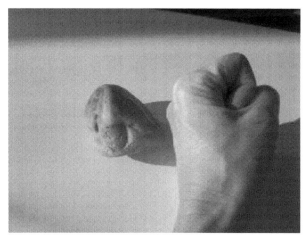

One of the hundreds of agates Vince collected before he was incarcerated

***

So far, it's been raining all day. This is the first time that it's a rained on a Saturday while I've been at boot camp.

If it's raining, we don't have to go out and do work crew stuff. I don't mind working, I never have, but this is a good opportunity to catch up on a lot of things, including writing.

One of my friends sent me a picture of my dog Willie. I instantly became sad. I miss him so much. It's amazing how close we can get to an animal. He has been through so much with me. He's about 12 years old now. I can't wait to see him again.

Who knows how or what dogs think about. Somehow, I know he misses me, and we will both be just as excited to see each other, only I will have tears in my eyes.

79 days and a wake up, and I will have the ability to start figuring out how to get him back in my life.

***

-Anne-

At first read I thought these passages of Vince's were not very interesting. After typing them and re-reading them, several things struck me. 1) He is capable of reviewing the past and remembering both good and bad things. Most of us need to live more in the now, but addicts need to be able to reflect back on the past before they can move forward. 2) He has at least one hobby, agate collecting. Hobbies will be important diversions for him once he's released. 3) He has someone (his dog) he misses; he can't wait to be reunited. Someone to miss, and who misses you—I would hope that'd be a strong deterrent to ever being locked up again. I hope Willie lives a very long time.

Super Best Friends

-Vince-

When I was arrested in December of '13, Willie wound up living with my friends in the Fillmore County area. He has spent over half of his life there and his dog friends are there, so I know he's happy, and that soothes me.

The people that are taking care of him I miss just as much. They were not just a part of my life, but they were my life, for years. And although we were all pretty good at drinking, we bonded with each other, and I stayed out of legal trouble for many years. Then, of course, I made a quick decision one night to use meth, and it took only a few months for me to separate from the pack, then leave altogether.

I miss you guys. I think of you daily. Not just you, but your families, who were all good to me.

Seth, our trip to Florida to watch [the Minnesota Twins] baseball spring training games was comparable to the best vacations I've been on. We had more fun in seven days than most people have in a year. It was "the crippie."

Curt, you and I have had conversations that have not, and will never again, happen in this world. I cherish every minute we spent together.

Sara. You are a free spirit and a true friend to everybody you encounter. You taught me how to ride a horse. I failed to learn. But that's because your horses are stupid.

Those three plus me. We were the "Super Best Friends Group" for years. I abandoned them like I abandoned the rest. They belong to the short list of the people I feel worst about. I write to all of them constantly. Some reply, some don't. But I keep writing.

Seth, Vince, and Sara at a baseball game. It was about 101 degrees.

***

-Anne-

I made an effort to travel with Vince before he left home. I considered it an important part of his education—travel itself, different people and places. We went to Seattle, New York City, and Washington DC, among other destinations. We mostly got along well when we traveled.

When he turned 30 he seemed to be doing so well—as was I—that I offered to take him on a "big trip" somewhere. He had heard me talk about my friends in the Scottish highlands, and said he'd be interested in going there. I think he was attracted to the hunting and fishing, the six dogs and two cats, the meat-laden diet, and of course the whiskey. It was a wild, manly, rural place. I thought Vince and my friend Lynn's husband would get on well together. Maybe Richard would even inspire Vince to aspire to be more.

Before I sunk thousands into a trip, I thought I should make sure he was serious about going, so I told him to get his own passport. I mailed him the form. It would have cost $75. I realize that may seem like a lot when you're a cook making minimum wage. He said he would do it, then didn't. So the trip never happened. I was disappointed, but relieved that I hadn't forced it to happen if he didn't really want to go.

A few years later he asked me if my offer of a birthday trip was still valid. He wanted to go to watch spring training baseball games in Florida in February with his friend Seth. I said yes. I feel strongly that getting out of your comfort zone is vital to personal growth, and Vince had barely stepped foot out of rural Minnesota in years. Besides, I had enough frequent flyer miles that it didn't cost me much. So he and Seth went, and apparently had a good time. Don't ask me what a "crippie" is.

Funny Money

-Vince-

Less than a week until the one year mark. I think that a year ago today was the day I was robbed at knife point. Man, prison is way better than that.

I had a different kind of scare about a month before that. I was very nearly arrested for the federal crime of passing counterfeit money. It was very scary.

I had made a transaction through a friend of a friend. As a drug dealer, you don't want to be seen or known, so I set it up so there was a "package" sitting on a car seat. Later, when I walked by, there was a similar "package" with money in it (we commonly used empty cigarette packages). Done deal.

287

When morning came, I made a trip to the gas station. I gave the clerk a $50 bill. He used one of those pens and it turned black. Uh-oh. He said, "We have to call the police." This would be bad. I was out on bail, my pockets were full of meth, pills, weed, cash, and baggies. Running would make me look guilty. I couldn't empty my pockets in a public place, too risky to lose the $3,000 worth of everything I had (funny we won't ditch something that could imprison us for years). All I could do was stand there like I was confused, and be honest (lie like crazy).

I went into the bathroom and ditched all of the small baggies in the toilet. Then I told the employee I was going out for a smoke. He didn't entirely believe me so he told me to write my info down. Somehow I knew this could help me later on. I wrote down my real info.

I went out to my truck and I frantically emptied my pockets onto the seats. The windows were tinted so it would be difficult to make anything out from the outside.

That's when two squad cars pulled up. They had been given a description of my vehicle so one came right up to me. The other officer went into the store. Officer 1 asked me for my info and I gave him the same as I had given the clerk so when Officer 2 came out, it would match. Establishing honesty.

Officer 1 asked how I got the bill. On the spot, I made up a story about drinking with someone I didn't know at a bar, him winning some money on pull tabs and giving me a $50 bill. He asked which bar, and I started to choke up a bit, and Officer 2 came up behind me.

He saved the day. He told Officer 1 what info I had given the clerk, giving me time to think of a bar where I knew a customer of mine who bartended. So my story was believable enough. My info checked out. Then Officer 1 went to the truck and looked through the window. He cupped his hand to block out the light. At least four felonies right on the seat. And one still in my pocket that I had just remembered.

He backed away from the truck, turned toward us, and said he wanted to have a word with the other officer before deciding what to do.

They left me standing in the sun. So many thoughts: Why am I so stupid? Why me? I'm gonna go to prison forever!

I was trying not to tremble. They walked back to me and said that because I was honest with them, they weren't even going to fill out a report. I was free to go. I just stood there, in shock, then turned around and opened the door to the truck, so I could just barely get in, blocking any view of the inside, got in, and drove away.

That incident was scarier to me than any time I was ever arrested. I've been pulled over many times holding substantial amounts of drugs but I always had a good poker face, remained calm, and never got even a ticket.

After a close call, I always began to shake, adrenaline pumping. Ready to do it all again. I will not miss those moments.

Je Pay

-Vince-

I've been reading "Always Looking Up" by Michael J. Fox for a day or so during my short periods of free time. I've always been interested in reading about him. He was a good part of my entertainment when I was young, on Family Ties, and in movies such as Back to the Future. I don't believe he's acted since 2000, so when I saw his face on a book in our small library I picked it up.

He and I have a lot in common. He's a famous actor with Parkinson's Disease, and I'm a prisoner that takes medication for a condition related to Parkinson's Disease. It's like we're twins.

Anyhow, I don't really have anything more to say on that subject, except that I was just mentioning it's a good book so far. Inspirational is the word I think I'm supposed to use.

***

-Anne-

A few updates:
Someone from the Department of Corrections called and asked if I was indeed Anne Maertz, if I was willing to house Vince upon his release, if I owned my home. I said yes and yes and yes. Then she said, "I need to confirm that you have no firearms or alcohol in your home." I stifled a laugh because I have learned that DOC people don't like it when you laugh. "You mean when Vince comes to live with me, right? Not as of this moment?" She said yes and I confirmed that I don't have any firearms and my house will be alcohol free when Vince is released. But I could not resist saying, "You realize there are 50 bars and liquor stores within walking distance of where I live, right?" She said she did realize that but that this was their policy.

When I'm not feeling contrary, I can see the logic of the policy. Most suicides are committed with firearms found in the home. Without instant access, many suicides could be prevented. Same for chemical dependency relapses. Say Vince is feeling despondent at 3am. If there's beer in the fridge, it would be so easy for him to walk 10 feet down the hall and medicate himself. But with nothing in the house and no bars or liquor stores open at that time, he would be forced to deal with his feelings and cravings until morning, and as the AA slogan goes, "Each day a new beginning."

My other interaction was with the prison industrial complex. As I wrote a couple weeks ago, the Minnesota DOC has switched email vendors. This sent me into a tizzy because email is the one cheap, dependable system that actually had worked for us to communicate. I finally found time to set up an account with the new vendor. They asked for my address, phone number, credit card number, and date of birth. That last one seemed unnecessarily intrusive.

The new vendor, J Pay, has a slick website with photos of people who look like they are having the time of their lives:

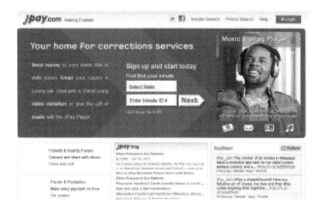

It calls account credit "stamps." Is that so you don't realize it's money? After multiple failed attempts, I was able to buy $2.00 worth of "stamps," which is the maximum one can purchase at a time.

It costs .40 per "stamp." The emails you can send are only about 1/3 as long–it's difficult to tell before you hit "send." Most people are not going to do the math, but I am not most people. The old system worked out to about 10 cents per page, while this one will be 40 cents per page. I would say, cynically, that they count on people being too overwhelmed or math-impaired to figure this out, but actually it doesn't matte –we are prisoners to J Pay and other such legal scams. The only other option is to send only postal mail. If I am realistic, that's just not going to happen. I like to send Vince newspaper articles about baseball, and those are not allowed to be mailed to prisoners. Don't ask me why.

At the bottom of the J Pay website were the usual social media buttons—"Like us on Facebook!" they implored. *Right*. As if J Pay is some sort of uber cool product I want to give free PR.

Concrete Thinking

-Vince-

My last post was about almost being arrested for counterfeiting. Another form of close calls happened much earlier in life. When I first started getting high regularly, I would come home to my dear Mother, the grand inquisitor, and have to answer a barrage of questions, all of them pertaining to me being high.

Well Mom, I can tell you now that you were right every time. What you don't know is how hard it was to control my words when the room was shaking back and forth. You see, in the early days, pot gave me vertigo. And somehow it came on strong after a walk home and sitting down in front of you.

Wave your hand back and forth in front of your face and imagine your hand is actually the room you are in. Scary.

I got vertigo for a few weeks during my sober years, too, but I don't know why.

***

Yesterday I was picked for the third week in a row to go out on a Restorative Justice Work Crew. This one was tough in comparison to cleaning windows at the nursing home last week. I'm sunburned and all of my muscles have had a good workout.

We went to Willow River School (K-12?) and tore up sidewalks and curbs. Some of us worked sledgehammers to break it up, some of us pushed brooms around, keeping all areas clean at all times, and I wheeled load after load of broken concrete—or cement—I don't know the difference, to the giant, metal garbage bins and dumped them out. Not always in the easiest way. I had to lift many pieces over the top, once the side door was closed.

At one point, four of us carried a piece that easily weighed 300 pounds about 60 yards quite awkwardly to its resting place in the bin. We did all of that for six hours.

Our boots were wrecked. Remember, our boots have to have a glass-like shine on the front two inches of the toe. Hahahahaha. I dropped at least three 100+ pound pieces on my toes throughout the day (thank you, steel toes) and my boots were battered. It took me three hours to break them down, re-apply two coats of wax, and get them looking good again.

After all was said and done, I felt pretty good about all of my hard work.

I had a small scare this morning when they announced that the running track has been repaired and we were going to run for the first time in 9 days. I was pretty sore from hauling concrete.

No worries. I completed the 4.5 mile run as usual.

As of today, we have eleven weeks left. 226 meals, 225 after dinner. 32 runs. 32 aerobics. Not that I'm counting.

Gigs, L.E.s, and Recycling

-Vince-

Today has been a rough day. It started with a run that was a bit faster than I'm used to. We ran seven laps with an average time of 8:50 and fastest mile at 8:14.

This was only the second time we have been able to run in the last two weeks because the track was under repair. I was proud of myself for finishing the 4.9 mile run. I would guess that 1/3 of the men that started it today did not finish it.

Our squad also took our blue-hat test today. I got 47/50 correct. My brain says that's 94% passing. Three weeks left of brown hat. I know that sentence is shady at best, but I can afford some bad grammar once in awhile.

Anywho, we will soon be seniors. This is the time for us to take the knowledge we've gained here and apply it. We will help train in the new guys when they get here, and will be held to the highest standards and expectations of the Challenge Incarceration Program.

I'm nervous, but only a little. The blue hat phase is where a lot of guys get kicked out or recycled into a squad a month behind, turning this into a seven month ordeal.

I have six total gigs. That's really, really good as far as discipline goes. I have no L.E.s (Learning Experiences, which are given out for major infractions, or accumulated gigs, which are minor infractions). If a guy has four L.E.s, he can be recycled. A few of our squad have three. I'm in good shape.

One thing they say is, don't get comfortable. Stay on your toes and follow all the rules. Avoid the "snowball" effect, piling on gigs and L.E.s in a short period of time.

**

I just got an uplifting email from my mom. It would appear that people out there are willing and able to help me out when I'm released. That is wonderful.

I know I'll have work soon after I'm out, but until the paychecks start coming it's going to be tough.

I'm beginning to feel better about leaving here. I'm one of the few in my squad that have been working hard to get everything we can out of this while we're here. We don't ever want to come back to prison, and we will put our all into that. As the old saying goes, "If we put half as much effort into staying sober as we did into getting high, we will succeed."

Well. I will succeed.

Life, the Universe, and Everything

-Vince-

I'd like to take a little time here once again to thank all of our readers for your support and words of encouragement. Survivor Grl, Hang in there. I wish I could have figured my life out when I was young. Actually, I tried when I was 22, but I had to do a little more research into addiction (ha ha) to make it clear to me again that my life was out of control.

I enjoy any comments and feedback I can get so keep it coming. I can't do this alone, and it appears I'm gaining support out there already.

***

Sunday. My down day. My lazy day. I've been reading nearly all day. For the second time in my incarceration I'm reading Nelson DeMille's The Lion's Game. I've read all of his books and a couple twice. I'm addicted to his writing, what can I say? It's better than being addicted to crack. I would know.

Here's something that still bothers me about this place. Many of the offenders here are here on convictions of gun charges or aiding and abetting a drive-by shooting. Since they didn't kill anybody—this time—they technically don't have a victim in their crime.

They also don't have drug problems, and they are forced into chemical dependency treatment with us. They don't identify with us, and even make fun of us every now and then for not being able to control our lives. Our counselor just tells everybody they're doing a great job, even when they hand in blank assignments, or openly argue with him.

Well just like every other aspect of prison, I use that as a reason not to come back. That's all I'm going to say on it.

***

I've mentioned before that we stand at the position of attention a lot here. Lately, I've been using that time to ponder time itself. When did time start? Was there always time? Is time infinite? My brain can't seem to understand it. How could there ever have been nothing anywhere?

I'll skirt around the God issue because that, to me, is even more unbelievable than the concept of infinity.

Then there is the big bang theory, which I believe to be true. Why was there a whole bunch of crap just sitting in the middle of nothing/nowhere? Why did it explode? Where did it come from?

If you are a scientist and are reading this, please answer all of these questions so I don't go crazy.

Bad Willie

-Vince-

We're sitting in treatment in a windowless room, when all hell breaks loose. We know the clouds were darker than usual when we came here. The chemical dependency building is about 150 feet away from the barracks. We march over.

It sounds as if a million woodpeckers are searching the corrugated metal roof for their dinner. It's deafening. I know it's a hail storm, but others don't because they can't see it.

Our counselor leaves the room briefly and comes right back, to tell us we can go look outside. And what I see is cool as hell. The ground is covered in what looks like those 1 cent white mint-flavored gum balls and golf balls. The ground is being bombarded by these in the millions. It's been only two minutes since I heard the first one hit the roof, and already they're three inches deep.

Accompanying the hail is a rain so heavy that it, too, appears white and forms a wall that blocks our view of everything else. It's beautiful. I've never seen anything like it in my life.

Ten minutes later … heavy rain continues. Something tells me I'm going to be very busy tomorrow on Restorative Justice Work Crew. If there's any damage from the storm such as downed trees or even flooding, we'll be there to clear debris, make sandbags, and do whatever else we can to help. I'll write more after treatment. (Treatment is really boring today.)

***

Back in the barracks. I can see out of a window again!

The sun is out, the ground is still covered with hail, but it's melting and creating fog, so it looks like the hail is slowly crawling its way back up to the clouds.

***

The hailstorm nearly wiped out our entire crop. Over four acres, no, maybe six acres … dang. I don't recall. But it destroyed a lot of organic matter. It also caused some minor flooding in Willow River so today myself and eight others swept and shoveled all of the sand and dirt left on Main Street. Six hours of sand removal. Ugh.

It was another exhausting day. As it turned out, wet sand is just as heavy as cement. Who knew. I'm happy that this day is over. 69 days and a wake up.

***

-Anne-

There's been a lot of buzz lately about Obama's clemency program. As of this writing, he has commuted the sentences of 68 prisoners, some of whom had been sentenced to life in prison for nonviolent drug offenses.

As I understand it, the program is only available to federal prisoners. I don't know the total pool of prisoners who were eligible, but 30,000 applied. So 68 were granted clemency out of 30,000, and that doesn't take into account prisoners like Vince, who are not federal prisoners.

The intention is good, and it's a start and just one part of the overall momentum to reform drug and sentencing laws.

What they are really afraid of on the Democratic side is another Willie Horton. He's the prisoner who was furloughed for a weekend while serving a life sentence for murder. He decided to spend his weekend committing assault, armed robbery, and rape. The incident torpedoed the presidential campaign of Massachusetts Governor Michael Dukakis. Such an incident couldn't be pinned on Hillary Clinton, but it would feed into the Republican narrative that Democrats ar eweak and soft on crime.

Starting Life Over / A Life Over

-Vince-

As of yesterday I have a total of $238.90 in my gate saving account. So, double that, and you have roughly what a prisoner makes in a year through our various jobs. The most I made was 50 cents per hour sewing underpants together in Moose Lake. The least I've made was here, in Willow River. Divide $2.50 by 16 hours. I'm horrible at math. [15.6 cents per hour]

It's not much to work with. I've mentioned before that half of our pay goes into savings and half we can spend on items that for the most part, are well over retail price. My current paycheck is $35 even, every two weeks. So I get $17.50 to spend on envelopes (61 cents each), shoe insoles ($2.10 for two pair that last exactly two weeks), paper, pens, pain relievers, muscle rubs, and all the stuff we need/use, we pay for. But, our food, bed, heat and AC, electricity are provided at no cost to us, so I'm okay with it.

It's July fourth. We will have a three-day weekend starting tomorrow (Friday). That does not mean we have the day off. In fact, we work extra hard, so that we won't want to be incarcerated for holidays next year. Well, that seems to be working for me.

***

Every time I catch myself thinking or saying that I'm tired, I think back to a year ago when I could be awake for days at a time. Paranoia would set in after day three or four, and I would often take things out of context and think people were out to get me.

I would hear my name in groups of people, or thought I did. Casual conversations would, in my mind, be people plotting to steal from me or turn me over to the cops. I would flash them an angry face and storm out of wherever I was. This was often when I would go out behind the wheel of two tons of steel.

On day five, the visual hallucinations kicked in. Often I would see the same vision. Snow coming down from a cloudless sky on a summer day. I knew it wasn't real, and I knew I shouldn't be out in public like that. But I had to keep "working." No more. I'm so glad I got arrested.

Actually, I'm glad they sent me to prison. I believe it's the only way I could have quit. Not just using, but the lifestyle that accompanied it. I had to get away. Most users/dealers just keep on racking up charge after charge. Then end up with 10 year sentences because they showed career criminal tendencies. I took the deal I made for prison time and at the same time let my co-defendant off the hook. Now I'm ready to start life over.

***

-Anne-

Not everyone can start over, like Vince. As delightful as snow falling on a summer day sounds, drugs and drug crimes ruin lives, families, and communities. Here is just one story about a man who was found unconscious in a hotel room while his toddler daughter wandered crying into the lobby with a soiled diaper and his infant son slept on the floor near his methamphetamine pipe. Meth, which is so highly toxic that people who sell their homes now have to sign statements swearing they have not used or made meth on the premises. How will this father ever, ever get over the guilt? What will social workers tell the toddler when daddy goes away to prison for years? How will the father and son ever make up for the lost opportunity for early attachment? How will the mother and father ever repair their relationship, if they aren't already divorced? Maybe now you won't think I'm hard when I say Thank God Vince never had children.

All Lives Matter

-Anne-

I have been avoiding the story of Sandra Bland since it broke about 10 days ago. I was afraid it would be too heartbreaking. I think I'm overwhelmed—a sure sign is that I switched to classical Minnesota Public Radio from the news version. The case of Freddie Grey, the black man who died of a broken neck after being handcuffed, put into the back of a police van, and driven all over Baltimore while he was tossed around helplessly, was my (heart)breaking point.

But this morning I switched back to the news and caught this story about Sandra Bland. It contains audio clips of the interaction between Bland and the officer who pulled her over for not signaling a lane change. In case you aren't aware of what happened next, the interchange escalated, she was arrested and thrown in jail, where she allegedly hanged herself.

It was really, really hard to listen to, but not for the reason I'd expected. I had assumed I would feel angry and powerless because yet another African American was dead after an interaction with a police officer. And I did feel that.

But Sandra Bland reminded me so much of me—specifically my confrontation with a correctional officer that got me ejected from Moose Lake and banned from visiting Vince for six months. You can hear it in her voice, and in her pauses. She is sick and tired of kowtowing. Bland didn't lose it as quickly as I did, but she was probably trying to put the brakes on herself since she is black, after all.

I wonder what would have happened to me if I had been black? Would I have been thrown to the ground, arrested, and taken to jail?

***

I struggle with the race issue. I know that black men, especially, are arrested, convicted, and incarcerated at a higher rate than white ones. After a police officer shot and killed a black teenager, Michael Brown, in Ferguson, Missouri, the U.S. Justice Department conducted an investigation which found a pattern of racial bias between 2012 and 2014 violating the Constitution and federal law. For instance, while the population of Ferguson is 67% black, 93% of arrests were of black people. You could say, "Maybe black people commit more crime," but for even minor offenses like jay walking, nearly 100% of the arrests are of black people. And when whites are arrested for jay walking, they are 68% more likely to have their charges dismissed than blacks are.

***

So why do I struggle with "the race issue" when it seems so clear cut? It's not that I doubt that black men are arrested and incarcerated at higher rates than white ones. It's that my son—despite the fact that he is white—is still in prison. He is still serving a way-too-long sentence for his crimes and he is still being exploited for nearly free labor. We are still paying through the nose for things like stamps, emails, and ramen. It remains to be seen, but I am afraid he will be released with very, very little in the way of support or resources. And he's one of the lucky ones—he's got me and others who are rooting for him and offering to buy him bedding or pants.

Yes, blacks are incarcerated at higher rates than whites;currently at St. Cloud they represent 31% of the prison population while they represent only 5% of Minnesota's overall population. But since whites make up 85% of Minnesota's population, their *numbers* in Minnesota prisons are higher—there are 627 white men in St. Cloud, compared with 335 black men.

Do people think Vince shouldn't be where he is—because he's white? Would some people dismiss him as a loser because, being white, he has no excuse not to be a mid-level manager by now with a wife and two kids and a house with a white picket fence in the suburbs? Do people think all white men have it made by virtue of white privilege, and therefore the only explanation when they fail is that they're bad seeds?

Bill Clinton Confesses

-Anne-

No, it's not what you think! But Bill's confession at the end of this July 16 editorial in the New York Times is a positive thing, and I think the piece is worth publishing verbatim, even if it is a bit long [4].

President Obama Takes on the Prison Crisis
On Thursday, for the first time in American history, a president walked into a federal prison. President Obama was there to see for himself a small piece of the damage that the nation's decades-long binge of mass incarceration has wrought.

Mr. Obama's visit to El Reno, a medium-security prison in Oklahoma, capped off a week in which he spoke powerfully about the failings of a criminal justice system that has damaged an entire generation of Americans, locking up millions — disproportionately men of color — at a crippling cost to them, their families and communities, as well as to the taxpayers and society as a whole.

Speaking to reporters after touring the cells, Mr. Obama reflected on the people he met there. "These are young people who made mistakes that aren't that different than the mistakes that I made, and the mistakes that a lot of you guys made. The difference is they did not have the kinds of support structures, the second chances, the resources that would allow them to survive those mistakes."
This indisputable argument has been made by many others, most notably former Attorney General Eric Holder Jr., who was the administration's most powerful advocate for sweeping justice reforms. But it is more significant coming from the president, not just in his words but in his actions. On Monday Mr. Obama commuted the sentences of 46 people, most serving 20 years or more, for nonviolent drug crimes. It was a tiny fraction of the more than 30,000 people seeking clemency, but the gesture recognized some of the injustices of America's harsh justice system.

On Tuesday, in a wide-ranging speech to the N.A.A.C.P. [National Association for the Advancement of Colored People], Mr. Obama explained that people who commit

303

violent crimes are not the reason for the exploding federal prison population over the last few decades. Most of the growth has come instead from nonviolent, low-level drug offenders caught up in absurdly harsh mandatory minimum sentences that bear no relation to the seriousness of their offense or to the maintenance of public safety.

"If you're a low-level drug dealer, or you violate your parole, you owe some debt to society," Mr. Obama said. "You have to be held accountable and make amends. But you don't owe 20 years. You don't owe a life sentence." Mandatory minimums like these should be reduced or eliminated completely, he said. Judges should have more discretion to shape sentences and to use alternatives to prison, like drug courts or community programs, that are cheaper and can be more effective at keeping people from returning to crime.

Mr. Obama also put a spotlight on intolerable conditions, like overuse of solitary confinement in which more than 80,000 inmates nationwide are held on any given day. Many are being punished for minor infractions or are suffering from mental illness. "Do we really think it makes sense to lock so many people alone in tiny cells for 23 hours a day, sometimes for months or even years at a time?" Mr. Obama asked. He said he asked the Justice Department to review this practice.

He talked about community investment, especially in early-childhood education and in lower-income minority communities, as the best way to stop crime before it starts. And he spoke of the importance of removing barriers to employment, housing and voting for former prisoners. "Justice is not only the absence of oppression," Mr. Obama said, "it is the presence of opportunity."
As Mr. Obama acknowledged, however, his powers are limited. Any comprehensive solution to this criminal justice catastrophe must come from Congress and the state legislatures which for decades enacted severe sentencing

304

laws and countless other harmful measures. In recent years, the opposite trend has taken hold as lawmakers in both conservative and liberal states have reduced populations in state prisons — where the vast majority of inmates are held — as well as crime rates.

It's time that Congress fixed the federal system. After failed efforts at reform, an ambitious new bill called the SAFE Justice Act is winning supporters, including, on Thursday, the House speaker, John Boehner, and may have enough bipartisan support to pass. It would, among several other helpful provisions, eliminate mandatory minimums for many low-level drug crimes and create educational and other programs in prison that have been shown to reduce recidivism.

One sign of how far the politics of criminal justice has shifted was a remark by former president Bill Clinton, who signed a 1994 law that played a key role in the soaring growth of America's prison system. On Wednesday, Mr. Clinton said, "I signed a bill that made the problem worse. And I want to admit it." It was a long overdue admission, and another notable moment in a week full of them.

Vince Maertz, PhD

-Vince-

Today we got to play tug-of-war with our brothers in Hotel squad. They came in the same day as us, India squad, about an hour before we arrived, so they have seniority on us for everything. We lined up on the volleyball court. 16 men on each side and a thick red rope travelling the length of the court.

The rules were simple, no tying knots and no letting go. It was a best of two out of three contest in which we did not need the third try, we were stronger. We all cheered and felt pretty good about ourselves.

305

I also saw myself in a mirror today in just a T-shirt. It's been a while. We are nearly always in our full khaki uniform and I couldn't believe my eyes. I looked good. Defined pecs, trim stomach, and powerful arms. I could have been a model for a boot camp ad in my khaki pants, grey T and shiny belt buckle. I really am beginning to see the results of all my hard work.

Happy.

***

On the opposite pole, there is negativity all around me. People just don't want to do any work to get an early release.

I've written before that everybody here is in chemical dependency treatment even though not everybody here has or had a problem with drugs. So, on occasion, I hear people talking about the fact that they aren't weak-minded pu*#@s that can't control their own lives, and other such comments. I understand that life isn't fair, and that part of this program is about punishment, but these guys get released into the general public at the same time too. They do minimal work, minimal exercise, and they always have bad attitudes. It sucks.

***

I got to go to the library. That's why Fridays are my favorite day. I say that, to say this: The other day I wrote that I had been pondering such things as the existence of time and space and life and what not. Well, today a book caught my eye, A Short History of Nearly Everything, by Bill Bryson. I read the thing on the back of the book that makes you want to read a book and it basically said it would answer all of my questions in a sort of simple, sometimes humorous way. I've only read the introduction so far but it has me captivated. I even read the first two paragraphs of Chapter 1 which starts to explain what a proton is and already can tell that I will be able to understand it. So I'm a scientist now. Wait, are scientists Doctors? Maybe this book will tell me.

***

-Anne-

I love Bill Bryson, who is definitely not a scientist. I just re-read his book about traveling around Europe, Neither Here or There, because I am going to Germany in a couple weeks. I think I'll pick up this book Vince is reading and see if I too can become a scientist. I tried reading Stephen Hawking's A Brief History of Time and couldn't get past the second page.

Arrrrrrs

-Vince-

Yesterday our squad had our AARs. I don't recall what that acronym stands for but I do know it's where we turn in our addresses for release to our case manager.

Now it is of my opinion that my mother moved from her apartment to her condo to avoid having to tell (or ask) a landlord for permission to have a felon living in the apartment. Well, it may still come up.

You see, my mother may own a condo, but somebody else may own the land that it's on, and they would still have to be informed of my situation.

I only get one phone call every two weeks so I can't tell her until Sunday but I think she may worry about having to do that. I suppose I could have waited to write this until I spoke with her but I'm in study hall right now and I'm all caught up with my assignments.

This will all work out. In fact, everything that I worried about or was afraid of since I arrived at boot camp has worked out just fine. I look back almost four months when I thought I could never run more than a mile, or go through 182 days without a nap. Well, the no nap part is still hard some days. Enough on that.

***

Holding it all together. Almost. That's the way I look at the year prior to my arrest in December 2013.

I had a full time job in Lanesboro. More often than not, I still showed up early and held it together for 11 hours at an outdoor grill working in front of people. Some days I was able to keep standing only through heavy concentration because I hadn't slept for days and I had been driving around all night selling drugs. Being a short-order/line cook is one tough job, and I could still do it but I made a lot of mistakes. Some nights I would have to look at a ticket over and over because I couldn't commit it to memory. I was wasting moves, as we call it.

Arms flying all over the place but not actually doing anything. So much stress. Nobody knew about my other life. Nobody knew that the power was out in my apartment, or that I had to use the bathroom a lot so I could hit my meth pipe to keep going. Or that I didn't have vision because I didn't have any more contact lenses and I literally could not see more than three feet away with any clarity, part of the reason I had to move back and forth so many times to read tickets.

I was a hot mess. I can't believe nobody ever asked me what was wrong with me. But it was all over in mid-October. At that point I began selling full time and it just got worse.

I spent the next couple months in various hotel rooms so I wouldn't have to face the music back at my apartment in Fountain. Hotel hopping, so nobody would see a pattern of in and out, in and out. All my drug profits went to my personal high, scratch offs, and gas. And food every now and then if I thought about it. Somehow, for reasons unknown, I didn't care. I didn't care about me, my family, or my real friends. And I showed them by abandoning everything.

I am so grateful for this place. And I'm proud of myself for sticking it out. Nothing about boot camp is meant to be easy. And it's not.

But I have pushed myself harder and farther than I ever have. Even when nobody else is looking.

An Inspector Calls

-Anne-

The Department of Corrections sent an agent to inspect my condo and interview me. Her title on her card is "CIP/ISR Agent." She is one of four agents monitoring 80 boot camp participants across five or six counties.

The agent (I'll call her Holly) was one of those tall, corn-fed, blond Minnesotans with ruddy cheeks. She was late because she'd come from visiting another mom whose son had been in for murder since he was 15—that was 22 years ago, which makes him the same age as Vince now.

"So she had a lot of questions," she said. Yeah, no kidding. I had a lot too. Holly walked through the condo but didn't open the fridge or closets as I'd been told she has the right to do. If I told you where I had stashed my beer and wine during her visit, I'd have to kill you. (I will honor the "no alcohol/drugs/firearms" policy once Vince is here, but he's not here for over a month.)

She seemed awed by the condo. "This isn't like the typical house we see," she said. "Most of them are pretty run down."
She explained that they would come to the house three times a week at random times. It could be 5am or 3pm or 3am. They can search the premises without a warrant at any time. I guess I hadn't realized that Vince will technically still be a prisoner, just one who is serving out his term in the family home.

She said Vince can't leave town, have any other ex offenders over (whew!), or possess booze, drugs, or guns. He won't be released with an ankle bracelet but they will slap one on him if he makes a misstep. During their three weekly visits they will do urinalysis tests and if they aren't clean Vince will go straight back inside.

Holly told me I would need to get a land line but she backed off from me having to install a doorbell, which was a relief. "We'll just rap on the front window," was her solution.

Vince will be allowed to search for work from 10am to 2pm weekdays. He can go to a workforce center or do it from home. I went to a workforce center when I was unemployed a few years ago and they are great resources but they are depressing because they are full of unemployed people.

I asked if they would help Vince find a job, or give him leads. She said they do pass along information, like the fact that Target refuses to hire ex offenders so he shouldn't bother with them.

I told her I was planning to let Vince use my car to look for work and she reminded me that he would have to be added to my insurance. So we'll put that plan on ice until I find out how much it will cost, and until Vince has a job and can pay for it.

I asked if Vince would have health insurance and she said he could apply for Medical Assistance.

I asked if it was a problem if I traveled, especially outside of the country, and she said no.

I asked her advice—should I set a time limit on how long he should live with me and if so how long? She said they don't give advice; that it's up to Vince and me to set ground rules.

At the end of the visit we talked about his graduation ceremony and actual release and I fessed up that I had been banned and wasn't sure if I'd be allowed in. She was shocked and said she'd never heard of such a situation. "The ceremony is really cool, so I hope you'll get to see it," were her parting words.

Softball, Kitten Ball, Hard Ball

-Vince-

It's my down day again. They keep coming so fast, and only nine to go.

Today, I chose to be lazy. I'm going to play cribbage as much as I can, and not do any treatment work. I may sound like a rebel there but I don't actually have any treatment work to do.

***

It's been a huge boost to my confidence hearing from my mother that people are so willing to help me out. I think it probably has a lot to do with the fact that they know a lot about my situation vs. just being some ex-convict in need.

Right now I'm sitting in my chair and everybody is being loud. It's so hard to concentrate sometimes. In a few minutes though, I'm going outside to play kitten ball which is exactly like softball except for the ball is even bigger and actually soft.

-Anne-

I filed a request for aid with the ACLU (American Civil Liberties Union). One of my neighbors (before I moved twice) is the executive director of the Minnesota chapter. I took a risk and told her about Vince. It always feels like a risk, doing that, although I've never received anything but kind words of support.

I had just received my BAN notice, and I specifically asked her if she thought I had any legal recourse.

She responded via email:
> *I am so sorry to read your email, your blog, and then think about you dealing with all this pain while at the same time looking for a place to move, packing and moving.*

Prison administrators have a great deal of latitude in how they deal with inmates and visitors, so there may not be an infringement of constitutional rights here. However, if there is a hook we can find that would indicate that your denial of visiting rights is retaliation for what you said, we might be able to do some advocacy for you.

I would suggest that you go on line and fill out an intake form. Our process is all volunteer driven and we get far more requests than we can take on, but it would be worth your time to try.

Again, I am so sorry. I hope that we can help.

***

So I filed the complaint, and forgot about it.

Four months later. I got a letter from the ACLU saying they couldn't take my case. Basically, due to their limited resources and all-volunteer attorneys, they have to prioritize cases that they think they can win, that won't drain a lot of resources, and that will have an impact on lots of people.

My case ... well it was really a case of "he said/she said." I understand completely and I'm not surprised except that it took them four months to respond.

***

The six-month ban will end on July 30. I will submit (the perfect word) my request for visitor's privileges next week. I am nervous that it may be rejected. I still don't know if they're aware of the blog and may decide to "teach me a lesson" and "show me who's boss." If I am denied, then by the time Vince is released in September it will have been over eight months since I've seen him. He's excited about his graduation ceremony. If I'm not approved to visit, I'll have

312

to just sit in my car out in the parking lot, I guess, until the ceremony is over and they send him out the gate.

A Simple Plan

-Vince-

This morning we had another weigh in. This time on the fancy scale in the Health Services. My math was a little off I think when I last mentioned my weight because I had used the scale in the weight room. Anyhow I weighed in at 181 pounds with 11% body fat. That's eight pounds less than last time.

I wasn't sure what to make of that, but then the Physical Trainer said it was very good. I've lost 20 pounds since I got to boot camp and 35 pounds over the last year.

My goal which I set for myself is only six pounds away, and I have two months to reach it. I will succeed.

***

62 days and a wake up. Some days, it seems too far, some not. I'm exhausted. Must keep going.

We had our brown hat reviews today. I did as well as I expected I would. I will be getting my new hat as soon as the two graduating squads leave this coming Tuesday.

This is the final phase in the incarceration part of the program. We've made it through 18 weeks. Eight weeks to go of the highest level of expectations.

Not all of us earned out hats, but they will over the next two weeks. As a squad, we did pretty well. And, as a 17 man squad, we have already lost over 300 pounds!

Summer is here. I don't remember every day being so humid as a child. Maybe it just didn't affect me as much. Who knows. I'm sitting at my "desk" (my desk is my lap with a folder on which I write.) and the A.C. is on full blast but my clothes are still sticking to me. Yuck. Always wearing our full khaki uniform has its disadvantages.

The book I started last week, A Short History of Nearly Everything by Bill Bryson, is amazing. It explains everything clearly that I never understood in biology, chemistry, astronomy, mineralogy, etc. Ok I never took some of those classes. Anyhow, I'm learning a lot about how much it took for me to be in existence, and how lucky we are to be here now. And, in relation to everything around us, how little time we have to enjoy. I don't ever want to waste any more time being locked up. Such a waste. All I have to do is never get high or drunk again and I should be alright. So, that's my plan.

Addiction: Disease or Habit?

-Anne-

I chanced upon an article, Addiction is Not a Disease, by Laura Miller in Salon. It describes how addiction used to be considered a moral failing, then was reconsidered as a disease with the rise of 12 step programs, and now neuroscientists are thinking it's more of an extreme habit.

Miller bases her article on the book Biology of Desire by Marc Lewis, a neuroscientist who is a former addict himself. He posits that addicts have a "particular 'emotional wound' the substance helped them handle, but once they started using it, the habit itself eventually became self-perpetuating and in most cases ultimately served to deepen the wound."

The disease model has been supported by the fact that addicts' brains are different.

"The changes wrought by addiction are not, however, permanent, and while they are dangerous, they're not abnormal. Through a combination of a difficult emotional history, bad luck and the ordinary operations of the brain itself, an addict is someone whose brain has been transformed ....

"More and more experiences and activities get looped into the addiction experience and trigger cravings and expectations like the bells that made Pavlov's dogs salivate, from the walk home past a favorite bar to the rituals of shooting up. The world becomes a host of signs all pointing you in the same direction and activating powerful unconscious urges to follow them. At a certain point, the addictive behavior becomes compulsive, seemingly as irresistibly automatic as a reflex. You may not even want the drug anymore, but you've forgotten how to do anything else besides seek it out and take it."

The good news is that habits can be unlearned. AA and NA and other 12 step groups do work for a lot of people. Others may need cognitive behavioral therapy, or meditation, or something else, or all of these things. It's kind of like how I fought long-term depression by trying everything, until something broke through.

I'm all for understanding the causes of things, in case that knowledge points to new solutions. I'm also big on measuring success to discover what works. This article in Scientific American basically concludes "we don't know" whether AA works because (in my lay language) it's too loosey goosey to study with the gold standard of the randomized clinical trial. It works for some people and not for others, and there are probably as many reasons for both outcomes as there are members.

***

On a long drive a few evenings after reading the article about how addiction is not a disease, I caught a podcast about the history of

Alcoholics Anonymous. I knew most of the story already, how two chronic inebriates, Dr. Bob and Bill W., found each other and developed the AA program based on something called the Oxford Group, which had gotten started in England and which was overtly religious.

The story is poignant. Both Bill and Bob were headed for early graves. Instead, they met each other. Talking about their problem with someone who also had it worked some magic that no amount of nagging by their wives or warnings from doctors could. Bill's wife Lois and another recovering alcoholic's wife, Anne, founded Alanon, to help them recover from their own insanity caused by living with alcoholics.

***

There are lots of "gurus" out there who will tell you that you have to go to AA or Alanon every week for the rest of your life, or that you have to give up every mood-altering substance—from heroin to caffeine to sugar—or that "real" meditation is only done in the early morning, for a minimum of 45 minutes, sitting in the lotus position.

I say, be open to trying a variety of solutions, and equally willing to stop using things that aren't working. Why would you want to limit your options when you're up against something that could make your life miserable, kill you, or land you in prison?

Empathy 101

-Vince-

Tired. Sometimes I don't even notice it until about this time of day because we're so active then we eat a huge dinner then come to study hall or an AA meeting for an hour. I've been sitting down for five minutes and it's really kicking in. Exhaustion. But we are not only not allowed to sleep from 0520 to 2120, we are not allowed to have the appearance of sleeping. We cannot have our eyes closed for more than a three count (the speed of which is determined by any correctional officer) or we get formal discipline. Yesterday, they caught somebody with their eyes closed who was going to be graduating and leaving tomorrow. Well, not now. They added a week stay at boot camp. That's not something I want to do. So, I tell myself over and over that I have plenty of energy, and find a task, like writing, to keep my brain going.

Over the past week, our squad has been working on victim impact letters. Our job was to think of five people, places, or things that have been directly affected by our crimes, and write a letter from them, to us. This is the first time in four months that I actually saw some real emotion. A few guys chose society, a few their children. I chose my Mother. And my mother is a good writer.

I write a lot. For every post you see out there, I write an equal amount in here. Most of what I write in here will never be seen, most of which is mundane and would not provide anything entertaining. Some of what I write I will eventually share with you, just not until I leave here.

I shared my letter in class today and it was very well received, especially by the people that care about things and can understand big words.

If I had written this a year ago, I think I would have felt like a piece of $@*t. But I've become close with her and I've changed a lot of my behaviors and thinking patterns and am heading in a very good direction which I know is a huge part of making amends. Am I just rambling on? I really want a nap.

Long story short: I love you Mom. I'm sorry I was a crappy son for so long. I am fixing it now. I'll be home in 56 days!

***

-Anne-

I am dying to know what "I" wrote to Vince, but he hasn't sent me a copy of the letter. I have had a lot of ups and downs over the last 20 years of his addiction. The worst was when he relapsed after nearly five years of sobriety. During those five years, even though he wasn't using, he still had some really big attitude problems and unproductive ways of thinking. Now he seems changed. I am really excited for him. Our relationship feels transformed. Whether it is real and lasting once he is released remains to be seen.

Rip Van Winkle

-Vince-

India squad (that's my squad) got to watch a graduation ceremony today. It was pretty cool. Every month, two squads graduate, and two squads that are two months away from the door get to watch. So, now we know what to expect.

It's a huge deal, being released from prison. It's literally the only day most prisoners look forward to. The big difference for us is that we aren't leaving through locked doors and razor-wire fences. Going home for us means the beginning of a new challenge: Phase II.

"Mastery items": that's a synonym with hobbies. You're right Mom, agate hunting is a good diversion. So will be running, weight lifting, cooking, and meetings. All things I enjoy doing. We've spent some time going over our mastery items in treatment and they will be on our daily/weekly schedule that I have to submit before I leave, and every week thereafter. They don't want us getting bored out there.

Another batch of new guys arrived less than an hour ago. They are fun to watch. They're so scared, many of them shaking so hard they have trouble buttoning up their shirts. Four months ago, I was the same. We started out as squad number 12 of 12. Today, we are 4 of 12. And we (most of us) got our blue hats yesterday! We are now a senior squad.

318

We can now teach what we have learned. This is a very dangerous position to be in for some of us as we are held to the highest standards. Mistakes are punished no longer with pushups, but with interventions (gigs) or Learning Experiences. Most people that get kicked out of boot camp are blue hats. I don't think I will have any trouble. I've been a good boy so far. I've done all I can to show that I'm paying attention here. I will most likely be the leader of our squad during graduation march. Some of our squad still can't call right on their right foot. Officers will be paying more attention to them now.

***

-Anne-

A friend sent me a story from the New York Times Magazine: "You Just Got Out of Prison, Now What?" It follows a couple of ex-cons who volunteer to pick up men being released, then spend a day trying to ease them into a world very different from the one they left when they were incarcerated.

They pick up a guy named Dale Hammock. He had been pulled over for not wearing a seat belt and the cops found a bag of meth in his car. Since it was his third offense, he was sent away for 21 years.

Twenty-one years.

It's got to be overwhelming to walk out the gates. The volunteers take him to Target to buy jeans. Have you noticed how many choices there are for jeans? In 1994 it was Levis, Lees, or Sears jeans. Now there are dozens of brands and styles—boot cut, skinny, extra long, straight leg, relaxed, low rise, and on and on. I haven't been in prison but I feel overwhelmed by all the choices. The same is true in chain restaurants, which now make you sift through five menus with hundreds of options, and in the grocery store. A couple times I have walked out of a store without buying anything because I was too paralyzed by the choices to make a decision.

Then of course there is technology. The volunteer showed Hammock something on his smartphone and Hammock asked, "Everything now, you just touch it, and it shows you things?" God help him.

Squad Squabble

-Vince-

We start Flag Detail tomorrow. We had a two hour training session yesterday on how to raise, lower, fold, carry, and store both the Minnesota State Flag and the American Flag. I will be involved in the process roughly every three days as we rotate. I'm a little nervous about it. Not because of punishment for doing something wrong, but because I have respect for the flags and I want to look good doing the job.

If somebody, even by accident, lets any part of either flag touch the ground, and staff finds out about it before we front-and-center about it, our sister squad and ours will owe 2,000 blue-hat pushups. That's 2,000 sets of 40 divided up between 34 guys that need to be documented and completed over the next however-many days are left when the potential event occurs. So needless to say, we're going to be careful.

If it does touch the ground and we admit to it we split up 200 sets. EZ

***

It's been a long day. I've run 4.2 miles, lifted weights for an hour, sat through three hours of treatment, cleaned the treatment building (my job), eaten three terrible meals, read the last 100 pages of my Bill Bryson book (awesome!), written four pages for you guys, written four pages on cross-addiction for treatment, and ... well, that's good enough right? My wrist is sore, so I say good day.

***

Less than 24 hours after writing the post about the Flag, somebody in my squad dropped it. The whole thing. Right on the ground. I was not in that five-man formation so I'm not feeling the heat, but I will be responsible for some pushups. The officer in charge of the detail isn't here today so I can't tell you much more.

***

As a squad we owe 200 sets of boot camp four-count push ups. That's 40 each set. That's 8,000 divided by 17 of us. That's for one squad member dropping the flag, then being honest about it. Yesterday we knocked out 37 sets as a squad. We should be done in a couple days.

What surprised me is that a few of us quite vocally stated that they didn't want to help at all. Their argument was based on the fictional idea that we wouldn't help them if they had dropped Old Glory themselves. I feel a lot of anger toward them for that. We are over four months in and should be working as a squad, but some continue to have negative attitudes and no desire to change.

All that said, I know that I can only control my thoughts, feelings, and actions. And I am not staff. I just wish staff would do something about these people instead of pushing them through the program and back out on the streets. I've worked so hard to be where I am now, and it just doesn't seem fair. And it isn't, is it?

Pistoled Off

-Vince-

A curious thing happened last night while we were all sleeping. There was a large boom. That is all we have been able to come up with. An incredible, loud boom that woke up everybody in all three barracks.

From where I lay, I could not see a clock. And even if there was one in my view my glasses were stored for the night. I could tell right away that everybody else seemed spooked. None of the usual elements associated with a noise you can feel were present. No soft tapping of rain on the roof. No creaking of window frames from wind. No random bright flashes of light. And no fading echo of thunder.

We do know that somewhere nearby is some sort of military facility. On occasion I've seen those gigantic helicopters with the twin propellers flying by low, enough to get our attention. So that is possibly the source of last night's disturbance. Nobody here knows what a sonic boom sounds like so here we sit confused. That's the whole story, I hope somebody out there can tell me with certainty what happened out there.

***

I have another favorite author. Bill Bryson has a way of reeling in my attention from page one. This week I picked up "In a Sunburned Country." Cool. The first and only nonfiction book I had ever read prior to "A Short History of Nearly Everything" (my first Bryson experience) was six or seven years ago. Anthony Bourdain's "Kitchen Confidential."

I should say that I've read many books I suppose in school that would be nonfiction thus negating my last paragraph.

Anyhow. "In a Sunburned Country" is amazing for the first 77 pages I've been able to squeeze in since last evening with my busy schedule. It makes me want to travel, especially to Australia. I mean, who wouldn't want to go there? If you've never read Bill Bryson, give him a shot.

***

51 days to go. 131 already down.

Last night the four blue-hat squads had a marching test for a chance to perform in a parade on National Night Out on August 4th. Well, the same people that didn't want to help us out with pushups also didn't care about marching. We didn't do very well. Four months in and the same guys still have significant difficulty with left and right turns. They also happen to be the only guys in our squad that are here on pistol-related charges and/or don't have drug problems. They have one more thing in common but it would be rude to mention it.

Prison News Round Up

-Anne-

I am leaving for Berlin in two days, so I'm going to review a pile of prison-related articles that I've accumulated—over a period of one weekend—that's how often prison is in the news. I'll give you the downers first, then the positive ones.

Ohio is having trouble obtaining drugs used to execute people, so the Ohio DOC has obtained an import license from the Drug Enforcement Administration to buy sodium thiopental and pentobarbital from overseas. Wow. Where overseas, I wonder? They "decline" to name the countries. I'm thinking China, North Korea, Iran, or Yemen, since these are our fellow members of the death penalty club. In case that doesn't work, Ohio legislators passed an "execution secrecy law" (I am not making this up) in hopes it would get small-scale drug manufacturers called compounding pharmacies to sell them the drugs. These are unregulated companies that have been in the news for sickening people with contaminated pharmaceuticals. But hey, if you're trying to kill someone, who cares what the quality of the drug is?

In Wisconsin, there is a prison guard shortage that has prompted two correctional facilities to call in guards from other institutions and pay overtime. So let me get this straight—we pack our prisons full of nonviolent drug offenders, which costs us taxpayers an arm and a leg, then we have to pay overtime to get guard coverage, which costs us more. Great system!

Which leads me to this editorial in the Minneapolis Star Tribune, "Finding solutions for overcrowded prisons." I like the opening line: "Either Americans are the most evil-people on Earth or there's something terribly wrong with their criminal-justice system." They mention something that's news to me: "It's a stretch to suggest that the bloated prison population is due mainly to the sentencing of nonviolent drug offenders. It's not. Most of the increase comes from locking up greater numbers of thieves and violent criminals and keeping them behind bars longer. Even if all nonviolent drug offenders were set free today, the prison population of 2.2 million would drop to only 1.7 million. Still, on the margin, granting early release to nonviolent offenders and shortening sentences to better match crimes seems a sensible step."

This information is new to me, and I wonder why I haven't read it elsewhere. Everywhere else, the narrative is that, if we just release all the nonviolent drug offenders, our prison population will be drastically reduced. But if there are more violent criminals in America than elsewhere, maybe we *are* the most evil people on earth.

Still, 2.2 million total prisoners minus 1.7 million nonviolent drug offenders is half a million people—not insignificant. And when you figure it costs (on average) $31,000 a year to keep someone in prison, that's over $1.5 billion a year.

On the same day, there was this feature article about Damon Thibodeaux, an 18-year-old who was wrongly convicted of rape and murder who spent 16 years on death row before being exonerated and freed, in large part due to the efforts of Minneapolis attorney Steve Kaplan. Thibodeaux had been raped and beaten on a regular basis by his stepfather since the age of five and so he was easily bullied and manipulated into confessing to the crime. It's a heart-rending story, but it has a happy ending. As I've written before, an important element of recovery from anything is feeling that you belong. And Kaplan has gone the distance to help Thibodeaux adjust to life after prison by including him in family and other social gatherings.

And there was this little factoid in The Week: that every day, on average, a dozen people die behind bars. The leading cause? Suicide, in local jails; cancer in other facilities.

Below are some prison-related images. The bully one made me shudder, because it's how I felt when I was kicked out of Moose Lake. It wasn't about my clothing; it was a power trip. Related to that is an interview with Richard Zimbardo, who led the Stanford Prison Experiment in which students were assigned to be prisoners or guards. The "guards" quickly became sadistic. "I lost my sense of compassion, I totally lost that," said Zimbardo.

Now, the good news.

Prison News Round Up Part II: The Good News

-Anne-

In the same weekend as all the depressing news stories I just listed, there were these two uplifting ones.

The Week published an excerpt of an article in Runners World. Yes, Runners World—about a program at the Oregon State Penitentiary that allows outsiders (even women) to go inside and run with prisoners. They even race half marathons. For some inmates, the outside runners are the only visitors they see. I am not a runner, but I've always been an exerciser—I go nuts if I skip my daily walk and I've been pretty faithful to weight training for 25 years. I swear by exercise as the best medicine for everything from depression to anxiety to all sorts of physical ills. So way to go, Oregon!

Second good news article: The good old New York Times can be depended on to run something about American prisons almost daily. Usually it's extremely depressing, but this past weekend there was this one about dogs in prisons [5] that will make you dog lovers out there weep. It made me weep, when I got to this line: "One older inmate cried when he met his puppy. 'I haven't touched a dog in 40 years.'" It made me wonder how heart-wrenching it must be when these guys have to turn their dogs over after they've been trained to detect bombs, which is what the program does.

Vince and I wrote about the dog-training program at Moose Lake, where he was before boot camp. Only about six prisoners out of a thousand get to participate, so it sounds good but it's not exactly at scale. As I've mentioned, I do foster care for kittens through the Humane Society. Every day from about April through August, I get dozens of emails a day from them looking for fosters for cats and kittens. Below are just two photos from the 13 emails I received today. For some reason the world doesn't seem to be flooded with stray puppies or dogs so much, except those taken in from domestic violence situations, which require months of special care. Could it work to have prisoners foster kittens? Is that a cray-cray or a win-win idea?

I got some good news—my visitor request was approved! That means that after I get home from Berlin I can visit Vince. By that time, it will have been eight months since I've seen him. The ban was for six months, but due to me being denied a visit, and to two chunks of travel, it's stretched out to eight. And yet on every visitor application and in the information for families that the Department of Corrections publishes online, they tout the importance of family connections. Ha.

Whole Lotta Saggin' Goin' On

-Vince-

My blue plastic chair, when in its proper place with me sitting properly in it, faces the bathroom. Luckily for me, there is a shower curtain that usually is pulled over the eight foot entrance. Usually. Well, say 50% of the time. So, anytime I look up from reading, writing, or reflecting, I have little choice but to see inside the bathroom. And every time there's a lot going on in there as you can imagine there would be with three urinals, three toilets, and eight showers. I see a lot more skin than I ever want to see again.

I say that to say this: I'm glad that in no point in my life was I morbidly obese. It's no secret that our country is fat. Well, there are a lot of fat criminals, too. Unfortunately, at a place like this, people tend to lose a lot of fat, but not a lot of skin. It's … unsettling. It makes me cringe.

And now a short list of things I want to eat my first day out: An avocado, sushi, a Dairy Queen Blizzard ® with both Reese's® cups and Butterfinger®, and although I don't believe it's technically edible, a large cup of quality coffee.

***

50 days to go. Have I ever mentioned my fear of needles? I must have. Well, my name was called to go to health services and when I walked down the corridor and rounded into the room, I froze. On the table in front of the bad man wearing blue latex gloves was a pile of syringes. I couldn't speak and I knew he could see my color draining away so he said, "It's just Mantoux, to screen for tuberculosis." This was about the best news there could have been. I can handle a needle going almost anywhere as long as it isn't a vein.

Only twice in my life has a needle entered directly into my bloodstream. Once in Hazelden in 2001, and once when I went to the hospital when I thought I was dying. I was actually angry when my blood work came back clean. It took four nurses to do the blood draw: one to remind me to keep breathing, two to talk to me while the fourth stole my blood. I don't think I heard much of what they were saying. After testing my feces, they found out I had Salmonella.

I'm also afraid of surgery. I can't listen to people talk about it. I can't watch it on TV, or look at pictures of it. I don't think I will ever have surgery, however necessary, because it combines my two least favorite things.

-Anne-

I too hate having blood drawn, and I have fainted a couple times, once hitting my jaw on the side of a table while I was going down. Vince fainted once, just listening to someone talk about surgery. I don't know if it's a physical or psychological thing (would Vince have learned or inherited this aversion from me?). I've learned to ask for three things: 1) a "butterfly" needle, which is thinner than the standard one; 2) that I lie down while they do the draw; and 3) that they talk to me to distract me. Health care folks are always happy to do these things; they don't want me falling onto the floor any more than I do.

Small Comfort

-Vince-

My squad mates made it official. I will be the caller for the graduation march on September 8. It's a good feeling. I've been working hard in many areas including marching in our squad formation. It's tough to get 17 men to turn at the same time on the correct foot, while singing our cadence. But I know I'll do well.

***

Yesterday I worked K.P. for only the third time since my arrival. I didn't go as much as most people because I've had a job that interfered with the scheduling, blah, blah.

330

I actually enjoyed it. I worked about 14 hours in the back of the kitchen. They were excited to have somebody that knew what he was doing. I got to use the big Hobart slicer and was happy to discover that I still had good form. And, I did not cut any fingers off.

This morning after our run we came back inside our barracks to discover that it had been "inspected." It happens about once a week. If anything is wrong, they take the drawer out and empty it out on the bed. In my case, I didn't roll one of my underpants correctly so I had to re-fold my shirts, socks, sweats, and undies. I'm usually one of the few that doesn't get flipped but I knew I had been slacking for a few days. It was just a little friendly reminder.

***

Flag detail is going well. I've been on it three times and we haven't dropped it. I was the safety today. My arms stay under the flag while it's being folded. It's pretty cool. I always wondered how the flag was put into such a nice triangle. Now I know.

I'm in study hall right now. Every Mon, Wed, and Fri we get an hour at night where everybody is quiet. So quiet. I can't wait until I'm able to just go find a quiet place—and read, write, or do nothing at all. I can't wait to sit in a comfy chair and kick my legs up. We have to sit straight up with the entirely of the bottom of our boots flat on the ground. All day. Every day. Well, I mean when we're sitting.

-Anne-

I received a postcard from Vince informing me that my last three letters to him had been destroyed. There was an explanation given for only one: it had contained an image of a website. All I could think of was that he had been urged to ask me for a list of AA meetings in our neighborhood, and I had copied a list off of the AA website, printed it, and mailed it to him. I checked the Department of Corrections website and it said nothing about images of websites not being allowed in letters.

Man, was I upset! Especially since I have an upcoming visit with Vince—the first in eight months. Did they know about the blog, and were they pissed off about it? Did they just not like the content of my letters for some reason? Or was it totally capricious? Would they find some reason to deny me a visit, after I drove for two hours to get there? Would I be able to keep my mouth shut if they did? I don't have answers to these questions. All I can do is try my best to suck it up if the guards give me any grief. Trouble is, I am really bad at kowtowing to authority.

A Visit, at Last

-Anne-

I went to visit Vince on Sunday, for the first time in over eight months.

Given my last experience with visiting, my subsequent six-month ban, the fact that my last four letters to him were destroyed, and that he'll soon be released, I thought I could skip this visit. But he really wanted me to come. I'm his only visitor, so he hasn't seen anyone from the outside for a long time.

Friends made suggestions for what I should wear to prevent a repeat of the unfortunate "low-cut blouse" episode. A nun's habit, suit of armor, a sleeping bag, a burqa … the list went on and on and it was all very ha, ha, ha but I was really very anxious. It's indescribable unless you've experienced it firsthand—the feeling of being at the mercy of a stranger in uniform—the powerlessness, uncertainty, and fear. And I'm not even in prison.

Problem was, I don't own a T-shirt or a button-up shirt or a turtleneck. I don't like clothing that constricts around the neck. I was inspired to put on one of my uncle's dress shirts—the uncle who died in December whose shirts I took for Vince. I could have fit two of me inside it. The sleeves fell down six inches below my fingers and the shirt tails fell to my knees, but it I could button it up to my neck. Maybe it would bring me good luck.

The hour-and-a-half-long drive to Willow River went smoothly and I arrived a few minutes before visiting hours. The gate was closed so I pressed the intercom button. A voice told me to leave the grounds and wait on the highway until visiting hours started.

I looked at my cell phone and said, "You mean, in four minutes?"

"Yes," he answered.

A year ago I would have made a sarcastic remark but I wasn't going to take any chances. I said, "Okay" and backed down the drive. I killed the engine and reflexively reached for my cell phone, then realized I had not left the grounds so I started the car up again, drove out to the highway, and sat there on the side of the road with my emergency lights on as cars and trucks zoomed by me.

After four minutes I drove back in and the gate was open. This facility is much smaller than St. Cloud or Moose Lake. There were no bars, metal doors, metal detectors, or guards behind plexiglass. My hand was shaking as I filled out the visitor-request form, but within 10 minutes I was waved into the visiting room and there he was. When I hugged him I could feel how much weight he had lost.

"People would pay to come here!" I said, laughing.

"I know, mom, I've never been in such great shape in my life," he said.

"And by the way, I just got a demerit because you arrived early."

What a splash of cold water! Vince got a demerit because I arrived four minutes early. It would be one thing if I had known this was a no-no, but I had checked the visiting rules online the day before and they said nothing about it. "Don't worry about it, mom. That's just how how it is. There's no way of knowing what the rules are until you break one. They're looking for a reaction, and I won't give it to them. Just don't show up early when you come to pick me up on my last day."

"If I were staying in longer, you could do a video visit," Vince told me. "They're promoting it heavily—one hour for only $99.95!" We burst out laughing at the absurdity of it, but he explained that a hundred bucks was cheap for the many families who had to drive from Chicago and pay for hotel rooms.

Our two hours together flew by. I drove home and felt completely drained. Two hundred miles, two hours with my son, two weeks til he comes home.

Here are a couple images of Willow River I found online:

Welcome to the Country

-Vince-

To say that alcohol lowered my inhibitions would be an understatement. It pretty much rendered me retarded. That said, here are a few things that I probably thought were funny at the time. Keep in mind that these are only things I remember doing or people told me I had done in a blackout.

- To impress "the ladies" I once downed an entire bottle of bubbles. You know, the kind you put the wand in and blow through it. What followed must have been amazing to see because several people stated they couldn't believe I had done that. Within one minute I started throwing up (with considerable distance) a clearish-pink foam that expanded even more once it hit the ground. The carbonation in the beer accelerated the bubbling process in my stomach and became fairly painful. I groaned in pain while heaving, making a noise no animal on earth would use as a mating call. After a few minutes it was over, I was surrounded by foam. Without hesitation I grabbed a fresh beer.
- Standing by a river with friends down in Iowa, I found a dead fish and took a bite out of its belly and spat it out at one of them at which point I started throwing up, he started throwing up and in no time at all we were all on the ground doing the same and trying not to laugh which was not easy.
- Passed out, blacked out on a canoe trip I was responsible for not only tipping a canoe, but sinking it forever along with the oars, cell phones, cooler, cigarettes, and clothing. I don't know why I was naked, but I do know that it was a long walk back to my friend's truck. Hey, at least we didn't have to carry a canoe back!
- Nothing makes a better combination than alcohol and shot guns. Especially when I don't have any glasses or contacts. So, one day a few of us went "hunting." We would usually look for squirrels, crows, or anything that moved. I saw a crow circling overhead and decided it was mine, even though

335

we were using slugs. I "aimed" and fired four times, missed, reloaded and missed four more times. I saw one of my friends running toward me to I smiled and waved at him. He didn't look too happy. He informed me that I had actually been firing wildly at a bald eagle. We put the guns away.

-Anne-

I got a postcard from Vince, in which he wished me a fun trip. Then he couldn't resist adding, "Germany sounds like a lovely place where they have loved people of our faith for a long time. Just remember, if somebody asks you to take a shower in a large metal room, run!" Vince has always been a joker. One of my favorites was the time he got kicked out of Hebrew School for writing his name on a name tag as "P. Ness." I had to act serious in front of Vince and the rabbi, who was humorless and thus terrible with teenagers, but I laughed out loud when I was out of earshot.

Boring but Important

-Anne-

This blog touches on a lot of issues related to imprisonment, like addiction, drug laws, mental illness, and intergenerational poverty. One thing I've been meaning to address is class, and historically, a four-year college degree has been the way for Americans to propel themselves from the "working class" to the middle class and beyond.

We talk a lot about race in this country, but we like to think we're a classless society because we don't have an aristocracy. We also like to believe that in America, anyone can overcome poverty or even become a millionaire if they just work hard enough. It's exactly because of this myth, I think, that our class divide is so hard to overcome, because we don't acknowledge that it exists or that the deck is stacked against many people.

***

In my last job I was the communications manager for a consulting firm that specialized in enrollment management for private colleges. What we did was this: our clients would send us the data on their freshman applicants, we would analyze it, then tell them which applicants to accept and how much money to offer them to come. These financial "awards" were really mostly just discounts to entice desirable students to come to a particular college.

When we analyzed the data—no matter whether it was Occidental College in L.A. or Loyola University in Chicago or St. Olaf College in Northfield, Minnesota—there was one thing that students with the highest grades and test scores had in common. Race? No. High school attended? No. These things were factors but really it all boiled down to parental income.

Colleges often offered discounts to the richest families. They call these awards things like "Presidential Scholarships" in hopes of flattering parents and beating their competitors.

Why do kids from high-income families do so well? It's not rocket science. They have grown up in safe, lead-free homes with toys and books. They went to preschool and well-resourced elementary schools. Their parents attended every parent-teacher conference and made sure they did their homework. They went to summer camps in the Adirondacks where they were on a lacrosse team, were immersed in French, or learned to play the marimba. Colleges love these well-rounded students.

Wealthy families can also afford SAT/ACT prep classes. They can afford to fly/drive to campus visits to the remote, pastoral towns where the most exclusive colleges are located. They can hire tutors and college admission coaches. These coaches do a brisk business in helping kids write the perfect application essay and advising parents on which colleges will give the biggest discounts.

But sometimes I think the biggest factor in driving kids toward academic success is that wealthy parents have expectations of them.

***

I don't recall anyone having expectations of me, or talking to me about college when I was 17. They may have, but I was so busy partying that I may not remember. Our neighborhood was blue collar—every mom was a housewife and every husband was a car mechanic, a roofer, or worked in a can factory. The only reason I even knew what a college was, was because there was a Catholic college nearby and my aunt had married a professor—the one "white collar" guy on the block.

I didn't want to work in a can factory or be a housewife, and that college was my ticket out. I applied to one college—Bemidji State University. Bemidji State is in an extremely poor part of northern Minnesota near the White Earth Indian reservation. It has a 90% acceptance rate and a 17% graduation rate (compared with around 7% and 99% for Harvard). All I knew was that it sounded as far away from home as anything I could imagine.

By the time I got my acceptance letter, I was pregnant with Vince. I wrote "deceased" on the envelope and threw it back in the mail.

***

I sometimes wonder what trajectory my life would have taken if I'd had some guidance about college, but on the whole I've made the best of it and have had a great life.

LeCordon Blue

-Anne-

My last post looked at the reasons that kids born into poor or blue collar families have a hard time negotiating the college admissions process. Low expectations, parents who know nothing about the admissions system, day care instead of preschool, and a lack of exposure to enriching opportunities like music lessons or travel.

Everyone's situation is different, but I have to write at least one more post about what happens when kids from poor families do aspire to attend college. It should be easy, if they start at a community college for their first two years, then finish at a public university, Pell Grants should cover their cost of attendance. Students can take up to six years to complete their degree, which allows them time to work, which covers their rent and other living expenses. Even private colleges can be a good deal for lower income kids, if they have good grades, because private colleges tend to offer more financial aid than public institutions. They should have to borrow minimal, if any, in student loans.

But what can happen is that low income kids get all excited about for-profit colleges that are national chains and advertise heavily on TV, the radio, and the web. These are places like LeCordon Bleu School of Culinary Arts, where Vince wanted to go when he was 16 and had dropped out of high school. He stopped in to get information and they pounced, completing all the paperwork for him to take out student loans to cover the $40,000 tuition.

That's $40,000 per year, for a two-year program. That's how for-profit schools make their shareholders very, very happy. LeCordon Bleu has a graduation rate that's better than Bemidji State University, but at 48% that still means 52% of students drop out under the worst possible circumstances: no degree, which means no prospects for a decent job, and on the hook for tens of thousands of dollars of student loans. That's U.S. Government money–aka tax dollars–going to subsidize for-profit colleges. It makes me sick. Back when Vince was jazzed about LeCordon Bleu I knew very little about college financial aid but I understood that $40,000 was a ridiculous amount to pay to get a degree as a pastry chef. I refused to sign the forms for Vince and he was furious, but maybe some day he'll thank me.

Recently Vince asked me to send him information about culinary schools. He was interested in earning a degree in the work he's been doing for 20 years. I checked out our local community and technical college and their tuition for a full-time student was a little over $3,000 per year.

But unsophisticated students can get into trouble even at community colleges.

Fast forward. Vince has completed four months of treatment at Hazelden and a year living in a Hazelden-sanctioned halfway house in West Palm Beach, Florida. He has settled in Rochester, Minnesota and is working at Spencer Gifts. He decides to pursue a degree at Rochester Community and Technical College.

I offered to help him figure out the financial aid picture. He seemed to think this was intrusive and unnecessary.

To make a long story short, he took out over $30,000 in student loans and dropped out a few credits shy of earning his associate degree. What was going on in that financial aid office? Wasn't anyone tracking that no student needed that much in federal loans to attend a college that cost $3,000 a year? Wasn't there an underwriter to flag that this was a high-risk borrower?

He subsequently defaulted on those loans. The penalties and interest piled up astronomically. Unlike other debt that can be discharged in bankruptcy, student loans are inescapable. As Vince would say, "Ugh."

It probably feels overwhelming to him; not what he needs as he is about to be released to make a fresh start.

Reading, Writing, Ready

-Vince-

Today is one of our work crew days, but they haven't had much work for us to do of late. They sent us out for an hour to do drill and ceremony but so far that's it. I haven't lifted a splitting maul, a saw, or a rake since my first month here. Don't' get me wrong. I do plenty, but some days I get bored with sitting in my blue plastic chair.

On the plus side, I have two new Bill Bryson books to keep me occupied. A Walk in the Woods and Neither Here nor There. I've read 117 pages of the former since I checked it out last night and I'm completely immersed. I now want to hike the Appalachian Trail, just like I wanted to visit Australia when I was reading In a Sunburned Country, and I wanted to visit outer space and a lot more when I read A Short History of Nearly Everything. I don't know what I'm going to do for reading next, I've exhausted all the authors I know and I still have weeks to kill.

***

I finished the 276-page A Walk in the Woods in just under an hour. I may have to start reading less. I sat in my blue plastic chair nearly all day, neglecting my body by getting zero exercise. Maybe it's okay to do nothing once a week.

I read these books and wonder about my ability to write my own. I have certainly lead a life worthy of writing about but I don't know how I could put it all together with all of my missing memories, lack of proper punctuation and rather short vocabulary compared to any book I've read. In the last book there must have been a dozen words I have never seen before.

I've been writing this blog for nearly a year, and I wonder if it would even fill in a hundred typed pages in a book. When I'm out I can finally check out this blog for myself and type instead of write. But who knows, I kind of like writing by hand.

***

Thinking back to when I started writing, I had no clue what boot camp was about. I heard so many things from so many sources, none of them very accurate. But I wrote them down as if I was an expert on the subject.

341

I say that to say this, everything I write is written as I remember it. And although my life has been crazy enough to have no need to embellish the truth, I'm sure some of the people involved in some of the stories might remember things differently. One thing I can tell you is that every word since the first post has been written by me completely sober. Sometimes it's difficult to look back through the fog for details. Sometimes I don't want to.

***

Another Sunday in the bag. Days seem to last forever, yet the weeks fly by. I hope I'm ready for the real world. It scares a lot of people. Prison scares me, so I am going to make sure I never come back. I will be a success. I am ready.

***

Here's the deal: I'm going to wind this thing down. I want to write, and I will. Unfortunately, I'm very restricted here in what I write. I can't say bad things or bad words. I can't give unfavorable opinions about any aspect of this program. I simply don't feel free to be expressive and explicit. So, I will write a couple more posts then take some time off.

I've enclosed a picture of myself from when I arrived at Moose Lake in November. I wish I could show you a picture of me now. The difference is substantial.

For Sale By Owner

It's been quite a journey. I can't wait to apply the knowledge I've gained here out in the world. I've worked hard on so many levels. I am lucky to have had the opportunity to be immersed in such an intense program. It's like Hazelden on steroids.

Thank you for reading.

An Exception to the Rule

-Vince-

I remember working at the Kemps Ice Cream plant in Rochester for roughly a year. Possibly significantly more or less, I have no idea.

I worked in the wrapper room. Seven lines of different flavors, brands, and styles would come through a Plexiglas wall from the production line and into one of the various machines to be individually wrapped, then bundled in four or six packs, then shrink-wrapped together before going into the deep freeze for several hours.

I worked a machine called an Amerio. Sort of a recycling freezer. 31 levels high, the ice cream would be pushed in from the front and out the back came the now frozen bricks onto a conveyor belt that flowed down to a separate room for wrapping.

I worked with a guy I'll call Bill. Often we worked 12 hour shifts in the summer time. We got to know each other pretty well. We joked around a lot, had some serious conversations, and once we even went out for a beer (just after I had started drinking again after five years sober).

Very shortly after that I lost my job and never saw or talked to him again.

Years later, while looking at the Olmsted County Sheriff's Office In Custody roster online, looking for anybody I knew in the meth world, I saw his name. Just below his name was a charge that even criminals despise.

It turns out Bill had a fairly long-standing relationship with a 12 year old girl. The police had letters he had written to her, and her to him, describing, in too much detail, their love.

I sit here now and am a little upset that I ever spoke to him, not that I knew anything about it. I would like to write a lot more about it but I can't. I will someday, when my mail won't be read before it's sent out.

***

I had a one-on-one with my CD counselor just a moment ago. We talked for a half hour about my worries and wants and my thoughts about employment upon release. His advice, go out and live life. He said he had full confidence that I would be good at being sober, but he wanted me to go out and be a good person.

Then he threw me a curve-ball. He thought I could make a great CD counselor within five years, by which time I would have gotten my Bachelor's in Social Work and then on to a LADC or something like that. I tend to daydream and space out a lot even if things are really important. But he made me feel like I was really capable of doing something with my life, even if it takes a while. So, I have that going for me.

***

Today our squad had our re-entries. What's that? Where we go into a room and one by one we talk to our CD counselor and case manager. It's really scary for the people that have not been doing any hard work. All my counselor said to my caseworker was, "He's doing exceptional work, and he facilitates the NA meeting on Friday nights. No worries." She smiled (nobody has seen her smile) and told me I was also the exception to the rule on her end. I have been approved to move to St. Paul upon my release! No more worries. I was the only one in my squad to be approved so far.

-Anne-

I felt nervous when I read that last paragraph. I say I'm not superstitious but I am a Midwesterner, and we have superstitions that go like this: 1) "Never saying anything good about yourself because you'll sound like a braggart, and everyone will look askance at you but not say anything" and 2) "Never say anything optimistic because that will immediately bring back luck down on you."

Or was it that I've known a lot of addicts and alcoholics, and they tend to be Janus faced in many ways—in this case grandiose today and ripping themselves to shreds the next?

I think I'll just be proud of how well he's doing.

Froggie Went a Courtin'

-Vince-

I just came back from a lawn mowing where I took the life of an innocent frog. It was a cold-blooded murder in the most literal sense.

Wait. Are frogs cold blooded? Hmm. I may be wrong but it sounded funny in my head.

I don't like to kill things, so I felt bad for a few minutes. I didn't do it on purpose, but when his (her?) severed head was staring into my eyes, I could still see life and I've been thinking about it ever since. Now that I've written about it, I can let it go.

I once killed a deer, for meat, and I once killed a deer with a Pontiac Sunfire. Oh, and some squirrels, which I also ate.

***

After months of no formal discipline, I got an intervention today. That is my sixth in five months, not bad. The guy with the most discipline in my squad has 21 and three Learning Experiences.

An intervention is basically a military gig, not a rehab intervention like you might see on TV. Mine was for not sleeping under one of my two sheets. It's very petty. If I do it two more times which I won't, I will get an LE.

***

I redeemed myself today for killing the frog. I saw him/her just in time while I was pushing the Frog Killer 2000 over the grass, and helped him along into the garden. Oh, yea, there were two of them. So if I ever kill another frog, I'm even.

***

We've been working lately in CD on the "ripple effect" of our crimes. Well, most of us have. The guy who shot at somebody several times but missed still claims his offense has no victim.

I never denied that selling drugs hurt society, people's lives, families, and of course the children. I'm sure the money given to me for meth could have been better spent on food, clothing, and shelter.

346

My criminality has affected my family as well. I didn't directly try to bring harm to them, other than stealing some money from My Mom years ago, and borrowing money more recently without, so far, paying it back. But I see my Mother, now in her 50s, still beautiful, energetic, kind, and unbelievably patient, without a husband, and I wonder if I am indirectly or directly responsible. Is that where the shame took hold? Am I such a black sheep that she didn't even bother?

She's had boyfriends over the years but they didn't stick. I see myself in the same boat. 37 with no wife and kids, no girlfriend waiting for me out there. Maybe together, we emit a powerful toxic odor that that repels potential mates. Hmm … I hope not.

The point is, even if I am not responsible for her mating habits, I am seeing that my choices affect more than just me. And it can ripple a long way out. I'm not just staying clean for me, I'm doing it for the whole pond.

-Anne-

My heart sank when I read this. Vince is in no way responsible for me being one of the 7% of American women my age who have never married. Take out the lesbian women who weren't legally able to marry, and I am part of a really small club. I always wanted to get married. I assumed I would.

Like a lot of things, it's complicated. I wasted my 20s and 30s—the years when most people marry—on Kermit and other alcoholics, abusers, and just plain jerks. Then I took a break from dating to figure out how to stop doing that. Then came Vince's lost year, when I was too distraught to think of anything else. Then, the older you are, the harder it is to meet people. So it was a combo of bad choices, bad timing, bad luck and yes, Vince was a factor but far from the only one. Being single is far from the worst fate, so now I claim my spinsterhood as if it was my plan all along.

The End. The Beginning.

-Vince-

Everything seems to be falling into place. Maybe not in the order I want it to, but aligning nonetheless. I volunteered to be one of the two in-house facilitators of the AA meeting, in addition to the NA meeting. It's been awhile since I lead a meeting but it is something I enjoy and have a lot of experience doing. It's all about service work. Starting it here will not only make me look good with my caseworker but makes me feel good inside.

***

I'm sitting in study hall, nice and quiet, when a man starts banging loudly on a table, starts crying, and leaves the room. I finally saw somebody snap. That's the only explanation. He's been here as long as I have, I hope they don't kick him out. He's a good guy, but this place can make you revisit some pretty bad places in your head.

***

What a day. Restorative Justice has a way of making me feel good, even with seven oozing blisters on my hands from shoveling tons of wet sand.

After breakfast (which is after aerobics), nine of us donned our reflective vests and hopped in the van, trailer in tow, and headed for Hinkley. We love riding in the van. And we were treated to a 40-minute trip. We were told we would be working hard, and that we were going to work on a house for Habitat for Humanity. Both statements were true.

Essentially we dug a four foot moat around the 30' x 60' house, two feet deep, four feet wide. Then we put blue Styrofoam insulation down to guard against frost. Then, after three hours of shoveling the sand out, we shoveled it back in. Ugh.

In the middle of the operation, I did get a side job of varnishing six wooden doors. That's something I have some experience with and enjoy and, well, it's way easier. But I still ended my day with load after load on the scoop shovel. Each scoop no less than 50 pounds. Our uniforms were destroyed. We were bleeding. We were hungry and tired.

And after all of that, the man in charge gave us a tour of the house and said it was being built for a single mother of three who had been working for five years taking care of her mentally and physically disabled adults, but couldn't make ends meet and was now homeless. A tear came to his eye when he thanked us for our work. There may have been some tears in our eyes too, or maybe I just had some sand in my eyes.

He told us how generous Wells Fargo was to donate the property. 3M paid HFH for the opportunity to have volunteers come and insulate the entire house. Whirlpool donates appliances to every— every HFH house. And an unnamed source donates the highest quality and efficient furnaces, water heaters, and air conditioners. And countless people donate their time in any way they can.

For their house, the soon-to-be-owner must put in 260 hours of her own time on the house, put $100 down, and pay a mortgage of $300 a month, interest free.

Yeah, I feel good because I worked hard for somebody who is in need. I'd like to do more things like that when I get out.

-Anne-

This will be Vince's last post from inside prison because he is being released today! As you read this, I will be in Willow River watching his graduation ceremony. Then he will walk out the door, with the clothes on his back and about $300. I will have an avocado in the car for him. We'll drive straight to a 1:30 pm appointment in St. Paul with his ISR agent. Then I will bring him home. I got the landline phone, as required. Thanks to friends pitching in, I've got a bed for him and toiletries and some books and a few clothes that won't make

349

him stand out as an ex con. I am so excited. So happy. We'll post a report on how it went, with photos, next time.

Out

-Anne-

I pride myself on being highly organized, but I lost the letter Vince had sent me that outlined the schedule for the day of his release. I called the facility and asked what time I needed to be there. The guy I talked to was very nice, and said Vince was a "great kid" and a "known agate collector." It was my first positive interaction with the corrections system.

I found out later that Vince received a demerit because I made this call.

***

I left the house at 7:30 am to drive up to the little town of Willow River, population 403 plus 142 inmates at the correctional facility. Here are some photos of Willow River:

I had dug out a long-sleeved, high-necked shirt from my winter clothes so there would be no chance I could get either of us in trouble. After all, this would be their last chance to fuck with me in person. But when I arrived at the facility half the women there for the release of their loved ones were wearing plunging cleavage and skin-tight tights.

We were shown into a gymnasium with a long row of empty chairs in the front facing us. The warden or whoever she was made a short speech, then the two graduating squads marched in. The first one was led by a guy who could be a real competitor on American Idol. There were no cameras or cell phones allowed, which is too bad because he was really impressive. He lead Hotel Squad—17 guys—

into the room, belting out the boot camp slogans in an old timey, spiritual sort of call and response.

Then it was Vince's squad's turn—India Squad. He had told me that someone else had been chosen to lead them out, but there was Vince doing it! I'm still not clear on what happened to the other guy. And while Vince wouldn't make it to the finals on American Idol, I was very moved that he was the leader of his squad.

There were various speeches by the head of the chemical dependency and education programs, which no one could hear because of the crying and otherwise-noisy kids in the room. Then each prisoner stood up and stated the length of his original term (between 48 and 100 months), what he had learned (patience was the one I recall hearing most often), and who he had to thank for helping him make it through.

All the guys thanked their families and the boot camp staff. One guy thanked The Lord. Vince mentioned the boot camp counselors by name but didn't mention me or anyone else outside of the program.

I knew in that moment I needed to get myself back to Alanon and schedule some weekends away.

***

An hour later, we were on the road back to St. Paul. It's no exaggeration that Vince was released with only the clothes on his back, a folder full of papers, and one month worth of medication for his Restless Legs Syndrome.

He asked to stop at a gas station. "The first thing every one of us guys wants to do is play scratch off tickets," he said.

"I guess it's better than buying meth," I said. "And I saw a billboard for gambling addictions on the way up so you know that help is available." He laughed.

Twice during the graduation ceremony, they had said that this second phase of boot camp–house arrest–would be harder than incarceration. That'll be true for me, too. My first challenge is, now that I've made clear my low opinion of gambling, to let it go. I have a right to state my opinion—once. Saying it over and over would be an attempt to control and manipulate.

Here are some photos of Vince shopping at Walmart.

A great day for freedom

-Vince-

It's good to be home. After 15 months of incarceration, I'm finally able to type my own words. The first few days have been fairly uneventful. I've mostly been relaxing, healing, and setting up my schedule for this week. I took the train down a good portion of University Avenue and back. There were a lot of people everywhere. It's overwhelming. But I survived. I'll write a few more posts from my last few days in Willow River. Then it's on to the next phase of my life.

8-2-15 On day two, our first full day of boot camp, we had our initial weigh-in. I had arrived in St. Cloud at an alarming 216 pounds. I did a little better when I got to Moose Lake at 201, with a body-fat percentage of 14.4%. Today we had our final weigh-in. When I saw the numbers appear, I was shocked. 173 pounds and 9.5% body-fat. I succeeded in both of my fitness goals! Then we ran our test-out mile. My entrance mile was 11:14. I shaved off four and a half minutes. One mile in 6:45. I was breathless after I ran but it still felt good.

I feel good about myself in so many ways. I am so ready to get out of here.

OK, that's all for now. Typing is very frustrating for me. I need to work on that.

BeFUDdled

-Anne-

I am writing this on Sunday to post on Monday, which is Rosh Hashanah, the Jewish New Year. I will go to early services, then spend much of the day outside. I love the High Holidays because, for one thing, the weather is always beautiful—crisp and cool, with the leaves starting to change colors and the sky intensely blue. Even though I no longer believe in god, I feel it's important to participate in community, so I go to services. Now there's a new prayer book for my stream of Judaism, Reform Judaism, that acknowledges many people's disbelief. I think that'll make me feel more "legitimate" walking in the door.

In the evening some friends will come over for dinner. Vince is looking forward to making a real hearty, holiday meal.

***

Vince has been home for five days. There was so little information available ahead of time that I didn't clock on to the fact that he's on house arrest. I don't know the difference between probation and parole but I thought he'd be on one or the other and would be able to come and go as he pleased, as long as he was doing constructive things like job hunting or going to AA meetings.

But no, he is confined to the house 24/7 except for job hunting from 9-2 Monday through Friday and other things he has to clear with the agents. So for instance he proposed an AA meeting on Saturday night and that was approved but he hadn't researched how far away the meeting would be or, more important, that there was a meeting at that time—which there isn't. So he's looking forward to fine-tuning his schedule.

Yesterday he had a two-hour window approved to go shopping. I thought he would enjoy the farmers market, with all the colorful veg and people watching. Not to mention, it's cheap. I dropped him off with some reusable shopping bags and went to park the car.

A few minutes later I got a text from him: "I don't like it here. There are no instructions. And I'm the only one with purses."

He was overwhelmed. I joined him and explained that everything was "two dallahs." We consulted our list for the holiday dinner and he seemed to relax into the experience. Then we went into the adjacent Asian market, which was even more crowded and full of the smells of live fish. He got a kick out of some of the items:

Last stop, Aldi, also crowded. I am normally a very slow and deliberate shopper but even I was sick of the shopping crowds, so we threw a bunch of stuff in the cart and got back to the house with time to spare.

***

It is definitely a big adjustment for me to live with someone. The condo is 825 square feet, not large by American standards.

This morning we both got up and out of the house at 7:30am for exercise. He ran, I walked. I stopped in at the nearby YWCA to get membership info and picked up a scholarship form for Vince. I gave it to him when I got home and won't ask him every day, "Did you fill out that form?" It's none of my business.

On the other hand, when I walked into the bathroom and saw some clothing tags next to the wastebasket instead of inside it, that was my business.

"Vince, what would they have done at boot camp if you'd thrown trash on the floor next to the wastebasket?"

"Ah, someone would have picked up after me," he joked. I think he was joking. Anyway, the tags were gone next time I looked. No drama.

So far there has been no yelling, eye rolling, sighing, or crying. So all we have to do for a year is know when to say something, when to bite our tongues, and try to maintain our senses of humor.

No situation is ever hopeless. Love can survive, and perhaps even grow richer, despite or because we live through a terrible time.

Every Day is a Beautiful Day

-Vince-

It feels as if all of that was a lifetime ago. As of the time of this writing, it's been two years, 11 months, and 13 days since I left boot camp. When I look back on those old posts, I see somebody else: this is not me. I remember so little of my prison experience probably because I have focused so much of my life on improving myself and helping others. Or perhaps my mind has blocked much of it out as if it were a trauma. Either way, life for me now is good.

The second phase of the Challenge Incarceration Program or, house arrest, was much more problematic and it lasted for 13 months, seven months longer than the first segment. I ended up being restructured, placed on a 30-day lockdown, and having to serve another thirty days on Intensive Supervised Release, all for missing a couple phone calls and not getting home fast enough. That 13 months was the worst experience of my life, and I've been to prison!

My mother and I had a difficult time living together and our relationship became strained and there were days where I actually wanted to go back to prison because I couldn't handle life out here and I thought maybe structure was the key. But after some time, a move away from the nest, and really getting into the program of A.A., I found that life was not only practicable, it could be downright gratifying.

At this moment, I am sitting on a couch in a house. My house. Our house. I am keying these words on my laptop while a child is watching her favorite show on the big-screen t.v. Over and over I am astonished at all of my accomplishments of the past (almost) three years that I feel as if I am living the song "Once in a Lifetime" by *Talking Heads*. "And you may find yourself in a beautiful house with a beautiful wife. And you may ask yourself, well, how did I get here?" Well, I worked my ass off, and she isn't my wife, but I do love her and her children, and we did buy a house together. But it's still surreal that this is what happens when I stay sober.

You may have noticed that I have written briefly on just a few topics. That is because I have written so extensively on those and so many more over the years that it is best for me just to share tidbits, and leave you a link or two where you can pick up the rest of my journey. It's not easy to read sometimes. As I said, in the beginning, there was a lot more slipping back than moving forward. I lived in my head a lot and I was muddled by daily life especially in such a controlled environment. I wrote comprehensively on my growth in a twelve-step program and as I look back on those years it's literally like watching a butterfly emerge from a chrysalis. I spelled chrysalis without cheating, but then I had to look it up to be sure and now I've been reading up on stuff I forgot from whatever grade it is that they teach about cocoons and moths and butterflies and such. Anywho, obviously I've continued my voyage as a writer and I have stayed with a message of recovery throughout most of my material. I believe in the power of writing as a therapy, and I believe that this blog—actually, a book now—can be used as a story of triumph.

I was the hopeless variety. I was just a fall-down drunk until I found something else to light my fire. I loved hard drugs and I loved the life that came with them. I loved being down and out. I loved pain. I loved to feel it, and I loved to cause it. I wasn't happy until I could see sorrow in my eyes or the eyes of those who cared for me.

Then over a period of years I found the true meaning of love and realized I had been wrong for all of those years. I suffered an excruciating addiction, and it cost me everything I had ever come into contact with. I did drugs because I didn't like who I was, but that was only because I never tried to be anything. I found out that I was capable of real love. I don't just mean that I could love people; I mean that finally I could let people love me. Finally, I felt human. I felt alive.

Now, every day is a beautiful day. Challenges and hurdles are part of life, and I am capable of meeting them both with a clear head and fervor. I am off of I.S.R., parole, and all other involuntary forms of assisted living that I had to cope with. I haven't had a slip. I haven't had a drink in over four years and I maintain my program to ensure my daily reprieve from intoxicants.

Finally.

I am a responsible adult.

Pick up where this story leaves off...[6]

Going Forward

Our Breaking Free blog is at

Breaking Free - https://breakingfreeblog.org/

Vince's writing can be found at

Vince's Blog - http://vincentmaertz.blogspot.com

References

[1] Bob Barker. https://www.bobbarker.com/

[2] Sentencing guidelines. https://mn.gov/sentencing-guidelines/assets/Applying%20the%20Guidelines%20Presentation_tcm30-31740.pdf

[3] Alexandra Kennedy. http://alexandrakennedy.blogspot.com/2011/07/for-prisoner.html

[4] Obama in New York Times. https://nyti.ms/1e3BUiE

[5] Dogs trained in Prison. http://www.nytimes.com/2015/07/28/science/dogs-trained-in-prison-to-protect-lives.html

[6] Breaking Free Blog. https://breakingfreeblog.org/2015/09/16/my-worst-24-hours/

Made in the USA
Monee, IL
12 January 2020